Exploring Networked Urban Mobilities

Exploring Networked Urban Mobilities investigates different conceptual and theoretical angles between social practices and urban environments, culture, infrastructures, technologies, and the politics of mobility. The book introduces the concept of *networked urban mobilities* and lays out a research agenda for the future of mobility studies. Each of the contributors represents a specific approach in the field and each article provides cutting-edge theoretical and conceptual reflections on the topic. Mobility here is understood as a heterogeneous phenomenon that shapes modern societies and cities by emerging in different dimensions: as physical, social, cultural, and digital mobilities.

Malene Freudendal-Pedersen is Associate Professor in Sustainable Mobilities at Roskilde University, Denmark. She has an interdisciplinary background linking sociology, geography, urban planning, and science and technology studies which she has been using to investigate praxes of mobilities and their significance for (future) cities. She is the co-manager of the international Cosmobilities Network, and the co-founder and co-editor of the new journal *Applied Mobilities*. She is the author of the book *Mobility in Daily Life: Between Freedom and Unfreedom*.

Sven Kesselring is Research Professor in Automotive Management: Sustainable Mobilities and the director of the Master of Science program Sustainable Mobilities at Nürtingen-Geislingen University (NGU), Germany. His research focuses on the sociology of (auto)mobilities, social theory, and the impact of technology and digitalization on everyday and professional lives. He is the founder and co-manager of the international Cosmobilities Network and co-director of the joint PhD program Sustainable Mobility and Mobility Cultures of TU Munich and NGU. He is co-founder and co-editor of the new journal *Applied Mobilities* and Studies in Mobility and Transport. He has edited several books including *Aeromobilities* (with Saulo Cwerner and John Urry).

Networked Urban Mobilities Series
Editors: Sven Kesselring
Nürtingen-Geislingen University
Malene Freudendal-Pedersen
Roskilde University

The Networked Urban Mobilities series resulted from the Cosmobilities Network of mobility research and the Taylor & Francis journal, *Applied Mobilities*. This three-volume set, ideal for mobilities researchers and practitioners, explores a broad number of topics including planning, architecture, geography, and urban design.

Exploring Networked Urban Mobilities
Theories, Concepts, Ideas
Edited by Malene Freudendal-Pedersen and Sven Kesselring

Experiencing Networked Urban Mobilities
Practices, Flows, Methods
Edited by Malene Freudendal-Pedersen, Katrine Hartmann-Petersen and Emmy Laura Perez Fjalland

Envisioning Networked Urban Mobilities
Art, Performances, Impacts
Edited by Aslak Aamot Kjærulff, Sven Kesselring, Peter Peters and Kevin Hannam

"An odyssey of physical, social, cultural and virtual mobilities. Clear-eyed and compelling. The book really is a milestone."

Professor Anthony Elliott, Dean of External Engagement, University of South Australia

Exploring Networked Urban Mobilities
Theories, Concepts, Ideas

Edited by Malene Freudendal-Pedersen
and Sven Kesselring

NEW YORK AND LONDON

First published 2018
by Routledge
711 Third Avenue, New York, NY 10017

and by Routledge
2 Park Square, Milton Park, Abingdon, Oxon, OX14 4RN

Routledge is an imprint of the Taylor & Francis Group, an informa business

© 2018 Taylor & Francis

The right of Malene Freudendal-Pedersen and Sven Kesselring to be
identified as the authors of the editorial material, and of the authors
for their individual chapters, has been asserted in accordance with
sections 77 and 78 of the Copyright, Designs and Patents Act 1988.

All rights reserved. No part of this book may be reprinted or
reproduced or utilised in any form or by any electronic, mechanical,
or other means, now known or hereafter invented, including
photocopying and recording, or in any information storage or
retrieval system, without permission in writing from the publishers.

Trademark notice: Product or corporate names may be trademarks
or registered trademarks, and are used only for identification and
explanation without intent to infringe.

Library of Congress Cataloging-in-Publication Data
A catalog record for this book has been requested

ISBN: 978-1-138-70886-0 (hbk)
ISBN: 978-1-315-20107-8 (ebk)

Typeset in Sabon
by Apex CoVantage, LLC

To John and Ulrich

Contents

Notes on Contributors		xi
Preface		xiv
1	Networked Urban Mobilities MALENE FREUDENDAL-PEDERSEN AND SVEN KESSELRING	1
2	Globalizing Networked Urbanism: Entanglements of Elite and Subaltern Mobilities MIMI SHELLER	19
3	Mobile 'Pseudonymous Strangers': How Chance Encounters Constitute Sociality in Digitally Augmented and Location-Aware Urban Public Places CHRISTIAN LICOPPE	36
4	The Worlds of Offshoring JOHN URRY	50
5	Networked Urbanism and Disaster MONIKA BÜSCHER, XAROULA KERASIDOU, KATRINA PETERSEN, AND RACHEL OLIPHANT	59
6	Vertical Mobilities: Confronting the Politics of Elevators in Tall Buildings and Ultra-Deep Mining STEPHEN GRAHAM	80
7	Mobilities Futures VINCENT KAUFMANN	108

x *Contents*

8 **Performing or Deconstructing the Mobile Subject?
   Linking Mobility Concepts, Research Designs,
   and Methods**   124
   KATHARINA MANDERSCHEID

9 **Mobility and the Cosmopolitan Perspective**   140
   ULRICH BECK

   Index   153

Contributors

Ulrich Beck (1944–2015) was one of the most influential contemporary German sociologists. His work focused on questions of uncontrollability, ignorance, and uncertainty in the modern age, and he coined the terms 'risk society,' 'second modernity,' or 'reflexive modernization.' He also tried to overturn national perspectives that predominated in sociological investigations with a cosmopolitanism that acknowledges the interconnectedness of the modern world. He was a professor at the Ludwig-Maximilians-University in Munich and also held appointments at the Fondation Maison des Sciences de l'Homme (FMSH) in Paris, and at the London School of Economics.

Monika Büscher is Professor of Sociology at Lancaster University, UK, Director of the Centre for Mobilities Research, and Associate Director at the Institute for Social Futures. Her research explores the digital dimension of contemporary 'mobile lives' with a focus on IT ethics. She leads research on the informationalization of risk governance, exploring opportunities and challenges in national and international projects (BRIDGE, SecInCoRe). She edits the book series Changing Mobilities (Routledge) with Peter Adey.

Malene Freudendal-Pedersen is Associate Professor in Sustainable Mobilities at Roskilde University, Denmark. She has an interdisciplinary background linking sociology, geography, urban planning, and science and technology studies which she has been using to investigate praxes of mobilities and their significance for (future) cities. She is the co-manager of the international Cosmobilities Network, and the co-founder and co-editor of the new journal *Applied Mobilities* (Taylor & Francis). She is the author of the book *Mobility in Daily Life: Between Freedom and Unfreedom*.

Stephen Graham is Professor of Cities and Society at Newcastle University's School of Architecture, Planning and Landscape, UK. He has an interdisciplinary background linking human geography, urbanism, and the sociology of technology. Since the early 1990s he has used this foundation to develop critical perspectives addressing the politics of infrastructure, xii *Contributors*

mobility, digital media, surveillance, security, militarism, and verticality emphasizing, in particular, how these work to reshape contemporary cities and urban life. He is the (co-)author of several books including *Splintering Urbanism, The Cybercities Reader, Disrupted Cities, Infrastructural Lives, Cities Under Siege*, and *The City from Satellites to Bunkers*.

Vincent Kaufmann is Professor of Urban Sociology and Mobility at Ecole Polytechnique Fédérale de Lausanne (EPFL), Switzerland. After a master's degree in Sociology (University of Geneva) he earned his PhD at EPFL on rationalities underlying transport modal practices. He has been an invited lecturer at Lancaster University (2000–2001), Ecole Des Ponts, Paris (2001–2002), Nijmegen University (2010), and Université de Toulouse Le Mirail (2011). He is the (co-)author of several books including *Re-Thinking Mobility, The Social Fabric of the Networked City, Rethinking the City*, and *Slices of (Mobile) Lives*.

Xaroula Kerasidou is Research Associate at the Centre for Mobilities Research, Lancaster University, UK. Her research interests lie within the field of feminist science and technology studies where she focuses on the material and semiotic practices of technoscience. She works on the EU FP7-funded projects BRIDGE (http://bridgeproject.eu/en) and SecIn-CoRe (www.secincore.eu) and explores the social, legal, and ethical implications of technology.

Sven Kesselring is Research Professor in Automotive Management: Sustainable Mobilities at Nürtingen-Geislingen University, Germany. His research focuses on the sociology of (auto)mobilities, social theory, and the impact of technology and digitalization on everyday and professional lives. He is the founder and co-manager of the international Cosmobilities Network. From 2014–2016 he was vice-president of the International Association for the History of Transport, Traffic and Mobility (T2M). He is co-founder and co-editor of the new journal *Applied Mobilities* (Taylor & Francis). He has edited several books including *New Mobilities Regimes: The Analytical Power of the Social Sciences and the Arts* and *Aeromobilities*.

Christian Licoppe is Professor of Sociology at the Social Science Department at Telecom Paristech, France. He has worked in the field of mobility and communication studies for several years. He has used mobile geolocation and communication data to analyze mobility and sociability patterns of mobile phone users. He has studied extensively one of the first location-aware communities (the Mogi players in Japan, 2003–2008) and the rich configurations of augmented encounters its evolving culture supports. He has also developed ethnographic approaches of complex activity systems relying on innovative use of communication technologies, at the intersection of sociology of work, organization studies, and anthropology of activity. He is currently developing a general analysis of interactions in telepresence settings.

Contributors xiii

Katharina Manderscheid works as a senior lecturer in the Sociology Department of the University of Lucerne, Switzerland, teaching social science research methods. Her research in the field of mobility studies focuses on several aspects of automobility, methods for mobilities research, mobilities and social inequality as well as mobilities from a discourse and dispositif analytical approach. She is a board member of the Cosmobilities Network. She co-edited several books and special issues on mobilities studies, amongst which *The Mobilities Paradigm: Discourses and Ideologies* is the most recent one.

Rachel Oliphant is Research Associate at the Centre for Mobilities Research, Lancaster University, UK. Her work here has focused on two EU-funded projects, BRIDGE (http://bridgeproject.eu/en) and SecInCoRe (www.secincore.eu), where she has been part of a team exploring the ethical dimensions of IT-supported emergency response. More broadly she is interested in community responses to crises and the potential for collaborative design and community engagement.

Katrina Petersen is Research Associate, Centre for Mobilities Research (CeMoRe), Lancaster University, UK. Her research explores how diverse communities communicate and collaborate over time and space around complex notions of risk, especially the role of visualization tools, such as digital maps and satellite images. She has a PhD in Communication Studies and Science and Technology Studies, and a BA in Geology. She also worked in public engagement in science museums.

Mimi Sheller is Professor of Sociology and founding Director of the Center for Mobilities Research and Policy at Drexel University in Philadelphia, USA. She is President of the International Association for the History of Transport, Traffic and Mobility, founding co-editor of the journal *Mobilities*, and associate editor of the journal *Transfers*. She is author or co-editor of several books, including *Aluminum Dreams*, *The Routledge Handbook of Mobilities*, *Mobility and Locative Media*, *Consuming the Caribbean*, *Citizenship from Below*, *Tourism Mobilities*, and *Mobile Technologies of the City*.

John Urry (1946–2016) worked at Lancaster University, UK, as a distinguished professor of sociology after completing degrees at Cambridge. He was one of the most important British social scientists and his work had a high impact in many different disciplines. From 2003 to 2015 he was Director of the Centre for Mobilities Research (CeMoRe). He was co-founder of the *Mobilities* journal at Routledge and the Cosmobilities Network. From 2015 to 2016 he was Co-Director of the Institute for Social Futures at Lancaster University.

Preface

'Networked Urban Mobilities': This was the title for the conference and art exhibition that the Cosmobilities Network organized from the 5th to the 7th of November 2014 in Copenhagen. It was a big scientific event and the reason for it was the tenth anniversary of the international research network. The conference was jointly organized by a team from Aalborg University and Roskilde University.

About 160 participants came to Aalborg University's campus in Copenhagen and in this three-volume set many of them are presenting their work and ideas. The book you hold in your hand is the first volume and it compiles theoretical debates, conceptual considerations, and new ideas and perspectives which are prominent within the new mobilities paradigm. Volume two is edited by Malene Freudendal-Pedersen, Katrine Hartmann-Petersen, and Emmy Laura Perez Fjalland, and presents a wide range of contributions which have the ambition to illustrate the strength of and variety in subjects and empirical broadness within the mobilities paradigm. Its subtitle indicates this in a pithy way: 'Practices, Flows, Methods'. Volume three is edited by Aslak Aamot Kjærulff, Sven Kesselring, Peter Peters, and Kevin Hannam. It collects contributions from the conference on 'Art, Performances, Impacts', as the subtitle tells. By so doing it propels a topic which has been a significant element of the work within the Cosmobilities Network since the 2008 conference on mobility and art in Munich: to demonstrate the analytical power of art and social science.

The Conference in Copenhagen was a special event and a milestone for the network in many ways.

Firstly, the Cosmobilities Network celebrated its birthday. Ten years before a small crowd of people came together in Munich for a workshop on 'Mobility and the Cosmopolitan Perspective.' At this time no one considered this the birth of a long-lasting collaboration and research network. The name Cosmobilities was mostly a running gag on how to shorten cosmopolitan mobilities during these days. At some point John Urry laughingly said, 'This name calls for a network!' And more than a decade later, the Cosmobilities Network plays a substantial role within the mobilities turn in social science and beyond. At the tenth anniversary conference we were celebrating

Cosmobilities as an academic space, a place for encounters, and a synonym for cutting-edge research and scientific innovation. A huge number of individual scholars and research institutions worldwide have generated a new interdisciplinary literature and a new thinking on the social transformations of the modern mobile world, its risks, and opportunities. The 'new mobilities paradigm' has influenced work and thoughts of academic scholars as well as practitioners in public authorities, industry, and civil society.

Secondly, what we luckily didn't know at this time, it was the last Cosmobilities conference where two very important academic personalities and thinkers, who both played an important role in the 2004 workshop and the beginning of the network, were still with us.

German sociologist Ulrich Beck was invited to the 2004 workshop and in the aftermath he fostered the founding process of the Cosmobilities Network. In the 2014 Conference catalogue he wrote a welcome note to the participants, stating that Cosmobilities "has become a reflexive place and space for re-thinking the basic principles of modernity and for the future of modern societies."

John Urry's role since 2004 and up until a very sad day in March 2016 cannot be overestimated. In many ways he was and still is the 'spiritus rector' and the mentor of the network and of many, many mobilities scholars. Without his unique personality and his brilliant mind the network would not be what it is today. And this is said without any exaggeration. For the 2014 conference catalogue he wrote:

> Throughout the last decade Cosmobilities has provided a really brilliant space that has nurtured the emerging mobilities paradigm. As a horizontal network of many senior and junior colleagues you have done a great job in bringing together scholars from many different fields and theoretical approaches as well as research traditions. You have been bridging the gap between academia and practitioners, too. And hopefully Cosmobilities will long continue.

The book series *Networked Urban Mobilities* is dedicated to these two thinkers. Both of their words we consider as the assignment and the mission of the Cosmobilities Network. We hope that the book in your hand and all three volumes together will give an overview of the depth, the diversity, and analytical sharpness of the new mobilities paradigm and the potentials of the scholars of the network. Beyond this we wish you an exciting and illuminating reading experience.

We would be glad if this book aroused some interest in our work, and maybe we will see you at one of the next Cosmobilities conferences.

Malene Freudendal-Pedersen, Sven Kesselring
Copenhagen, September 2016

1 Networked Urban Mobilities

Malene Freudendal-Pedersen
and Sven Kesselring

In his 1903 seminal article on 'The Metropolis and Mental Life,' sociologist Georg Simmel made a point of defining cities as the incubators of societal—or in today's parlance: 'global'—transformations. As with much-analyzed metropolises, urban regions and increasingly the 'networked urbanism' (Graham and Marvin 2009; Kaufmann 2011) of globalized societies and economies give access to the general transformations of modern societies and their route into mobile risk societies. The 'urban field' (Lefebvre 2000) needs to be explored, experienced, and envisioned as nodes within global networks, scapes, and flows. Increasingly cities are being (re)produced by what flows *through* them rather than what is fixed *within* them (Derudder, Witlox, and Taylor 2013; Sheller and Urry 2006; Ritzer 2010). They function as 'spatial fixes' (Harvey 1990) in a space of global accumulation, constant mobilities, and transformation. To make cities places of lived social, economic, and ecological sustainability, it needs strong and socially coherent and inclusive mobility systems that are more than just transport systems and connections.

For this book, the urban perspective on mobilities and social change has not been chosen by chance; cities and regions constitute complex settings of social, technological, geographical, cultural, and digital networks of mobility (Urry 2000, 2007; Graham and Marvin 2009). The urban scale is an essential part of the global 'network society' (Castells 1996) with new forms of social and cultural life emerging and with strong impacts on ecological conditions. Mobilities research plays an important role in the future of cities by offering a strong approach that bridges research disciplines and traditions (Sheller and Urry 2006; Canzler, Kaufmann, and Kesselring 2008; Grieco and Urry 2011; Cresswell 2006). Mobilities encompasses the large-scale movements of people, goods, capital, and information, as well as the more local processes of daily transportation, communication, and the travel of artifacts (Urry 2000). These different mobilities are considered fundamental in framing modern social life and urban cultures. The mobilities turn offers analyses of societal consequences of path dependencies, funding decisions and technology policies, cultural transformations, the mobility practices and changing forms of sociality, embeddedness, social cohesion, and so forth.

2 Freudendal-Pedersen and Kesselring

In this introductory chapter we discuss some of the work that has had an impact on our understanding of cities today. The chosen excerpts will primarily be sociological perspectives on societal processes and how mobilities—even when only related to as a technical fixture called transportation—have had a defining role in the cities we know today. We write about the city, its planning and social life, and through this narrative we will also present a framework for the topics put forward by the contributing authors as they reach into the future of networked urban mobilities.

The City and Its Mobilities in a Historical Perspective

Even a cursory sketch of the story of the city and its mobilities would produce several books just by itself. When we start the story with Ebenezer Howard's vision of the garden city, it is because this has had a major impact on modern planning traditions. Ebenezer Howard (1902) created the utopia of the *Garden Cities of Tomorrow* as a solution to the big city's inhumane problems, as he called it. The issues facing cities in this early phase of modernization were: unhealthy living conditions; pollution from production; and heating and transport. Howard's utopia recognized this and focused solely on physical solutions and concrete problems, and less on the social happiness that could, and should, result from the realization of this vision. The planning ideal behind the Garden City was to create light, air, green spaces, institutions, and facilities to accommodate healthier living and work environments. It was thought of as creating rational and efficient localization, communication, and transport, to attract both factory owners and merchants, and with this a qualified and motivated working force that could reside in the neighborhoods with a balanced social diversity (Tonboe 1993). In many ways it was a re-ordering of the city, a way of creating rational systems for efficiency and development.

The Garden Cities of Tomorrow idea became an important inspiration in the development of the *Town and Country Planning Act* and the *Greater London Plan*, created under the leadership of Professor of Architecture, Sir Leslie Patrick Abercrombie. These plans were aimed at cleaning up the city, not only after World War II but also from the messy and unhealthy environment the city had become due to modernization. These plans became a big inspiration to the industrialized world and the functionalistic planning paradigm—still prevalent today—is largely an outcome of this. It has, for instance, inspired the development of the so-called Finger Plan in Copenhagen that has been the overarching planning principle for Greater Copenhagen from 1947 onwards (Freudendal-Pedersen 2015; Gaardmand 1993; Nielsen 2008). The Finger Plan consists of the inner city in the palm of the hand, and then transport, housing, and industry/business corridors along the fingers, and green spaces in-between. The Finger Plan (the fingers) also illustrates how the Garden City idea inspired the building of suburbs in cohesion with the spread of the family car. Howard's idea with the Garden City was not to make suburbs but instead to developed so-called 'New Towns' with the aim of building independent 'finished' towns, of limited size, located in close proximity to the city. Nevertheless the penetration of the family car and the opportunity to move away from 'the unhealthy city' meant that the overall idea inspired from the Garden City and 'New Towns' became the cornerstone in the growth of suburbs, and with this urban sprawl. Perhaps the significance of these ideas was that the big city—in the words of Jane Jacobs (1961)—was dying. She directly attacked the modernistic planning idea in her book *The Death and Life of Great American Cities* and not the least Howard for this development:

> The most important thread of influence starts, more or less, with Ebenezer Howard. . . . He not only hated the wrongs and mistakes of the city, he hated the city and thought it an outright evil and an affront to nature that so many should get themselves into an agglomeration. His prescription for saving the people was to do the city in. . . . His aim was the creation of self-sufficient small towns, really very nice towns if you were docile and had no plans of your own and did not mind spending your life among others with no plans of their own.
>
> (Jacobs 1961, 17)

And she continues by saying that "Howard made sense in his own terms but none in terms of city planning" (Jacobs 1961, 19). When this book was published, Jacobs was an active part of a campaign to stop Robert Moses' 'Lower Manhattan Expressway' that entailed tearing down Greenwich Village where she herself was living at the time. Jacobs was in strong opposition to the 'cleaning out' that the rationalistic planning paradigm entailed. You could say that she saw how this planning tradition was throwing the baby out with the bath water, when making the city too clean and too perfect. It also killed the life of the city—the places where people wanted to meet and to live. Her main argument was that the city holds opportunities to integrate people and places with different qualities. She suggested that the role of planning should be to support and balance the dynamics already existing and to establish equilibrium in the parts of the city where it was not present. Jacobs' book was also a direct critique of the planning ideals that Le Corbusier (1947) was involved in, in particular the CIAM planning doctrine and the Athens Charter. CIAM—the International Congress of Modern Architecture (1928–1959)—was where 28 European architects were engaged in formalizing the architectural principles of modernity and the functional city. This was later presented as the 'Athens Charter' where it was proposed that social problems could be resolved through strict functional segregation. Le Corbusier's utopian 'Radiant City' was composed of skyscrapers, zonings of mobilities, and functions, all placed within a park.

> Le Corbusier's Utopia was a condition of which he called maximum individual liberty, by which he seem to have meant not liberty to do

4 Freudendal-Pedersen and Kesselring

anything much, but liberty from ordinary responsibility. In his Radiant City nobody, presumably, was going to have to be his brother's keeper any more. Nobody was going to have to struggle with plans of his own. Nobody was going to be tied down.

(Jacobs 1961, 22)

Le Corbusier's ideas came to play a significant role in today's conception of urban mobility where zoning for the different mobilities and activities brings order to the urban territory (Debord and Wolman 1956, in Sadler 1999, 24). This conflict between the rationalistic planning paradigm (of cleaning up the city and zoning praxis of the people living there) and the fight for the lived city (where people can unfold and collaborate with each other and the materialities) is still going on today. In Copenhagen today, part of the story about why the city is often named as a very liveable city, is how 'lucky' it was that the city was so poor during the 1970s and 1980s. This meant that there was no money to follow the doctrine of a 'successful' city, meaning highways leading into the very center of the city, modern high-rises, parking facilities, and so forth. Due to these funding issues, Copenhagen has both blue and green elements (water and parks) as well as an infrastructure that doesn't focus solely on cars. In this sense, the fact that Copenhagen was so poor back then (and couldn't afford the planning ideas intended to propagate growth and prosperity) led to its success today.

The Social Fabric of Cities

Discussions of the social fabric of the city within science also took place alongside those of physical planning. Karl Marx and Friedrich Engels represented a historical materialism, where the urban and its mobilities were seen as a product of the economic-material development and process of production. The history of the working class was also the history of manufacturing and urbanization:

> A manufacturing establishment requires many workers employed together in a single building living near each other and forming a village of themselves in the case of a good-sized factory. They have needs for satisfying of which other people are necessary; handicraftsmen, shoemakers, tailors, bakers, carpenters, stonemasons, settle at hand. "The greater the town, the greater its advantages. It offers roads, railroads, channels . . . it offers a market to which buyers crowd."
>
> (Engels 1987, 66)

Marx also pointed out the connection between transport and growth for capitalism; or, in other words, that transport was an integral part of the process of production. When geographical distance is measured in time, and calculated in money, it becomes an important part of the circuit costs.

Networked Urban Mobilities 5

Thus the creation of the physical conditions of exchange—of the means of communication and transport—the annihilation of space by time—becomes an extraordinary necessity for it.

(Marx 1973, 524 (113))

During early modernization when these texts were written, the building of the physical infrastructure—to accommodate the necessary physical transport—was still in its early stages. This infrastructure could not be carried by the single producers alone—it required the community's help. The development of mobilities systems was part of defining the cities, as we know them today. At the same time it seems like we are now in the middle of a new turn due to virtual and mediated mobilities that enable new routines and systems for producers of the different elements that earlier made the city (Birtchnell 2016).

Like Marx and Engels, Max Weber (1958) was interested in investigating the macro scale with a specific focus on capitalism's institutional and bureaucratic foundation. Weber focused on the institutional scale—on the solidities and materialities of the city. But Georg Simmel chose another direction. He shifted the focus of sociological analysis away from the more general and objective (often hidden) pattern behind societies' metabolisms, which were dependent on the surrounding material world. He systematically investigated the micro scale of social relations and concentrated on individuals and groups, their social praxis and significant social phenomena, ideas, or trends. In his phenomenological approach, he considered the city not as "a spatial entity with sociological consequences, but a sociological entity that is formed spatially" (Simmel 1969, 178). Simmel analyzed the city as the place where a new social type emerged: the individualized, sophisticated, blasé, and superficial individual who needed a specific attitude to handle the strong positive and negative emotions condensed in the city. He considered being 'blasé' the logical reaction to economic and social transformations cities such as Berlin found themselves going through at the beginning of the twentieth century.

The Chicago School was largely inspired by Weber's and Simmel's sociologies. They defined the borders and limits of the growing city, and its urban socio-material structures, as their main frame of interest. Many of Chicago's social scientists paid close attention to the development of transportation and communication, and the movements of population, at an empirical level, and mobilities have been an essential part of this understanding of the city. McKenzie distinguished different kinds of mobility and documented their interrelations with urban changes and problems in his voluminous paper on *The Neighborhood* (1921). In the book *The City* from 1926, Park, Burgess, and McKenzie framed mobilities as significant in understanding the city:

Transport and communication, tramways and telephones, newspaper and advertising, steel construction and elevators—all things in fact,

6 *Freudendal-Pedersen and Kesselring*

which tend to bring about at once a greater mobility and a greater concentration of the urban population—are primarily factors in the ecological organization of the city.

(Park, Burgess, and McKenzie 1926, 2)

Also in this book, Burgess underlined in his chapter, 'The Growth of the City' (1926, 61), mobility as the pulse of the community and the city. He opens by distinguishing between movement and mobility in relations to growth:

Movement, per se, is not an evidence of change or of growth . . . movement that is significant for growth implies a change of movement in response to a new stimulus or situation. Movement of this kind is called *mobility*.

(Burgess 1926, 58)

This difference between movement and mobility has been recently discussed in relation to mobility potentials (Canzler et al. 2008) and aligns with Burgess' understanding of the difference between money and capital as described by Marx (1867). Mobility implies a change, a development bringing about diverse societal expansions and developments. Nevertheless Burgess' understanding of mobility—as essential in understanding the city—differentiates from the mobilities turn in its rationalistic view when he defines mobility as a tool to understand the expansion, as well as the metabolism, of the city. He suggests mobility as a tool that can be "susceptible to precise quantitative formulation, so that it may be regarded almost literally as the pulse of the community" (Park et al. 1926, 61).

This methodological, as well as theoretical, definition of mobility was used by Park et al. (1925) to create a rationalization on how to measure the city's expansion process and its effect on social systems. They suggested a concentric zone model, through which a city expands outwardly beginning in the central business district. Thereby the city is understood as consisting of many different sub-societies rather than one single environment. Through this human ecology perspective, the processes of stability, growth, and decline in various urban neighborhoods become related to economic resources, age, culture, ethnicity, and also mobility. In many ways this can be related to Jacobs' ideas that the role of planning should be to support and balance the dynamics that already exist within the city. Park et al. provided a sort of methodological toolbox to do this. The concentric zone model is still applied today within mobilities research—for instance when trying to understand the connection between mobilities and belonging (Jensen and Jørgensen 2016).

Mobilities as a Way to Better Understand the Urban

In more recent sociology, the approach of the Chicago School has been under critique for the human ecology ideas of a 'natural' determination of

Networked Urban Mobilities 7

social processes in the city. Castells (1976) asks, in a somewhat provocative essay, 'Is there an urban sociology?' with the intent to put focus on the lack of urban sociology interacting with societal relations. According to Castells the point is that spatial structure (the city) does not hold any independent explanative force in relation to social processes. Spatial conditional relations can have effects on the social dynamic but there is no naturalness in this relation. These discussions were part of what is known as the spatial turn, and as part of this the duality of structure and agency were considered. Giddens' (1984) structuration theory—in which the time-space dimension (inspired by Hägerstrand 1970) holds all action and social systems—enables us to understand the city as an agglomeration of time-space situated patterns of relational networks and the social praxes between actors or collectives. These discussions are a meeting between geography and sociology in an effort to meld social processes and spatial structures (Gregory and Urry 1985). Based on a Marxist understanding of political-economic structures as determining, David Harvey steps into this discussion and talks about the city from a perspective of uneven geographical development. Harvey says that it is important to distinguish between urbanism as a way of living and the urban form (Harvey 1973).

Concurrently new technologies, and the discussions they elicited, entered the scene. The introduction of information and communication technologies and the World Wide Web as every individual's possession (in the Global North) created a new inception for life and its urban(ized) mobilities. In the article 'Crisis, Planning and the Quality of Life' (1982), Castells is ruminating upon the apparent paradox existing between the enormous increase in mobilities and the rootedness of reproduction and social systems to space. He calls for "a new space' that based on the current historical process promotes city and regional government, gives opportunities for technological innovation, stimulates productivity, increases consumption and re-establishes communication. It seems that here Castells is searching for a 'new space' as the precondition for a different society, a space that can be used as a tool in the hands of those who dominate. In the article on offshoring in this book (Chapter 4), John Urry shows how mobilities have become this space, but with a less optimistic outlook than Castells imagined. Within the spaces and flows of mobilities, political-economic processes are disconnected from planning and government but nevertheless dominate the development of cities. As Bauman noted: "Mobility climbs to the rank of the uppermost among coveted values—and the freedom to move, perpetually a scarce and unequally distributed commodity, fast becomes the main stratifying factor of our late-modern or postmodern time" (Bauman 1998, 2).

Already in his early work, Urry searched for a different way to understand the time-space relations in cities, the connections between the materialities and the city and the ongoing social processes within the urban field. In his article 'Localities, Regions and Social Class' from 1981, he discusses how the effects of space are not stemming from the materialities of the space itself,

8   *Freudendal-Pedersen and Kesselring*

but from the causal power in the social elements occupying the relations in space. Yet he still emphasizes how "such spatial variations, of contiguity, or distance, or betweenness, do matter, and they matter in ways which social science has generally failed to recognize" (Urry 1981, 462).

In 2000, *Sociology beyond societies* consolidated these ideas and ignited a mobilities paradigm based on an understanding of mobilities as a specific process depending on, but also transgressing, space. In relation to the discussions on the spatial turn, Urry's approach can be seen as a way to overcome spatial fixity without taking the meaning out of space. In particular the triangle out of networks, scapes, and flows became central pillars of his analysis of the mobilized and cosmopolitanized world. As put by Mimi Sheller (2016) in her memorial article on the late John Urry:

> The new mobilities paradigm challenged the idea of space as a container for social processes, and thus brought the dynamic, ongoing production of space into social theory across many different domains of research.

Mobilities as Networks in the City

Within the mobilities paradigm there has been a lot of focus on the highly differentiated socio-material networks produced by mobilities (Elliott and Urry 2010; Larsen, Urry, and Axhausen 2006; Cwerner, Kesselring, and Urry 2009). Communities in pre-modern societies with low-pace mobilities was illustrated by Simmel (1923) as concentric circles, with the center being that of the individual's identity and belonging. In modern societies, mobilities' increasing speed and sheer extent have caused these circles to intersect, illustrating multiple identities in many communities. Kesselring (2008) elaborates on this through three models of networks: a centered model with a single core and different routes into other communities; a de-centered model with several cores with each of their additional routes; and lastly a networked model where different networks are overlapping, creating a myriad of routes. Kesselring's elaboration on Simmel's work shows the significance of virtual mobilities to social life. However, when Simmel points out that social interaction is significantly different depending on whether or not people are in spatial contact with each other, it seems he still has a relevant point today. According to him, some interactions can work for a period without personal interaction but in the end changes happen to the relationship (Simmel 1923, 641). The mobile lives and networks today are more significant for people living increasingly cosmopolitan lives, but still an everyday life that involves kids, work, leisure activities and so forth is often quite localized. Nevertheless, as Beck points out, we are all woven into a comprehensive process of the cosmopolitization through mobilities

> nobody can escape the global. This is because . . . the global—i.e., the cosmopolitized reality—is not just 'out there' but constitutes everybody's

strategic lived reality. . . . Even immobile people are cosmopolitized. People who have never left their villages, let alone ever boarded a plane, are still closely and commonly linked with the world: in one way or the other they are affected by global risks. And they are linked with the world not least because the mobile phone has come to be an integral part of the everyday across the globe.

(Beck 2016, 8–9)

Consumption is also increasingly mobilized today, in the sense that it is being grounded in mobility. This goes for shopping for groceries, clothes, electronics, furniture, etc., and also for cultural events, education, and so forth. Modern lives are increasingly based on mobility and communication, and increasingly on the Internet. As American science writer Jeremy Rifkin puts it, there is a transformative historical development at work that is fundamentally and irreversibly changing the (human) conditions of late modern culture:

In the nineteenth century, steam-powered printing and the telegraph became the communication media for linking and managing a complex coal-powered rail and factory system, connecting densely populated urban areas across national markets. In the twentieth century, the telephone, and later, the radio and television, became the communication media for managing and marketing a more geographically dispersed oil, auto, and suburban era and a mass consumer society. In the twenty-first century, the Internet is becoming the communication medium for managing distributed renewable energies and automated logistics and transport in an increasingly connected global Commons.

(Rifkin 2015, 28)

Despite the inventions in technologies within what we term mobilities systems, Castells pointed to the apparent paradox in the fact that neither production, reproduction, or social systems can be disconnected from space and its materialities. Here he warns about the regulated and politicized monopolistic-capitalist interests that dominate contemporary cities and points out that these developments will threaten human existence, the environment, civilization, and the legitimacy of democratic institutions (Castells 1983).

The Mobile Risk Society and the Urban Age

Today, cities are nodes in global networks—hubs to global space, and the flows running through them make them the power centers of the mobile risk society (Taylor 2004; Brenner 2004; Castells 1996). The urban has not lost any of its fascination since Simmel wrote his early twentieth-century essay on the world city. But since these times the ambivalent character of

10 *Freudendal-Pedersen and Kesselring*

the process of urbanization has become obvious as never before in history. Lewis Mumford's seminal writings on the modern city and urban dystopia have become part of the everyday discourse on the future: what is seen as a good (mobile) life; the sustainability of modern lifestyles; and ways of production and consumption. What has been called the 'urban age' (Burdett and Sudjic 2011) is not only occurring in megacities and global cities, it is a global phenomenon which does not stop at smaller cities but which connects urban spaces in a global pattern and structure. The urban field doesn't end at administrative borders, and through networks and systems of mobility, places all over the world are tied into spaces of global connectivity. There is a global process of urbanization at work, generated, sustained, and propelled by forms of worldwide-networked urban mobilities. The global connectivities of worldwide transport and communication networks are highly ambivalent (Kesselring 2009; Beck 2016). On the one hand they keep cities, with their institutions, actors, and forms of life, in the global 'space of flows,' yet on the other they are part of changing and threatening the very nature of what we used to consider the urban form or fabric. Urban lives, cultures, and economies are significantly challenged by different mobilities (Ritzer 2010; Urry 2011). Time-space compression, the digitization of the world, and the ongoing individualization process has a deep impact on all spheres of life. Every systemic, work-related and private element of interacting, collaborating, communicating, and social exchange has been affected by them—mobilized and cosmopolitanized. There is no such thing as local mobility any more. Every move, every journey, every communication is somehow connected and related to the global scale—be it through the interconnectedness of jobs to the global economy, through private and increasingly cosmopolitan social networks, or be it the logistics behind the food we eat, the beverages we drink, or the music we listen to and the products we buy, etc. Consumption is a global connector. Even if companies, restaurants, etc., try to use a high share of locally and regionally produced materials and ingredients, it is rare that the amount of 'local' products is higher than 40%.

Against this backdrop, the future of urban mobilities has become a key topic for the world risk society. We are not overestimating their relevance by saying that in the urban age the question of how cities and regions manage and plan their physical infrastructures (and, by doing so, the socio-material structures which shape and form social cohesion, interaction, participation, and social life) is one that is essential. Flow management—people, workforce, resources, knowledge, data, waste, energy, etc.—lies at the bottom of all social activity; it pre-structures cultures and all sorts of routines. Therefore, any talk about urban mobility cultures should include not only everyday culture, but also politics, business, planning, etc.

The question of how to structure the existing and future architectures, the technologies, the infrastructures, that is to say the *scapes* of cities, is in fact a form of 'designing'—if not somehow 'engineering'—the social layout and (at least) parts of human interactions, too (Latour 1991; Urry 2007; Law and Hassard 1999; Beckmann 2004; Tully 2003). Planners and engineers tend to focus on the feasibility, the societal and political acceptance and legitimacy of measures, when in fact this is the most durable form of materializing how societies consider the future of urban mobilities. Based on existing data, models, and calculations, planners and engineers mostly envision what, and how, decisions on spatial development, technology implementations, and other forms of regulations impact on CO_2 emissions, congestion, land use, the densification of cities and the consequences for ecosystems, etc. But the social consequences—the silent modifications of social configurations within neighborhoods, the interactive structures, and the social inequalities within cities—these aspects tend not to play a significant role when it comes to long-lasting decisions. And this is not because planners and engineers don't want them to be part of the decision-making process; mostly it is because the relevant data doesn't show up in the data sets, models, or simulations.

Networked Urban Mobilities

Discourses of urban futures are no longer locally embedded. The networked character of the urban field, the transnational and global connectivity and interdependencies in question of economic activities and work, migration, intercultural exchange relations, logistics, and transport, etc., almost ban local and even national concepts of cities and regions. Also, when rationalities of planning, urban design, and city marketing still play with the concept of place—of city identity and the brand character of cities—it shows that the 'container society logic' (Ulrich Beck) can't help to understand contemporary developments and transformation. The 'place' rationality still exists despite the fact that cities are part of global supply chains, global flows of workforce, interconnected through airline networks and global infrastructures such as airports, transnational rail connections, container networks and road networks, etc. The networked character of the cities of today can only be deciphered and understood when we acknowledge the fact that decisions, agency, and futures are shaped and reproduced by globalized and cosmopolitanized discourses. There is 'a power of the local' (see Berking 2006; Brenner 2004 and many more) and cities have many opportunities to structure and shape their futures. But at the same time they are embedded in globalized networks of power, which are transforming the future of urban lives and mobilities in an unchangeable and historically unique way. Against this background, Urry's statement hasn't lost any of its substance:

> Places are like ships, moving around and not necessarily staying in one location. In the new mobilities paradigm places themselves are seen as travelling, slow or fast, greater or shorter distances, within networks of human and non-human agents.

> (Urry 2004, 28)

12 *Freudendal-Pedersen and Kesselring*

And, as Beck writes:

> [The network of power] needs a mobility related research that focuses on places of flows and the power techniques and the strategies of boundary management that define and construct places and scapes where cosmopolitanization is possible. From these places we can learn how the cosmopolitan society works. The cosmopolitanization of modern societies does not happen in an abstract space of flows. It happens where and when the local meets the global and the channeling and the structuration of flows has to be made and organized. It is the hidden 'power of the local in a borderless world' . . . that structures and gives shape to global flows and mobilities.
>
> (Beck 2008, 34)

By starting out with Simmel's writings on the world city and referring to Howard's Garden City, we want to show the huge historical changes in the relationship between the urban, mobilities, and their socio-material networks. Throughout the last century—and with an extreme growth during the last decade—cities have become networked through diverse mobilities systems.

The contributing authors to this book illuminate, in many different ways, the challenges in understanding and analyzing the transformations of urbanism in a globalized, highly mobilized, and networked world. A lot of emphasis is placed on the virtual mobilities and how they change spaces, interactions, movements, communities, identities, technologies, and the materialities and the social fabric of the city.

Mimi Sheller focuses on how networked interaction is made possible through mobilities. She shows how this permeates urban lives and makes up a global 'third space' that we need to study in its entirety. The widespread wireless access to digital networks and location data provides a new potential to radically reconfigure urban mobilities, communication practices, and spatialities. This creates a new phenomenon of 'mobile medialities,' driven by concepts of smart cities, for example, or the Internet of things. It is composed of the massive generation of software systems speaking to each other and ensuring that particular mobilities or sortings take place. This goes for public services, for example health and social care, and also automated transportation, such as driverless cars and intelligent highways. Through location-aware smartphones, individuals are both part of virtual networks (while being guided through specific locations filtered by the settings on their phone) and the networks created.

In a highly political way, mobilities systems also allow for the presence of the security state's apparatus of surveillance and anticipatory anxiety. This is not only taking place in the Global North and the most advanced technologically advanced forms of urbanism, but also in the Global South and the excluded margins. Sheller frames this as the 'global shadows' where people

Networked Urban Mobilities 13

in the Global South or other spaces of exclusion find ways to tap into electric grids or wireless communication cells and create informal services and tap into networks. However, these processes are highly ambivalent. New possibilities are also emerging for people to create network capital and to work around infrastructural access to fix electrical power, or use phone companies as banks to make money transfers. Migrants arriving at the borders of Europe, who are highly connected through mobile phones, find maps and tips about the place they are arriving in or plan to travel to. Also, humanitarian workers can arrive at disaster areas packed with mobile informational technologies linking them to crisis informatics.

Christian Licoppe discusses an exciting aspect of networked urban mobilities. Like Sheller, he is touching upon discussions around 'mobile mediality.' He discusses some aspects of sociality in urban public places, which are especially relevant to the users of so-called 'locative media.' The availability of such technologies makes it possible to discover other people nearby using certain mobile apps and devices. While such 'discovered' fellow users may be previously unknown, they are not completely anonymous either, for some profile and personal information will usually be available digitally through the locative media. Licoppe describes encounters of this sort as encounters between 'pseudonymous strangers' and some of their specific features. 'Timid encounters' are thus a characteristic form of encounters between pseudonymous strangers in networked urban environments. They build on the different ways in which embodied, physical interaction in public places and online interactions on screen may be entangled. Finally he shows how the spread of locative media might reshape the urban experience, with the smart city of the future being a 'place for pseudonymous strangers' as much as the modern metropolis was, and still remains, a 'place for strangers.'

In his chapter on the worlds of offshoring, John Urry introduces us to a global phenomenon of mostly unseen, often unrecognized, but nevertheless powerful networks of semi-legal and illegal practices of money transfers and capital mobilities into so called 'treasure islands.' The recent publication of the 'Panama papers' by German newspaper *Süddeutsche Zeitung* and the British *Guardian* has generated a sad and disturbing publicity for it. The world of offshoring is highly relevant for the urban condition, mostly because the money transferred never lands in the environments where it has been generated or where the infrastructures, institutions, etc., that enable the actors of offshoring to be productive residents. Offshoring becomes a generic principle of contemporary societies, and it is impossible to draw a clear distinction between what is onshore and what is offshore. This has many consequences for urban relations, housing supply and prices, and the nature of work. In many ways the public has been privatized, enclosed, or commercialized at the outset in offshoring. The optimism rooted in globalization (as that which would create openness and various commons) has turned out to be its very antithesis. Instead, globalization has created diverse secret worlds of offshoring where resources, practices, people, and money

14 *Freudendal-Pedersen and Kesselring*

are secretly moved from one national territory to another. These worlds are made possible through new mobilities systems. The offshore world avoids taxation—money that could be used to maintain the commons of the networked city—for its urban relations, housing supply and price, and nature of work.

Seen here is a major arena of struggle between offshore worlds and various kinds of democratic and global organizations. In many ways cities are struggling with these phenomena and trying to find instruments to govern it and avoid being exploited by it. The stakes are indeed high as to how theses struggles will play out. And it is possible, as various dystopian futures remind us, that we may not have seen anything yet and the twenty-first century could be a century of 'extreme offshoring' with many further dark consequences for democracy and the possibilities of developing a post-carbon future.

Monika Büscher, Xaroula Kerasidou, Katrina Petersen, and Rachel Oliphant ask what it means to see disasters through the lens of networked urban mobilities. Their chapter aims to bring attention to which tools to consider in practices of risk governance. The practices around this constitute a particular form of networked urbanism characterized by interconnected infrastructures, netcentric organizations, and self-organized mobile publics. Mobilities, especially virtual mobilities, enable people affected by disaster to connect intensively with each other, the media, and emergency agencies. This often results in information overload, which hampers the emergency agencies ability to react, or the authorities ask people not to tweet locations of raids fearing suspects might monitor the communication. This creates landscapes of communication, interdependency, and responsibility that are difficult to handle, to react to, and be prepared for. They suggest that practices of information stewardship are central in establishing trust and coordinating information exchange, and point out that communities at risk are not static communities but dynamically evolving communities in relation to the specific event.

Stephen Graham focuses on in the crucial but often ignored role of vertical transportation technologies. He shows that elevators are by far not marginal urban phenomena but complex systems of mobility essential to the cultural politics of urban space. Innovations, especially in super-tall skyscrapers, interact with digital technologies to reduce overall movement by assigning potential riders to specific cars and thus increase speed. Elevator travel has long been a central component of cultural notions of urban modernity. The mobilities in elevators are unequally distributed; this goes for the design of the elevator but also, to a greater degree, with relation to the maintenance. The modernist dream of mass social vertical tower housing, inspired by Le Corbusier, was dependent on this vertical mobility. These housing projects are found in many cities today and generally occupied by people on low incomes, and the elevators have turned into "dystopian nightmares of extreme isolation and enforced withdrawal, especially for those with children or the less mobile." The super-fast elevators on the other hand stand as proxy indicators for urban growth and prosperity. The social inequalities in access to vertical transportation are carrying the same splintered geographies as, for instance, TVG trains or business flights. Even more invisible is the world of mining where elevators are not only essential but often a matter of life or death. Just as elevators are central to skyscrapers, faster and bigger elevators are crucial in systematically exploiting the resources in ultra-deep mines.

Vincent Kaufmann discusses the phenomenon that in recent decades mobility has become an increasingly important feature for social and professional integration. The ability to be mobile has become a key dimension of social position and success. In the past decade, car ownership and use has been declining in many European cities of over 500,000 inhabitants. This chapter aims to explore this apparent paradox based on a literature review, and outlines three ideal-type future mobility scenarios based on emerging trends. Based on these scenarios Kaufmann elaborates on the exciting observation that modern societies are on the threshold of radical changes in their relationship to mobility and transport.

Katharina Manderscheid engages in a methodological discussion on current work within mobilities studies and its ability to fully comprehend the interconnection between the human and the technologies and materialities that enable mobilities. She points out that research practices should not only be understood as descriptors of empirical worlds but they should also be considered as techniques to effect and coproduce these worlds. Against this background, she points out that mobilities research primarily draws on narrative qualitative work on the micro level. Manderscheid suggests it would be beneficial to look more closely at theories and methodologies interacting with technology (ANT, STS) as well as multilevel statistics. This would provide a contextualization of individual practices within broader structural backgrounds that could contribute to the way we conceive mobility and might be able to change it too.

The last chapter is a reprint of an article published first in Canzler, Kaufmann, Kesselring (2008) which can be read as a manifesto pointing out the challenges of mobility research in a cosmopolitan perspective. Ulrich Beck argues here that social science needs to abandon the analytical prison of 'methodological nationalism' and turn towards a radical 'methodological cosmopolitanism.' Only then can global risk dynamics, transnational relations, new inequalities, and the globalized images and symbols influencing everyday culture be brought into analytical focus. Two essential issues move to the fore: on the one hand the process of Europeanization; on the other the cosmopolitanization of cites and spaces. In both cases national patterns of explanation and legitimization fail. The questions elicited are: What is new about mobility viewed from the cosmopolitan perspective? How does the cosmopolitan gaze change the conceptual framework, the realities, and the relevance of mobility? Beck clearly sees that networks, scapes, and flows contain and generate powers that transform the mobilized risk society into a

16 Freudendal-Pedersen and Kesselring

constellation of cosmopolitanized societies. He asks what consequences this has for places and calls them 'places of flows,' localities and urban spheres where the cosmopolitanization of modern societies occurs. Only a mobility-related approach in social science can regain the power to understand the transformations that the late Ulrich Beck (2016) framed in his most recent work as the 'metamorphosis of the modern world.'

References

Bauman, Z. 1998. *Globalization: The Human Consequences.* Cambridge: Polity Press.

Beck, U. 2008. "Mobility and the cosmopolitan perspective". In *Tracing Mobilities: Towards a Cosmopolitan Perspective*, edited by Canzler, W., Kaufmann, V. and Kesselring, S., 25–36. Aldershot: Ashgate.

Beck, U. 2016. *The Metamorphosis of the World.* Cambridge: Polity.

Beckmann, J. 2004. "Mobility and safety". *Theory, Culture & Society*, 21, 81–100.

Berking, H., ed. 2006. *Die Macht des Lokalen in einer Welt ohne Grenzen.* Frankfurt and New York: Campus.

Birtchnell, T. 2016. "The missing mobility: Friction and freedom in the movement and digitization of cargo". *Applied Mobilities*, 1(1), 85–101. doi:10.1080/23800 127.2016.1148324.

Brenner, N. 2004. *New State Spaces: Urban Governance and the Rescaling of Statehood.* Oxford and New York: Oxford University Press.

Burdett, R. and Sudjic, D. 2011. *Living in the Endless City*, 1 Auflage. Berlin: Phaidon.

Burgess, E. W. 1926. "The growth of the city". In *The City*, edited by Park, R. and Burgess, E. W, 47–62. Chicago: The University of Chicago Press.

Canzler, W., Kaufmann, V. and Kesselring, S. 2008. "Tracing mobilities: An introduction". In *Tracing Mobilities: Towards a Cosmopolitan Perspective*, edited by Canzler, W., Kaufmann, V. and Kesselring, S., 1–10. Aldershot: Ashgate.

Canzler, W., Kaufmann, V. and Kesselring, S., eds. 2008. *Tracing Mobilities: Towards a Cosmopolitan Perspective.* Aldershot: Ashgate.

Castells, M. 1976. "Urban sociology and urban politics: From a critique to new trends of research". In *The City in Comparative Perspective: Cross-National Research and new Directions in Theory*, edited by Walton, J. and Masotti, L. H., 291–300. New York: John Wiley & Sons.

Castells, M. 1982. *Crisis, Planning, and the Quality of Life: Managing the New Historical Relationships between Space and Society.* Working paper/Institute of Urban & Regional Development, University of California, Berkeley no. 383. Berkeley: Institute of Urban and Regional Development, University of California, Berkeley.

Castells, M. 1983. *The City and the Grassroots: A Cross-Cultural Theory of Urban Social Movements.* California Series in Urban Development 2. Berkeley: University of California Press.

Castells, M. 1996. *The Rise of the Network Society.* Oxford: Blackwell.

Cresswell, T. 2006. *On the Move: Mobility in the Modern Western World.* New York: Routledge.

Cwerner, S., Kesselring, S. and Urry, J., eds. 2009. *Aeromobilities.* International Library of Sociology. London: Routledge.

Derudder, B., Witlox, F. and Taylor, P. J. 2013. "U.S. cities in the world city network: Comparing their positions using global origins and destinations of airline passengers". *Urban Geography*, 28(1), 74–91. doi:10.2747/0272-3638.28.1.74.

Elliott, A. and Urry, J. 2010. *Mobile Lives: Self, Excess and Nature*. International Library of Sociology. New York and London: Routledge.

Engels, F. 1987. *The Condition of the Working Class in England*. London: Penguin.

Freudendal-Pedersen, M. 2015. "Cyclists as part of the city's organism: Structural stories on cycling in Copenhagen". *City & Society*, 27(1), 30–50.

Gaardmand, A. 1993. *Dansk Byplanlægning 1938–1992*. København: Arkitektens forlag.

Giddens, A. 1984. *The Constitution of Society: Introduction of the Theory of Structuration*. Berkeley: University of California Press.

Graham, S. and Marvin, S. 2009. *Splintering Urbanism: Networked Infrastructures, Technological Mobilities and the Urban Condition*. Reprinted. London: Routledge.

Gregory, D. and Urry, J. 1985. *Social Relations and Spatial Structures*. New York: St. Martin's Press.

Grieco, M. and Urry, J., eds. 2011. *Mobilities: New Perspectives on Transport and Society*. Transport and Society. Farnham: Ashgate.

Hägerstrand, T. 1970. "What about people in regional science?" *European Congress: Papers*, 24, 7–21.

Harvey, D. 1973. *Social Justice and the City*. London: Arnold.

Harvey, D. 1990. *The Condition of Postmodernity: An Enquiry into the Origins of Cultural Change*. Cambridge and Oxford: Blackwell.

Howard, E. 1902. *Garden Cities of Tomorrow*. London: Sonnenschein.

Jacobs, J. 1961. *The Death and Life of Great American Cities*. A Vintage book V-241. New York: Vintage Books.

Jensen, H. L. and Jørgensen, A. 2016. "The life and influence of the 1925th Chicago-map". *Geoforum Perspekti*, 15(27), 33–47.

Kaufmann, V. 2011. *Rethinking the City: Urban Dynamics and Motility*, 1st edn. Milton Park: Routledge and EPFL Press.

Kesselring, S. 2008. "Skating over thin ice: Pioneers of the mobile risk society". In *The Social Fabric of the Networked City*, edited by Pflieger, G., Pattaroni, L., Jemelin, C. and Kaufmann, V., 17–39. Lausanne: EPFL Press.

Kesselring, S. 2009. "Global transfer points: The making of airports in the mobile risk society". In *Aeromobilities*, edited by Cwerner, S., Kesselring, S. and Urry, J., 39–60. International Library of Sociology. London: Routledge.

Larsen, J., Urry, J. and Axhausen, K. 2006. *Mobilities, Networks, Geographies*. Aldershot: Ashgate.

Latour, B. 1991. "Technology is society made durable". In *A Sociology of Monsters: Essays on Power, Technology and Domination*, edited by Law, J., 103–31. London: Routledge.

Law, J. and Hassard, J. 1999. *Actor Network Theory and After*. Oxford: Blackwell.

Le Corbusier. 1947. *The Four Routes*. London: Dennis Dobson.

Lefebvre, H. 2000. *The Production of Space*. Oxford: Blackwell.

Marx, K., ed. 1867. *Das Kapital: Kritik der politischen Ökonomie*. Hamburg: Meissner.

Marx, K. 1973. *Grundrisse*. Harmondsworth: Penguin.

McKenzie, R. D. 1921. *The Neighborhood: A Study of Local Life in the City of Columbus, Ohio*. Reprint. The Rise of Urban America. New York: Arno Press and The New York Times.

18 Freudendal-Pedersen and Kesselring

Nielsen, T. 2008. *Gode intentioner og uregerlige byer.* København: Arkitektskolens forlag.

Park, R. E., Burgess, E. W. and McKenzie, R. D. 1926. *The City.* With a bibliography by Louis Wirth. University of Chicago Studies in Urban Sociology, Vol. 1. Chicago: University of Chicago Press.

Rifkin, J. 2015. *The Zero Marginal Cost Society: The Internet of Things, the Collaborative Commons, and the Eclipse of Capitalism,* Palgrave Macmillan Trade paperback edn. New York: Palgrave Macmillan.

Ritzer, G. 2010. *Globalization.* Malden: Wiley-Blackwell.

Sadler, S. 1999. *The Situationist City.* Cambridge, MA: MIT Press.

Sheller, M. 2016. "Moving with John Urry". *Theory, Culture & Society,* April 20, 2016, at www.theoryculturesociety.org/moving-with-john-urry-by-mimi-sheller/.

Sheller, M. and Urry, J. 2006. "The new mobilities paradigm". *Environment and Planning A,* 38(2), 207–26.

Simmel, G. 1923. *Soziologie: Untersuchungen über die Formen der Vergesellschaftung.* München and Leipzig: Duncker & Humblot.

Simmel, G. 1969. "The metropolis and mental life". In *Classic Essays in the Culture of Cities,* edited by Sennett, R., 47–60. London: Prentice Hall.

Taylor, P. J. 2004. *World City Network: A Global Urban Analysis.* London: Routledge.

Tonboe, J. 1993. *Rummets Sociologi: Kritik af teoretiseringen af den materielle omverdens betydning i den sociologiske og den kulturgeografiske tradition.* Dissertation, Akademisk Forl. Univ., København, Aalborg, 1994.

Tully, C. 2003. "Growing up in technological worlds: How modern technologies shape the everyday lives of young people". *Bulletin of Science, Technology & Society,* 23(6), 444–56.

Urry, J. 1981. "Localities, regions and social class. *International Journal of Urban and Regional Research,* 5(4): 455–73.

Urry, J. 2000. *Sociology beyond Societies: Mobilities of the Twenty-First Century.* London: Routledge.

Urry, J. 2004. "The new mobilities paradigm". In *Mobility and the Cosmopolitan Perspective: A Workshop at the Munich Reflexive Modernization Research Centre (SFB 536),* edited by Bonß, W., Kesselring, S. and Vogl, G., 25–35, January 29–30. München: SFB 536.

Urry, J. 2007. *Mobilities.* Cambridge: Polity Press.

Urry, J. 2011. *Climate Change and Society.* Cambridge: Polity Press.

Weber, M. 1958. *The City.* Glencoe, IL: The Free Press.

2 Globalizing Networked Urbanism
Entanglements of Elite and Subaltern Mobilities

Mimi Sheller

Networked interactions increasingly permeate urban social lives, work practices, transport systems, and public spaces, whether in the technologically invested global cities of the 'developed' world or on the marginalized peripheries of the world's growing megacities and rural hinterlands, including the fact that state security agencies can sweep up every kind of data and track all kinds of movements. With the widespread wireless access to digital networks and locational data in many buildings and public spaces, in cars and in transit stations, in slums and in solar-powered rural villages, via phones, computers, cables, power lines, cell towers, and satellites, there is a constant remaking of the relation between urban and extra-urban im/mobility and communication practices, each with their entangled infrastructures, materialities, and spatial practices. Emergent networked urbanism therefore consists of uneven constellations of people, devices, systems, code, laws, regulations, and territoriality that together enable mobility and communication to be dynamically produced, distributed, and consumed, as well as contested, enforced, and circumvented (Parks and Starosielski 2015).

Through everyday mobilities around (and beyond) these networked infrastructures of global urbanizations—at a time of 'planetary urbanization' when the whole geography of urbanism as a fixed location is also in question (Brenner 2014; Brenner and Schmid 2014, 2015)—people across the planet are creating new ways of interacting with others, accessing resources, moving money, bypassing barriers, and building network capital. Studying mobilities today therefore means engaging with networked mobile communication technologies, locative media, and networked urbanism wherever they are found. And at the same time, urban studies requires an understanding of the changing and interconnected forms of mobility practices, materialized infrastructures, and mediated urban spatialities, both within and beyond the city and its urbanizing planetary (even extra-planetary) transects.

This chapter seeks to bring together the latest understandings of mobile locative media practices with an approach drawing on critical mobilities theory to better understand the material relations that connect elite and subaltern networked urbanism globally. It will sketch out three frames for thinking about global networked urbanism. The first concerns the global

20 Mimi Sheller

'kinetic elites' and how the day-to-day uses of mobile media and geoloca-tional data are producing new relations theorized as 'mobile mediality' and expressed through ideas such as 'sentient cities' and 'the Internet of things.' The second concerns the 'global shadows' and how technologies, infrastruc-tures, and models for networked urbanism 'from below' are being appropri-ated and mobilized across the Global South and other spaces of exclusion wherein people find new ways to tap into public electricity grids, access wireless communications cells, and create informal services such as mobile money transfer. The third frame, finally, attempts to show the frictions and connectivity between these two forms of networked urbanism, and the ways in which the kinetic elite and the subaltern shadows in fact make up one networked global 'third space'—encountered at fraught borders, danger-ous seam-spaces, and sometimes on common platforms—which we need to study in its entirety.

This analysis draws on 'materialist approaches' to media (influenced by Friedrich Kittler, James Carey, and Michel Foucault; see Packer 2003, 2013) which investigate the significance of communication as an embodied spatial practice that produces space/time and is itself constitutive of social orders and power (Packer and Wiley 2012); communication is not only performed, but performative. Critical mobilities theory likewise has elicited attention to the material infrastructures and 'moorings' of mobility and communication systems (Sheller and Urry 2006; Hannam, Sheller, and Urry 2006), including the deep time of media archaeologies based on oil, carbon, and the mining of metals, thus linking networked urbanism back to global political economies and geo-ecologies (Urry 2011, 2013). The study of contemporary networked urbanism therefore must encompass global geo-ecologies (such as appro-priations of metals, water, energy, and the resulting waste) and global geo-politics (such as governance of the movements of migrants, militaries, and humanitarian aid) if we are to understand the underlying interconnectivity of the im/mobilities at different scales that are remaking planetary urban spacialities and infrastructures.

In the following sections I describe the three frames for thinking about networked urbanism, the first focused on the most powerful urban centers and elites in (or connected to) the Global North; the second focused on more marginal global cities and 'shadow' populations in the Global South and other spatial peripheries; and the third suggesting a hybrid third space of globally networked urbanism embedded in planetary urbanization processes.

Networked Urbanism 1: Kinetic Elites

The first frame for thinking about networked urbanism concerns the ways it is imagined and brought into being in the global center of metropolitan hyper-connectivity envisioned and promoted (often by key corporate inter-ests like IBM or Google) as 'smart cities,' 'sentient cities,' 'connected mobil-ity,' or other such terms. As John Urry and I argued in *Mobile Technologies*

Globalizing Networked Urbanism 21

of the City, there "has been a massive generation of specific software systems that need to speak to each other in order that particular mobilities and 'sortings' take place" (Sheller and Urry 2006, 7). Both people and information, bodies and data, move through these technoscapes within the software— embedded and digitally augmented urbanism that various theorists describe as 'sentient cities' (Crang and Graham 2007), 'networked urbanism' (Graham and Marvin 2001, 30–33), 'networked place' (Varnelis and Friedberg 2006), 'net locality' (Gordon and de Souza e Silva 2011), or 'digital cityscapes' (de Souza e Silva and Sutko 2009), and as 'networked urban mobilities' here in this book.

What does networked urbanism mean in practice? How is it embedded in place and embodied in the experience of urban space and mobility? In "Place: Networked Place," Kazys Varnelis and Anne Friedberg argued more than ten years ago that:

> Contemporary life is dominated by the pervasiveness of the network. With the worldwide spread of the mobile phone and the growth of broadband in the developed world, technological networks are more accessible, more ubiquitous, and more mobile every day. The always-on, always-accessible network produces a broad set of changes to our concept of place, linking specific locales to a global continuum and thereby transforming our sense of proximity and distance.
>
> (Varnelis and Friedberg 2006, n.p.)

This global networking of place, they say, leads to "the everyday superimposition of real and virtual spaces, the development of a mobile sense of place, the emergence of popular virtual worlds, the rise of the network as a socio-spatial model, and the growing use of mapping and tracking technologies" (ibid., n.p.). If early accounts of such transformations were somewhat breathless and hyperbolic, they are nonetheless the jumping off point for subsequent technological trends and prognostications of a mobile sense of place. Screens and sensors were said to emerge everywhere, moving with users as they move, such that computing, according to Ash Amin and Nigel Thrift, will "become a pervasive part of the urban environment, with even the most mundane device having some computing power and some ability to communicate with other devices, so producing a constant informational hum" (2002, 102).

This informational hum is the basis for networked urbanism, and is increasingly the target of schemes for Open Data Cities and dreams for harnessing big data, which are supposed to improve governance. IBM Smarter Cities, for example, promotes a typical technological vision that "by 2020 all public services will be digitised and integrated transforming the way citizens interact with public services" such as emergency services, medical records, health and social care, driver assistance, and licensing.[1] High-density broadband is making Open Data Cities increasingly possible. Within a dynamic

22 *Mimi Sheller*

urban infrastructure, city-scale services like power in the form of smart grids with dynamic pricing algorithms, big data in the form of ubiquitous computing, and automated transportation (such as the potential for driverless cars and so-called intelligent highways) can adapt in real time through sensors, algorithms, and learning processes. As William Mitchell put it: "Now, nothing need be without processing power, and nothing need be left unlinked. . . . Networked intelligence is being embedded everywhere, in every kind of physical system. Code is mobile. Code is everywhere" (2003, 101). The various systems throughout a modern city are beginning to maintain persistent memories of their own use, communicate with each other about their status, and even reconfigure themselves based on dynamic needs, evolving into what Adam Greenfield (2006) dubbed a troubling 'everyware.' If this was the futurist vision, what has the practice been?

As user-generated maps and location-aware mobile devices became commonplace for smartphone users today, one's position, defined by latitude and longitude coordinates, became the entrance to the Internet (de Souza Silva and Sheller 2015). According to this logic, location works as a filter that determines the types of information one can access and the way one interacts with the spaces near and far. The pervasiveness of location-aware technology has made it possible to locate oneself and be socially networked while on the move, shifting the way one can connect to other people and to information while moving through connected physical places. We no longer enter so-called 'cyberspace' as a virtual realm—we carry it with us and are potentially immersed in it, 'always on' as a kind of augmented reality. We can access its diverse affordances even while moving, and locational awareness is increasingly integrated into transportation networks, including cars, airports, transit networks, and a range of new applications for accessing and sharing vehicles, determining walkability, or navigating amongst location-based transport options (Sheller and Urry 2006; see e.g. the popular Citymapper.com).

Mobile phones, GPS receivers, and RFID tags are only a few examples of location-aware mobile technologies that mediate our interaction with networked place and influence how we move in these spaces. Wearable computing brings this hum closer and closer to the body, incorporating our heart rates, steps taken, and stress levels into the computable code/space. As communication is extended by new mobile devices and accomplished in motion, it leads to everyday practices that I call 'mobile mediality' (Sheller 2013b), understood as a new spatiality formed by digitally mediated movement. Mobile mediality depends on the backgrounded array of satellites, cell towers, Wi-Fi, and Internet protocols, smartphones, smart buildings, and other interconnected communications infrastructure. New mobile medialities create the conditions for regenerative as well as degenerative cultural and spatial practices that are transforming fundamental dimensions of contemporary urban culture and urban space. They are also potentially presenting a challenge to the existing mobility regimes, which have dealt with movement, power, and control based on twentieth-century technologies and territorialities.

Ultimately there is a hybrid interface between physical and digital mobilities in the 'transduction' of 'code/space' which is increasingly automated, ubiquitous, and pervasive (Kitchin and Dodge 2011). Kitchin and Dodge define 'transduction' as "the constant making anew of a domain in reiterative and transformative practices" (ibid., 263). Space is animated and brought into being by this background of calculation and computation—which Nigel Thrift calls 'enacted environments.' Such systems are anticipatory rather than reactive. Pervasive data surveillance and forms of continuous real-time calculation—referred to by Nigel Thrift (2008) as 'qualculation'—create an artificial world that is said to be increasingly sentient, and potentially adaptive. This leads to the notion of 'networked objects' (Bleecker and Knowlton 2006), everything is embedded with sensors and is hooked into pervasive communication networks. Software is 'everyware' (Greenfield 2006) but is experienced as nowhere: a pervasive cloud, an invisible infrastructure, detached from its material basis in planetary resources, distant labor, repair and maintenance, and geopolitical power relations

This suggests a fundamental change in the everyday practice of mobility, as software invisibly delegates coordination to smart and intelligent environments, or imperceptibly leans on them to support already learned habits and routines. Code/space, in other words, taps into mobile habits. Thrift describes five key socio-technical characteristics of the contemporary moment: 1) "a structured continuity which always privileges the appearance of movement"; 2) gesture-awareness and interactive surfaces; 3) 'awhereness' in which "the continuity of motion becomes locative as the world is tagged with an informational overlay"; 4) constant feedback, enabling "interactive composition" in real time; and 5) that "cognition becomes even more of a joint experience between persons and things" (2011, 8–11). The networked urbanism of the future is still exploring all of these aspects of enacting hybrid space, but these appear to be the emerging qualities of this new code/space.

However, the 'sentient city' also offers a continuous immersive and pervasive presence of the security state's apparatus of surveillance and anticipatory anxiety, while 'splintering' the new 'awhereness' away from those whom it excludes, bypasses, and disconnects (Graham and Marvin 2001). In highly political ways, then, mobility systems become crucial points of anxiety, fear, and securitization—whether to search out terrorists, smugglers, undocumented migrants, or people with fevers. This is a sketch of a realm of networked urbanism as imagined from the seats of power in the Global North. Mobilities research offers new theoretical perspectives and new mobile methods to empirically investigate such mixed realms of physical and digital space, defining a global networked urbanism of the elite.

Nevertheless, urbanism is a complex emergent global system of networked connections, dominant mobility regimes, and critical counter-practices. It is

24 *Mimi Sheller*

not sufficient to deal only with the Global North and the most technologically advanced forms of urbanism. It is crucial that we understand how such emergent forms of networked urbanism are also connected with the Global South, with megacities, slums, rural peripheries, extractive industries, places of waste disposal, hidden labor, and the excluded margins. In the next section, then, I turn to this wider vision of networked urbanism as it emerges through subaltern appropriations of the technologies and infrastructures of mobility and connectivity.

Networked Urbanism 2: Subaltern Appropriations

In the Global South, on the margins of global cities everywhere, and in the regions that James Ferguson (2006) calls the global shadows of the neoliberal world order, the challenges of precarious access to mobility and communication produce the sharpest contours of uneven network capital. Another vein of mobilities research contributes new approaches to understanding the technological, social, and cultural developments in mobilities, border control, mobile communication, 'intelligent' infrastructure, and surveillance in the non-privileged zones of global networked urbanism. In particular, some researchers focus attention on how these networked infrastructures are extended and appropriated by forces of both governance and resistance (e.g. Graham and Marvin 2001; Packer 2008; Vukov and Sheller 2013). How do the denizens of urban informal districts outrun control and build 'cities from scratch' (Fischer, McCann, and Auyero 2014)? How do marginalized people and relegated places insert themselves into 'signal traffic,' whether seizing it for themselves or disrupting its logics, its territorialities, and its exclusions (Parks and Starosielski 2015)?

The mobility systems that constitute urbanism include ticketing and licensing of drivers, oil and petroleum supply, electricity and water supply, addresses and postal systems, road safety and public safety protocols, station interchanges, websites, money transfer, luggage storage, air traffic control, barcodes, bridges, time-tables, CCTV surveillance, and so on (see Sheller and Urry 2006, 5–6). Some of these systems engage physical infrastructure, while others concern informational systems, but all have a kind of global currency that flows across regions and striates territories. Some involve moving things like bodies, vehicles, oil, or water; while others involve moving things like data, code, and images. Physical and informational mobility systems are being tightly coupled into complex new configurations, such that mobility systems are becoming more complicated, more interdependent, and more dependent on computers and software, but also are deeply embedded in *global* physical and material contexts that are locationally specific. Thus there is an emphasis on materiality, difference, unevenness, and relations of power in recent work on the invisible

Globalizing Networked Urbanism 25

infrastructure of mobile networks and computer servers (Farman 2015), on the laying of undersea cables (McCormack 2014; Starosielski 2015), and the geography of satellites and signal transmission (Parks and Schwoch 2012; Parks and Starosielski 2015).

Dynamic constellations of global and local mobility and communication can be said to exhibit various kinds of uneven topologies, turbulence, disruptions, differential speeds, and frictions, which at the same time offer handles, channels, and frequencies for interruption 'from below.' The reconfiguration of complex mobility, communication, and information systems via the mobile phone, therefore, is not simply about infrastructures or control systems, but is about reconfiguring the public itself, its meanings, its spaces, its capacities for self-organization and political mobilization, and its multiple and fluid forms. It is the mobile phone's ubiquity and mobility that allows it to bridge public and private spaces in ways that are crucial to political mobilization—in Cairo as much as Manila or Kingston. What kinds of social and material practices allow some to remain highly connected even in the midst of general disconnection (see Sheller 2016a)— moving through the same physical topographies but connected to different Hertzian topologies? How do uneven mediations jump spaces, scales, and subjects? And if subaltern publics have already appropriated infrastructural possibilities, how might these be refashioned and built on to strengthen and democratize existing modes of social and political action and urban governance?

New possibilities are emerging for people to create network capital using new 'work arounds' that bridge demands for infrastructural access and possibilities for mobile connectivity. Some examples from the 'global shadows' include the use of transformers in Kibera, Kenya, that are, as described by *The Economist,*

> run by shady types who tap into the city grid. They are less than scrupulous when it comes to safety and they charge heavily. But at least Kibera has power, unlike many other parts of Africa. Soft drinks sold in shops are chilled. Rooftops are awash with TV aerials and mobile phones are as ubiquitous as in the West.
>
> (*Economist* 2013–2014, 11)

Likewise, when vendors close their shops,

> they deliver their cash receipts to nearby mobile-phone stores. Kenyan phone companies double up as banks; they take deposits and transfer funds. After decades of being excluded from banking, slum-dwellers now move their money fast and often; they no longer keep it under the mattress.
>
> (Ibid., 13)

26 Mimi Sheller

And in another example of infrastructural appropriation a company called Sarvajal, meaning 'water for all' in Sanskrit,

> sells clean drinking water to more than 70,000 people in rural India. . . . In small villages it installs solar-powered water dispensing machines that can be topped up just like a mobile phone. The machines send data to a central server via SMS, which helps Sarvajal ensure regular supply of clean water.
>
> (Ibid., 23)

In the first case energy infrastructure is appropriated for other needs such as powering television and phones; in the second case mobile phone companies are appropriated to serve as banking and money transfer conduits; and in the third case an entirely new kind of connected network is built to provide clean water. Other examples abound. Energize the Chain, for example, is a project that uses power from cell towers to refrigerate blood-bank deliveries brought by motorcycle to parts of rural Africa.[2] These examples all offer a different vision of networked urbanism, blending digital access and material needs in innovative ways. However, just as the hype surrounding the 'smart city' shaped the visions of the globally networked elite, so too do outlets like *The Economist* feed into the 'for good and for profit' hype around harnessing Information and Communications Technologies for Development (ICTD). As Lisa Parks trenchantly asks, "How can ICTD research be used to stage interactions geared toward the introduction of technological potentials and possibilities [that reorder political relations] as opposed to idly advancing deterministic agendas of technological integration, adoption, and revelry?" (Parks 2015, 133).

As I have explored elsewhere, even Haitians in small rural villages may have pretty sophisticated mobile communications technology at hand (Sheller 2016a), which may serve many important purposes including organizing financial remittances from abroad through the innovation of 'mobile money' (Baptiste, Horst, and Taylor 2011). These remittances, as well as the circulation of various other kinds of locational information across the Haitian diaspora, were hugely significant elements of the recovery effort after the 2010 earthquake. Mobile money is itself an important appropriation of cell phone networks for remote banking and person-to-person money transfer purposes—which depend on the locatability of the recipient and the conversion of data into money at specific physical locations. There is always an ongoing struggle between control 'from above' and efforts to appropriate, hack, or game the system 'from below' (Horst 2013), through various appropriations of technology that redirect infrastructure into everyday social practices (McFarlane, Desai, and Graham 2014). Through these struggles over 'infrastructuring' (Star 1999) users may create fissures and new possibilities for connection, which may have important effects on national space, on scalar relations, and on governance and control (Horst and Miller 2006; Baptiste et al. 2011).

As wireless broadband becomes more accessible and affordable, a growing number of people across the world has access to these kinds of mobile interfaces, and increasingly the Internet is being accessed by mobile smartphone, not by computer. Being able to consistently and persistently locate ourselves and be located (or perhaps cloak one's location) within this mobile digital network through location-aware technologies fundamentally changes how we understand both the Internet and the physical space around us (Gordon and de Souza e Silva 2011; de Souza e Silva and Sheller 2015). More and more forms of moving (as well as staying still, waiting, pausing) combine and mix together aspects of physical and digital locatability at the same time; moreover both people and things are locatable and can trade in the currency of locational information—thus creating a new kind of hybrid environment. Of course the choice to go off-grid or disconnect, to become hyper-local, also becomes a position within this field of possibilities.

In their work on mobile gaming, Christian Licoppe and Yoriko Inada (2012, 2015) note that the concept of hybrid ecologies was introduced within the Human-Computer Interaction (HCI) research field to describe new classes of digital ecology that merge multiple environments, physical and digital together. In the broadest view, the concept of *hybrid ecologies* covers all kinds of screen-mediated situations that switch between on and off screen in the course of activities, whether mobile gaming, smartphone use, navigation, or 'ambient play' (Hjorth and Richardson 2014).

Yet few have studied how such hybrid ecologies unfold in the Global South. What if navigating through such hybrid ecologies were also joined with the entrepreneurial practices that Clapperton Mavhunga (2014) has described in the African context as 'transient workspaces'? In such cases, micro accounts of the phenomenology of proximity-aware walking intersect with deeper macro histories of mobilities, colonial power, and difference. Mavhunga shows how forms of everyday innovation in Zimbabwe deepen our idea of technologies of mobility and communication. Likewise, Lisa Parks describes the 'walking phone workers' who provide access to mobile communication in Mongolia (Parks 2014), as well as the problematically maintained intersections of wireless cellular phone technology with water infrastructure and energy access in rural Zambia (Parks 2015). How are new technologies such as cell phones or mobile money being creatively incorporated into the existing cultural practices of such transient workspaces, fleeting material infrastructures, and fragile practices of urban/rural improvisation?

Mobilities research reminds us that culture, lived experience, and meanings are all crucial elements of technological systems (Cresswell 2006). Any network of planetary urbanization is made up of technologies, practices, infrastructures, networks, and assemblages of all of these—as well as narratives, images, and stories about them—which together inform its mobility culture. Critical mobility thinking in the field of urban studies calls for "re-conceptualising mobility and infrastructures as sites of (potential) meaningful interaction, pleasure, and cultural production" (Jensen 2009, 139), where people engage in 'negotiation in motion' and 'mobile sense making'

28   *Mimi Sheller*

(Jensen 2010). We therefore need a more extensive and complex understanding of how such meaningful interaction, cultural production, and mobile sense-making takes place in the contexts of networked urbanism across the Global South. What other global stories can we tell about the meanings of such hybrid, transient, and networked urbanism?

Networked Urbanism 3: Hybrid Global Third Spaces

In the third frame for networked urbanism we can begin to recognize that the first and second forms described above are in fact interconnected and symbiotic, rather than separate terrains. The empowered networked urbanism of the kinetic elites in the centers of global metropolitan power rubs up against and confronts the subaltern networked urbanization of the global shadows, where laborers, farmers, slum-dwellers, refugees, undocumented migrants, and various other marginalized and possibly vulnerable populations seek access to and seize mobility by any means necessary. Subaltern networked urbanism hacks into infrastructures, flows across borders, and connects remote peripheries, resisting the divisive territorialities of elite-exclusive infrastructures. In the view from above, this becomes a matter of securitization and management of such global networked urbanism, a question of 'governmobility' (Bærenholdt 2013); in the view from below, this will be a matter of escape, resistance, serious play, and capillary power in the Foucauldian sense (cf. Sheller 2016b).

For example, Peter Adey argues in *Aerial Life* (2010) that the "emergence of biometrics in contemporary airports, border zones, security spaces and everyday life sees the systematic use of biological and bodily data as a means to identify and manage risky mobile populations, focusing upon not territory but vectors" (Adey 2010, 88–89). These are vectors of global networked urbanism in which forms of enrollment, self-selection into 'trusted traveler' programs, and passenger responsibility to present the data-ready body all build on colonial practices of mapping, visioning, and surveying (Amoore 2006; Amoore and Hall 2009; Salter 2008). Data-veillance enables (neo) colonial governance not only through the mapping of territories and the regulation of mobilities across borders, but also through the biopolitical management of disciplined and racialized bodies enrolled in self-disclosure at the border check-point. Yet as borders become increasingly mobile and controlled via software there are also new potentials for smuggling, trafficking, and 'no border' activist resistance (Mountz 2010; Vukov and Sheller 2013). Recent migrants arriving at the borders of the European Union, for example, have been described as highly connected via mobile technologies through which they stay in touch with family, download maps and local information, and find social media tips on where to go, where to find shelter, and how to avoid danger. The refugees from the wars of the Middle East and North Africa who cross national borders are well-equipped transnational denizens with flexible skills in using mobile technology.

Globalizing Networked Urbanism   29

Secondly, we can think of global networked urbanism that embeds itself in the fabric of urban infrastructure and 'sentience.' Building on Georg Simmel's ideas of 'urban metabolism' and Henri Lefebvre's 'rhythmanalysis' (Lefebvre 2004), mobility theorists argue that bodies and objects shape cities, and in turn are shaped, through their rhythms of movement, their pace and synchrony (Edensor 2011, 2014). At the same time, big data is increasingly being embraced as a way to capture, visualize, and act on such urban rhythms, in the constant predictive algorithms of qualculation. So we see networked urban infrastructures of communication becoming sites for tracking mobility, easily tapped into by security agencies and mined for their rich locational data, but also open to the possibilities of counter-practices and alternative uses.

Historians of mobility and place-making emphasize the rhythms, forces, atmospheres, affects, and materialities that are assembled around various modes of transport (Edensor 2014; Adey 2010). This approach to global metabolism can now be extended to the rhythms, forces, and atmospheres of the rubber dinghies arriving from Turkey on the Greek island of Lesbos, or the buildup of pressure at Calais where migrants seek to enter the Channel Tunnel, or the dismal loss of life as boats leaving North Africa sink in the Mediterranean, just off the island shores of tourist 'places to play' (Sheller and Urry 2004). In cases of migrant detention and refugee camps we can see clearly how containment and mobility are coproduced. As Alison Mountz and collaborators put it:

> We find paradoxical issues of containment and mobility, as well as bordering and exclusion built into national and transnational landscapes of detention. . . . Detention functions as part of a rationale to *regulate* mobility through technologies of exclusion rather than to end mobility altogether.
>
> (Mountz, Coddington, Catania, and Loyd 2012, 524)

And so there emerges "a principle of managed mobilities, mobilizing and immobilizing populations, dislocating and relocating peoples" (Loyd, Mitchel-Eaton, and Mountz 2016, 4) forming a kind of global metabolism of networked urban and ex-urban mobilizations and demobilizations.

Thirdly, along with spatiality and materiality there is also a growing interest in temporalities within mobilities research. Temporalities of slowness, stillness, waiting, and pauses are all part of a wider sensuous geography of movement and dwelling in which human navigation of embodied, kinaesthetic, and sensory environments are crucial (Bissell 2007; Jensen 2010; Vannini 2014). There are interferences between the rhythms and temporalities of the kinetic elites (Birtchnell and Caletrio 2014) and those of the global shadows who may have to work in their employ, vacate land for their use, or seek to circumvent them. Sometimes the fast temporalities of capital circulation slam into the slow pace of getting things done in faraway places;

30 Mimi Sheller

other times the conscientiously slowed temporalities of tourism conflict with the hustle of people selling goods and services for a living. The rhythms and sensations of the burgeoning megacities of the Global South spill over into global networked urbanism. Mobile communication technologies and the innovation around practices such as mobile money also allow for new temporalities and rhythms of networked urbanism that bridge the shadowy peripheries and the metropolitan cores and their corridors of security.

Fourthly, especially in cases of disaster where one group's mobilities have been severely disrupted while others seek to bring aid, there can be strange effects of uneven physical and communicational connectivity and disconnectivity. As I have described elsewhere, based on my own empirical research in post-earthquake Haiti (Sheller 2013a, 2016a), humanitarian responders, researchers, engineers, and armed forces arrived equipped with various kinds of mobile informational technologies for communicating as well as gathering, geotagging, and mapping information. In addition, the United Nations peacekeeping force had bases with very strong communications infrastructure, including satellite dishes and radio or cell towers. The humanitarian responders held meetings on the UN base and used mobile phones and laptop computers with Internet connections to communicate and share information. Yet they also excluded local people, territorializing their own mobility power through physical, linguistic, and infrastructural barriers to access.

This mobile, locational, communicational infrastructure connected the emergency response to an entire field known as 'crisis informatics' involving 'digital humanitarian organizations,' crowd-sourced information, and open-source mapping. Groups like Ushahidi worked to aggregate, verify, and curate the data into open-source GIS mapping platforms (haiti.ushahidi. com). This kind of open mapping project potentially makes micro-level disaster news and information accessible and searchable by location, so that interested parties can zero in on specific sites or types of information. Such networking tools are now considered crucial for crisis mapping and global humanitarian organization in response to disasters, and indeed have been described as a kind of bottom-up 'social collective intelligence' that can complement more top-down orchestration (Büscher, Liegl, and Thomas 2014). But how can such resources be appropriated by the marginalized?

Perhaps there are other ways in which the kinetic elites of the Global North can seek to extend mobile resources to the excluded margins. Birtchnell and Hoyle argue that the use of 3D printing for development projects, known as 3D4D, "offers a solution to the disconnected supply chains, collapsed economic markets, and vulnerability of the citizenry characteristic of disaster settings and clusters of poverty in the Global South" (2014, 7). They offer inspiring examples of how it is being used as "a bottom-up development option in the Global South," including the case of iLab/Haiti[3] which 3D prints recycled plastic into goods like prosthetic hands and umbilical cord clamps. Yet bridging such hybrid spaces of electronic interactivity requires paying closer attention to the capabilities that people already have and how these might be built on in ways that might strengthen their network capital and extend their existing modes of action (Sheller 2016a).

Using communication technology to build grassroots development networks only works if there are communities organized to appropriate technology and adapt it to their needs, rather than the imposition of high-tech solutions from outside. Democratizing digital access is not simply about creating open maps and crowd-sourced data. It requires meeting people half-way, at the connected locations where they join mobile connection to energy, undersea cables, cell towers, and satellites; where they transport bodies, goods, and information to physical and virtual places; and where they turn mobile money into access to actual land, water, and shelter. Only then will planetary urbanization improve lives.

Conclusion

This discussion of three different visions of globally networked urbanism has tried to show some of the prevailing discourses and cultural practices around emergent hybrid ecologies of physical/digital connectivity as they impact on and produce different kinds of planetary urban spatialities. In the first instance networked urbanism is assumed to refer to the most technologically advanced locations of the Global North, used by the kinetic elites of the (over)developed world. In the second instance, though, we see that there is also an appropriation of such technologies of mobility and connectivity in the Global South, as well as in certain corporate and humanitarian projects to 'save the world' with new networked technologies. Finally, though, I have suggested these two forms of networked urbanism must be seen in relation to each other, whether in friction-filled conflict or symbiotic cooperation. Ultimately we exist in one globally networked process of ongoing urbanization, however splintered and uneven its infrastructural access may be.

What lessons can be learned from this argument? I conclude that we need both a deeper historicizing of mobilities research in terms of colonial histories, global geographies, and neo-imperialism, as well as a deeper ecologizing of the material resource bases of mobility in extractive industries (Sheller 2014). This brings me to argue for bringing in Foucauldian perspectives on uneven mobilities (Sheller 2016b), including:

- 'Genealogical' attention to histories of the colonial, imperial, and military apparatus that forms a *sovereign terrain for movement* in which there are divergent pathways, differential access.
- 'Archaeological' attention to the deeper geo-ecologies of resource extraction and energy use that support the splintered infrastructures and uneven materialities of (im)mobility.

All kinds of mobilities—whether corporeal, communicative, imaginative, virtual, or the physical transit of objects (Urry 2007, 47–48)—are always

32 Mimi Sheller

grounded in earthly materialities which do calamitous damage to the natural environment, and to settled ways of life, which in turn often drives further migration, urbanization, and displacement.

Thus I would advocate for a deeper planetary and geo-ecological perspective on mobilities and communication, showing how human and non-human mobilities are deeply interconnected, and part of complex extensive systems of planetary urbanization. Networked urbanism is not simply about 'building a better world,' as some corporations describe it, but is part of the transduction of planetary spaces of uneven livability and the struggles from below to re-imagine the whole world as a more just and egalitarian hybrid ecology.

Notes

1. https://youtu.be/p3qOpU7QttY.
2. www.energizethechain.org/.
3. www.ilabhaiti.org.

References

Adey, P. 2010. *Aerial Life: Spaces, Mobilities, Affects*. Chichester: Wiley-Blackwell.

Amin, A. and Thrift, N. 2002. *Cities: Reimagining the Urban*. Cambridge: Polity.

Amoore, L. 2006. "Biometric borders: Governing mobilities in the war on terror". *Political Geography*, 25, 336–51.

Amoore, L. and Hall, A. 2009. "Taking bodies apart: Digitized dissection and the body at the border". *Environment and Planning D: Society & Space*, 27(3), 444–64.

Bærenholdt, J. O. 2013. "Governmobility: The powers of mobility". *Mobilities*, 8(1), 20–34.

Baptiste, E., Horst, H. and Taylor, E. 2011. "Earthquake aftermath in Haiti: The rise of mobile money adoption and adaptation". *Lydian Journal*, 7.

Birtchnell, T. and Caletrio, J., eds. 2014. *Elite Mobilities*. London: Routledge.

Birtchnell, T. and Hoyle, W. 2014. *3D Printing for Development in the Global South: The 3D4D Challenge*. Basingstoke: Palgrave Macmillan.

Bissell, D. 2007. "Animating suspension: Waiting for mobilities". *Mobilities*, 2(2), 277–98.

Bleecker, J. and Knowlton, J. 2006. "Locative media: A brief bibliography and taxonomy of GPS-enabled locative media". *Leonardo Electronic Almanac*, 14(3).

Brenner, N., ed. 2014. *Implosions/Explosions: Towards a Study of Planetary Urbanization*. Berlin: Jovis.

Brenner, N. and Schmid, C. 2014. "Planetary urbanization". In *Implosions/Explosions: Towards a Study of Planetary Urbanization*, edited by Brenner, N. Berlin: Jovis.

Brenner, N. and Schmid, C. 2015. "Towards a new epistemology of the urban?" *CITY*, 19(2–3), 151–82.

Büscher, M., Liegl, M. and Thomas, V. 2014. "Collective intelligence in crises". In *Social Collective Intelligence Computational Social Sciences*, edited by Miorandi, D., Maltese, V., Rovatsos, M., Nijholt, A. and Stewart, J., 243–65. Zurich: Springer.

Globalizing Networked Urbanism 33

Crang, M. and Graham, S. 2007. "Sentient cities: Ambient intelligence and the politics of urban space". *Information, Communication & Society*, 11(6), 789–817.

Cresswell, T. 2006. *On the Move: Mobility in the Modern Western World*. London: Routledge.

De Souza e Silva, A. and Sheller, M., eds. 2015. *Mobilities and Locative Media: Mobile Communication in Hybrid Spaces*. New York: Routledge.

De Souza e Silva, A. and Sutko, D. M., eds. 2009. *Digital Cityscapes: Merging Digital and Urban Playspaces*. New York: Peter Lang.

The Economist. 2013–2014. "Transforming cities special edition". *The Economist*.

Edensor, T. 2011. "Commuter: Mobility, rhythm, commuting". In *Geographies of Mobilities: Practices, Spaces, Subjects*, edited by Cresswell, T. and Merriman, P., 189–204. Farnham and Burlington, VT: Ashgate.

Edensor, T. 2014. "Rhythm and arrhythmia". In *The Routledge Handbook of Mobilities*, edited by Adey, P., Bissell, D., Hannam, K., Merriman, P. and Sheller, M., 163–71. New York: Routledge.

Farman, J. 2015. "The materiality of locative media: On the invisible infrastructure of mobile networks". In *Theories of the Mobile Internet: Materialities and Imaginaries*, edited by Herman, A., Hadlaw, J. and Swiss, T., 45–59. New York and London: Routledge.

Ferguson, J. 2006. *Global Shadows: Africa in the Neoliberal World Order*. Durham: Duke University Press.

Fischer, B., McCann, B. and Auyero, J., eds. 2014. *Cities from Scratch: Poverty and Informality in Urban Latin America*. Durham: Duke University Press.

Gordon, E. and de Souza e Silva, A. 2011. *Net-Locality: Why Location Matters in a Networked World*. Malden and Oxford: Wiley Blackwell.

Graham, S. and Marvin, S. 2001. *Splintering Urbanism*. London: Routledge.

Greenfield, A. 2006. *Everyware: The Dawning Age of Ubiquitous Computing*. Berkeley, CA: New Riders Publishing.

Hannam, K., Sheller, M. and Urry, J. 2006. "Mobilities, immobilities, and moorings". *Mobilities*, 1(1), 1–22.

Hjorth, L. and Richardson, I. 2014. *Gaming in Social, Locative and Mobile Media*. New York: Palgrave Macmillan.

Horst, H. 2013. "The infrastructures of mobile media: Towards a future research agenda". *Mobile Media and Communication*, 1(1), 147–52.

Horst, H. and Miller, D. 2006. *The Cell Phone: An Anthropology of Communication*. Oxford: Berg.

Jensen, O. B. 2009. "Flows of meaning, cultures of movements: Urban mobility as meaningful everyday life practice". *Mobilities*, 4(1), 139–58.

Jensen, O. B. 2010. "Negotiation in motion: Unpacking a geography of mobility". *Space and Culture*, 13(4), 389–402.

Kitchin, R. and Dodge, M. 2011. *Code/Space: Software and Everyday Life*. Cambridge, MA: MIT Press.

Lefebvre, H. 2004. *Rhythmanalysis: Space, Time and Everyday Life*. London: Verso.

Licoppe, C. and Inada, Y. 2012. "When urban public places become 'hybrid ecologies': Proximity-based game encounters in Dragon Quest 9 in France and Japan". In *Mobile Technology and Place*, edited by Goggin, G. and Wilken, R., 57–88. London: Routledge.

Licoppe, C. and Inada, Y. 2015. "Mobility and sociality in proximity-sensitive digital urban ecologies: 'Timid encounters' and 'seam-sensitive walk'". *Mobilities*, 11(2), 264–83.

34 *Mimi Sheller*

Loyd, J., Mitchel-Eaton, E. and Mountz, A. 2016. "The militarization of islands and migration: Tracing human mobility through US bases in the Caribbean and the Pacific". *Political Geography*, 53, 65–75.

Mavhunga, C. C. 2014. *Transient Workspaces: Technologies of Everyday Innovation in Zimbabwe*. Cambridge, MA: MIT Press.

McCormack, D. P. 2014. "Pipes and cables". In *The Routledge Handbook of Mobilities*, edited by Adey, P., Bissell, D., Hannam, K., Merriman, P. and Sheller, M. London: Routledge.

McFarlane, C., Desai, R. and Graham, S. 2014. "Informal urban sanitation: Everyday Life, poverty, and comparison". *Annals of the Association of American Geographers*, 104(5), 989–1011.

Mitchell, W. J. 2003. *Me++: The Cyborg Self and the Networked City*. Cambridge and London: MIT Press.

Mountz, A. 2010. *Seeking Asylum: Human Smuggling and Bureaucracy at the Border*. Minneapolis: University of Minnesota Press.

Mountz, A., Coddington, K., Catania, R. T. and Loyd, J. 2012. "Conceptualizing detention: Mobility, containment, bordering and exclusion". *Progress in Human Geography*, 37(4), 522–41.

Packer, J. 2003. "Disciplining mobility: Governing and safety". In *Foucault, Cultural Studies and Governmentality*, edited by Bratich, J., Packer, J. and McCarthy, C., 135–61. Albany: State University of New York Press.

Packer, J. 2008. *Mobility without Mayhem: Safety, Cars, and Citizenship*. Durham, NC: Duke University Press.

Packer, J. 2013. "The conditions of media's possibility: A Foucauldian approach to media history". In *The International Encyclopedia of Media Studies*, Vol. 1, edited by Vadivia, A., 2–34. London: Blackwell Publishing Ltd.

Packer, J. and Wiley, S. C., eds. 2012. *Communication Matters: Materialist Approaches to Media, Mobility and Networks*. New York: Routledge.

Parks, L. 2014. "Walking phone workers". In *The Routledge Handbook of Mobilities*, edited by Adey, P., Bissell, D., Hannam, K., Merriman, P. and Sheller, M. New York: Routledge.

Parks, L. 2015. "Water, energy, access: Materializing the internet in rural Zambia". In *Signal Traffic: Critical Studies of Media Infrastructures*, edited by Parks, L. and Starosielski, N., 115–36. Urbana: University of Illinois Press.

Parks, L. and Schwoch, J., eds. 2012. *Down to Earth: Satellite Technologies Industries and Cultures*. New Brunswick: Rutgers University Press.

Parks, L. and Starosielski, N., eds. 2015. *Signal Traffic: Critical Studies of Media Infrastructures*. Urbana: University of Illinois Press.

Salter, M., ed. 2008. *Politics at the Airport*. Minneapolis: University of Minnesota Press.

Sheller, M. 2013a. "The islanding effect: Post-disaster mobility systems and humanitarian logistics in Haiti". *Cultural Geographies*, 20(2), 185–204.

Sheller, M. 2013b. "Mobile mediality: Location, dislocation, augmentation". In *New Mobilities Regimes in Arts and Social Sciences*, edited by Witzgall, S., Vogl, G. and Kesselring, S., 309–26. London and New York: Routledge.

Sheller, M. 2014. *Aluminum Dreams: The Making of Light Modernity*. Cambridge, MA: MIT Press.

Sheller, M. 2016a. "Connected mobility in a disconnected world: Contested infrastructure in post-disaster contexts". *Annals of the Association of American Geographers*, 106(1), 330–9.

Sheller, M. 2016b. "Uneven mobility futures: A Foucauldian approach". *Mobilities*, 11(1), 15–31.

Sheller, M. and Urry, J., eds. 2004. *Tourism Mobilities: Places to Play, Places in Play*. London: Routledge.

Sheller, M. and Urry, J., eds. 2006. *Mobile Technologies of the City*. London: Routledge.

Star, S. L. 1999. "The ethnography of infrastructure". *American Behavioral Scientist*, 43(3), 377–91. doi:10.1177/00027649921955326.

Starosielski, N. 2015. *The Undersea Network*. Durham, NC: Duke University Press.

Thrift, N. 2008. *Non-Representational Theory: Space, Politics, Affect*. New York: Routledge.

Thrift, N. 2011. "Lifeworld Inc: And what to do about it". *Environment and Planning D: Society and Space*, 29, 5–26.

Urry, J. 2007. *Mobilities*. Cambridge: Polity Press.

Urry, J. 2011. *Climate Change and Society*. Cambridge: Polity.

Urry, J. 2013. *Societies Beyond Oil*. London: Zed.

Vannini, P. 2014. "Slowness and deceleration". In *The Routledge Handbook of Mobilities*, edited by Adey, P., Bissell, D., Hannam, K., Merriman, P. and Sheller, M., 166–24. London and New York: Routledge.

Varnelis, K. and Friedberg, A. 2006. "Place: Networked Place". In *Networked Publics*. Cambridge, MA: MIT Press. Accessed 9 July 2017 at http://networkedpublics.org/book/place

Vukov, T. and Sheller, M. 2013. "Border work: Surveillant assemblages, virtual fences, and tactical counter-media". *Social Semiotics*, 23(2), 225–41.

3 Mobile 'Pseudonymous Strangers'

How Chance Encounters Constitute Sociality in Digitally Augmented and Location-Aware Urban Public Places

Christian Licoppe

The modern, industrialized metropolis of the twentieth century has been described as a 'city of strangers' (Lofland 1998), in which the paths of large-scale fluxes of mobile bodies unknown to one another mingle in the course of their daily mobilities (Whyte 1980). For twentieth century sociology, one characteristic and constitutive feature of urban mobilities in metropolitan public places was the expectation that encounters in public places would mostly involve unknown and anonymous strangers (which made unplanned encounters with acquaintances an unusual and noticeable event). 'Stranger' does not involve here the kind of alterity implied for example in Simmel's early use of the concept (Simmel 1971), but highlights the fact of being unacquainted with the persons with whom one crosses paths. This was a transformation from the village or small community perspective, in which the default expectation would be the reverse, that is that one would mostly encounter familiar faces and known people (which would make encounters with outsiders highly noticeable). Goffman has analyzed systematically the organization of focused and unfocused encounters between anonymous strangers in public places and highlighted the importance of normative expectations regarding the preservation of face and leaving others mostly alone. In that respect, Goffman's civil inattention appears as a moral expectation and a crucial practical resource in the management of encounters with strangers in urban public places (Goffman 1971).

An implicit assumption in this representation of the modern metropolis as a nexus for a swarm of anonymous strangers is that those are mobile, unconnected bodies, with no means to acquire, or to have acquired, some prior knowledge about one another. However, urban denizens today can be expected to be equipped with connected mobile devices, which mediate new forms of awareness of their surroundings. I will pay special attention to the case in which they also have access to mobile locative media. By locative media we will mean here any kind of application or services which uses and indexes the position of its user, implicitly or explicitly, and evolves dynamically with it. Locative media applications are currently very diverse, with the kind of location awareness or proximity awareness they provide varying greatly in its explicitness from one application to another: mobile

Mobile 'Pseudonymous Strangers'   37

games, location-sensitive recommendation applications, location-sensitive social networks, mobile dating, or dynamic car-sharing applications. However, all these kinds of locative media share a common core feature: They are designed so as to augment digitally one's knowledge about one's current urban environment, in a dynamical way (meaning such knowledge is updated as people move around in the city). As such, and even if existing locative media have either failed or succeeded mostly in niche markets, and been making only slow and irregular headway in our everyday practices as shown by communication research (de Souza e Silva and Sutko 2009; Wilken and Goggin 2012; Farman 2013; de Souza e Silva and Sheller 2014; Hjorth and Richardson 2014), and Human-Computer Interaction (HCI) research (Benford et al. 2003; Brown and Laurier 2012), one may wonder what kind of social behavior would develop in cities, should their use become pervasive, for passersby might not be expected to be anonymous strangers anymore.

To pursue this sort of thought experiment, I will consider first situations in which, disregarding the use of mobile locative media, people may meet strangers about whom they have some prior knowledge. I will in particular argue that, before the development of locative media, such encounters between what I would call 'virtual acquaintances' had to be planned, and to involve some form of earlier reference or interaction at a distance. While such encounters are becoming more frequent with the development of digital networks and the 'Uberization' of urban services, I will try to show that mobile locative media bring a distinctive twist in making us aware of people around us and providing us with sources of knowledge about them (by making available some profiles, or allowing us to chat on screen with them). With mobile locative media, such encounters do not have to be planned anymore, for they allow their users to 'discover' the presence of what we could call 'pseudonymous strangers' (people we have never heard about but that we can check online as we happen to become aware of them for instance) close to them wherever their urban mobilities take them. Therefore, if mobile locative media should develop and become pervasive, we must reconsider a fundamental tenet of urban studies: The city should not be treated as a place for strangers, but as a place for pseudonymous strangers, that is the kind of public place where the default expectation underlying encounters would be that they will involve pseudonymous strangers.

To give an empirical basis to this argument, I will rely on examples taken from the fast growing state of the art in this domain, and my own extensive ethnographic fieldwork, considering in more detail three types of mobile locative media. The first set of applications I will discuss are location-aware games, from early experiments (Benford et al. 2003) to current and emergent large-scale platforms of location-based gaming (Hjorth and Richardson 2014), such as the Google-based Ingress (Morel 2014), with a particular focus on the pioneering Mogi game in Japan (Licoppe and Inada 2006; Licoppe and Inada 2010). I will also consider a proximity-based gameplay

38 *Christian Licoppe*

in which, unlike in the fully location-aware games which provide dynamic on-screen maps of the current gameplay, players only become aware of the proximity of one another through notifications of their Wi-Fi- or Bluetooth-sensitive terminal, such as the Dragonquest 9 game (Licoppe and Inada 2016). Second, we will take the example of social networking applications, which combine checking in one's location and various forms of spatial recommendations, from the insights provided by the seminal Dodgeball (Humphreys 2007, 2010) to current mobile social networking platforms and particularly Foursquare (Frith 2013, 2014; Licoppe and Legout 2014). Third and last, we will discuss recent forms of proximity-sensitive dating applications such as Grindr in the gay community (Blackwell, Birnholtz, and Abbott 2014; Brubaker, Ananny, and Campbell 2014), and the emergent Tinder and Momo. In the case of Grindr, proximity awareness seems to be used in a way which promotes casual hookups (Race 2015), and therefore occasions many sexually-oriented encounters with pseudonymous strangers (Licoppe, Rivière, and Morel 2015). This extensive empirical spectrum is enough to provide a broad enough basis on which first to provide some examples of encounters between pseudonymous strangers and their characteristic features, and second to draw generalizable conclusions about the possible transformation of a networked urban sociality with the spread of mobile locative media, which is the purpose of this chapter.

Planned Face-to-Face Encounters With 'Virtual Acquaintances'

To analyze such encounters, it is useful to consider first a very particular kind of encounter between unknown parties, namely collocated encounters in which two persons who have never met before (and are therefore usually unable to identify one another) but who know something about one another actually meet. Such encounters involve others who are both strangers and acquaintances of sorts. He/she is a stranger because we have never met him/her in person and we would not recognize one another by sight. He/she is an acquaintance because there has often been some form of communication between us from a distance, even if we have not met in person. In older times, such remote interactions could have been accomplished through written correspondence, but today it would rely on phone or electronic communication. With respect to the distinct criteria of visual familiarity and acquaintance, such a virtual acquaintance (previously unseen, but heard of or talked to) can be contrasted to the 'familiar stranger' (Milgram 1972). The familiar stranger is that unknown person the face of which may become familiar in the course of repeated mobilities and encounters, but with whom interaction remains non-existent or minimal, precluding the sharing of personal information. The virtual acquaintance is visually unfamiliar, but some personal knowledge about him/her has been made available, either through prior interaction or by references from other parties.

Mobile 'Pseudonymous Strangers'   39

This could be some unknown person whom a well-intentioned friend has recommended you meet for a job or any kind of personal service, someone whose ad you answered to exchange some goods, or a virtual relationship constituted online and with whom you eventually arrange a face-to-face meeting.

The experience of meeting face to face such virtual acquaintances used to be a rather rare occurrence. Such encounters would almost always involve careful planning (and therefore the project to meet): Since such protagonists have never met in person before, it would take very special circumstances for them to be able to discover they are collocated by chance, without planning for it. A typical early twentieth-century example would be people meeting through personal ads in newspapers and organizing a first date in some public place (Cocks 2009). Such an example highlights (1) the role of media in making possible and relevant such encounters and (2) a typical and central concern of the parties concerning a first face-to-face encounter between virtual acquaintances: recognizing someone one has never met before but already interacted with, among a crowd of strangers, with an element of possible misdirection at play. In the interview excerpt below, a woman who has been using a web-based dating site describes such an encounter, including how she relied on environmental cues to identify and recognize her unknown partner, and how some mismatch between her expectations and his appearance became a significant issue.

Extract From an Interview (A Is the Interviewee, Q the Interviewer)

A. So er, him (she smiles), I met him after work, in the Halles. We were supposed to meet, we had made an appointment . . . we did not know one another so we counted on the fact that we would be the only two people waiting there and . . .

Q. Was it outside or inside a café?

A. It was outside at the corner of . . . it was in the Halles at the corner of Place du Chatelet and . . . ah I was disappointed because I had fantasized him . . . I said to myself . . . well I was fantasizing about his first name, I loved his first name, I loved his voice. He had seemed interesting in the small talk we had made on the phone. And er well he did not match what I expected physically.

The common practice of pre-arranging visual cues such as clothing details is a testimony both to the relevance of identification concerns and to the difficulty of managing such identification practically. With respect to the previous section, such special situations can be said to be 'folded' by design. Because a collocated encounter has been scheduled with an unknown acquaintance, one 'knows' that some unmet party may be around, so that one's surroundings, here and now, can be inspected for her visual discovery, while some

40 Christian Licoppe

representations and expectations of that unmet other are available from a prior history of remote earlier interactions. This duality of access and the joint relevance of both direct perception of the other and of what transpired from previous exchanges at a distance is characteristic of these situations, which can be described as 'folded' (Licoppe 2016). A consequence of it is a constant orientation, in the course of identification, to try to match what is perceptible to expectations emerging from a prior story of remote interactions or references *in absentia*. It highlights and makes highly noticeable potential mismatches and misalignments, which may threaten the potential unity of the situation and make relevant some alignment work and requalification of expectations of the persons involved.

Coming back to the importance of media, and especially digital media in a networked world, it is interesting to note that in the extract above, the interviewee was a user of a web-based dating site. All the digital platforms which connect strangers online to make them able to interact around relational or commercial issues offer opportunities for them to build online virtual acquaintanceships before possibly meeting one another face to face. Such encounters have to be planned for when for the first time. The very first phases of such rendezvous raise issues of recognition/identification (because such people have not met in person) and of matching immediate sensorial evidence with expectations based on digital profiles and earlier interactions. The extension of such social networking platforms to mobile devices and the generalization of peer-to-peer collaborative approaches to all kinds of services are providing more opportunities for this particular kind of encounter to occur. For instance, in an ongoing ethnographic study of a French web-based platform for ride sharing, we recorded first encounters between passengers and drivers. Usually the passenger has checked the profile of the driver online before, and they have interacted when planning to meet somewhere to start the trip. On the appointed day and time for the travel, the passenger has to find and identify the car and the driver she has never seen (or only an online picture) around the meeting point. It is usual that she calls the driver on her mobile phone for guidance, sometimes remaining on the phone as she gets to the car. This highlights another characteristic feature of such encounters today, that is the possibility to interact with people close by 'directly,' in an unmediated way, and 'indirectly,' through mobile devices, a point to which we will come back later.

When interviewed, passengers describe how, in the final approach and early stages of such encounters, they try to fit their online reading of the driver's profile and their previous (mediated) interactions with what they can perceive now they are physically together. The situation is a bit different with respect to the other passengers, for they usually have not checked one another or interacted online before, and they usually meet as anonymous strangers around the car. The so-called 'Uberization' of the service economy provides increasing opportunities for such encounters between virtual acquaintances to proliferate in urban public places. However, whether for

Locative Media: Enabling Chance Encounters Between Virtual Acquaintances and 'Pseudonymous Strangers'

dating, ride sharing, or buying large things on eBay, the co-present rendez-vous have to be planned in advance. This is precisely where mobile locative media make a significant difference.

Because of the practical problems involved in identifying and recognizing one another, meetings with virtual acquaintances could only exceptionally happen by chance. You in general had to know beforehand that such a virtual acquaintance was around to be able to identify him/her. But with many kinds of locative media, users are provided with a sense of the proximity and location of other users. If you are a locative media user, a central feature of these devices is to allow you to 'discover' the presence or proximity of other users around you, thus allowing for the possibility of chance encounters with them. These encounters may involve virtual acquaintances, but most of them will concern what we might call 'pseudonymous strangers': these are other users with whom one may never have interacted or talked about before (unlike virtual acquaintances), but who are not complete strangers either, for the locative application usually makes available some info about them, such as an electronic tag name (which may be an actual name or an electronic pseudonym), together with some elements of profile and prior history of use (if privacy settings allow for it). This may happen as well with proximity-sensitive mobile games such as Dragonquest 9 or Ingress, location-sensitive mobile social networking applications such as the general purpose Foursquare, or the dating-oriented Grindr and Tinder.

With such devices, and even more so as they become more pervasive, chance encounters with virtual 'acquaintances and pseudonymous strangers become not only possible, but also commonplace. With proximity-aware and location-aware locative media, when two users of the same mobile platform get close to one another, their mobile devices may 'recognize' one another, so that the mobile application makes each one aware of the presence of the other under the guise of his/her digital persona (how they appear within the mobile application), either through notifications or real-time maps. If they choose not to ignore their mutual awareness of the presence of the other and initiate an encounter, they find themselves in the situation of recogniz-ing visually someone they have never met physically, but of whom they have some digital notion (through profiles in the mobile application, and/or prior communication).

Grindr, for instance, is organized around proximity awareness. If one con-nects to the application, gay contacts and their profiles become available on screen, and they are ranked according to spatial distance, with the closest first. Encounters with potential new partners (or 'casual hookups') may now occur by chance, unlike the online dating example above. In the excerpt below one user describes such an encounter, in which he connects to the application in

42   *Christian Licoppe*

a gay bar and 'discovers' another Grindr user, previously unknown to him, in the same place (Licoppe et al. 2015):

> Once I happened to see a guy near me in a bar, and between what he gave off and what he had put on his profile, I found that completely paradoxical and I told him so. He looked much better on the profile than he actually looked. But it was not a question of his physical appearance, but more of what he was emanating. It was (on the profile) like "open guy, kind and positive" and here was a guy who was scowling and did not appear to be easygoing at all. I sent him a message, he looked down and he did not even answer it. I was almost in front of him and he saw very well, and he did not have the balls to reply, even on Grindr.
>
> (C., 40 years old)

The main difference between this example and the previous one taken from an online dating interview is that, while in the earlier example the face-to-face encounter between pseudonymous strangers was the product of design (it was pre-arranged), here it happens by chance. Otherwise, one finds again the characteristic features of encounters between virtual acquaintances and pseudonymous strangers. The 'discovered' potential partner is available and 'known' on screen through his mobile application identifier and profile, so that the match between the digital impression which is made through the mobile application and his physical appearance becomes enough of a concern to be mentioned explicitly. The situation involves managing the articulation of the online profile and the co-present person. However, the Grindr user also describes how the situation was managed by using its seamfulness as a resource. Though face-to-face conversation was a possibility (since they had recognized one another), contact was made by text messaging, so that face-to-face interaction appeared to be missing or 'avoided.' Implicit here is the normative orientation that mutual awareness of co-proximity should be acknowledged in interaction through overt recognition and greetings (Licoppe and Inada 2010).

Locative media therefore make possible the 'discovery' of a pseudonymous stranger with whom one has some sort of online connection but has not met in person before, and may not even have interacted online before (as was the case with virtual acquaintances), as an unplanned and serendipitous occurrence. This is a general feature, which is not limited to dating applications. The next excerpt is taken from a field study of Foursquare users in Paris (Licoppe and Legout 2014). In this location-aware mobile social networking application where users may check into particular 'places' (as defined by geolocation and online descriptors), two Foursquare users who have been checking in and competing for the 'mayorship' of the same hotel thus describe their encounter.

> This summer I was having a holiday in la Réunion, and I spent one afternoon with an Air France stewardess, precisely because she was checking in on Foursquare, and she came to look for me at the reception of the

hotel, saying "Are you the Sandrine who just robbed me of my position of mayor for this hotel?" I said yes and we spent the afternoon talking about her job and many other things. And so these are real encounters I would not have made, she would not have talked to me if I had not been on Foursquare.

(Sandrine, 45 years old)

This is another instance of a chance encounter between pseudonymous strangers. They had never met, and knew one another only through their having previously checked in at the same Foursquare 'place,' that is an indirect form of interaction. Mutual awareness occasions an encounter. Unfolding the articulation between physical and online co-presence is limited here to recognition and initiation of talk (through direct queries). Matching online profiles and physical appearances is much less of an issue than with dating applications. The way the event above is told, there is also less playful exploitation of the seamfulness of the situation than in the dating examples. It is evoked in the initiation of talk, though, for the opening conversational gambit was supported by a reference to digital awareness (performed through checking in and competing for mayorship).

Some Characteristic Trajectories in the Unfolding of Encounters With Pseudonymous Strangers: 'Timid Encounters'

Though these chance encounters between pseudonymous strangers may unfold relatively straightforwardly in face-to-face interaction, participants are very much open to the interactional possibilities offered by the seamfulness of encounters unfolding in reflexive hybrid ecologies, as was already the case in the Grindr example above. For instance, the players of the proximity game Dragonquest 9 (a game played on mobile devices in which notifications occur and game actions become possible when players get within a few meters of one another) thus distinguish between 'brave encounters' and 'timid encounters.' In 'brave encounters,' a bit like in the Foursquare example where the air stewardess made herself known to the other Foursquare user competing with her for the title of hotel, mayor, players who become aware that they are close to other players they have never met (and only 'know' as characters in the game) make themselves known to them and initiate a face-to-face conversation (Licoppe and Legout 2014). In 'timid encounters' the same player will stay nearby but will not make himself/herself known in person. He/she will try to act so as to be recognizable as a passerby, while interacting with other players in his/her vicinity only through the gameplay. 'Timid encounters' exploit the 'seamfulness,' foldedness, and the 'evidential boundaries' (Goffman 1974) of the situation (bodies are visually available to people around but on-screen actions are not). The Grindr encounter in a bar described above was also a timid encounter of sorts. Both Grindr users possibly recognized one another as such but elected not to acknowledge it by

44 Christian Licoppe

acting upon it, and kept their interaction within the confines of the mobile screen. In a 'timid encounter' the timid party deliberately tries to elude visual recognition or avoid acknowledging explicitly while interacting with the other party on screen.

'Timid encounters' provide evidence for the fundamental categorical ambiguity of pseudonymous encounters with strangers in public places that are usually populated by a lot of pedestrians and a few other users of the same location-aware applications (therefore dwelling in the 'same' reflexive hybrid ecology). Two sets of categories are always available to these location-aware, connected urban denizens when their paths cross: that of ordinary mobile strangers, making relevant civil inattention in Goffman's sense, and that of connected users of the same mobile application, which make them aware of one another's proximity under a digital guise, and which projects the possibility of a more focused encounter and of exchanges through talk or digital resources. 'Timid encounters' play on such an ambiguity, which is also constitutive of other forms of conduct in pseudonymous encounters.

This also opens the way to various types of potentially transgressive behavior. A mild one would be a kind of mobile digital voyeurism, in which one would check the online profiles of other people around without making them aware that one is doing it. A future connected poet might be tempted to check the profile of the beautiful and unknown passerby who strikes his eye, and would probably not describe such an encounter in the same way as Baudelaire did. For the same reason, encounters with pseudonymous strangers entail specific forms of vulnerability. In the following example (Figure 3.1),

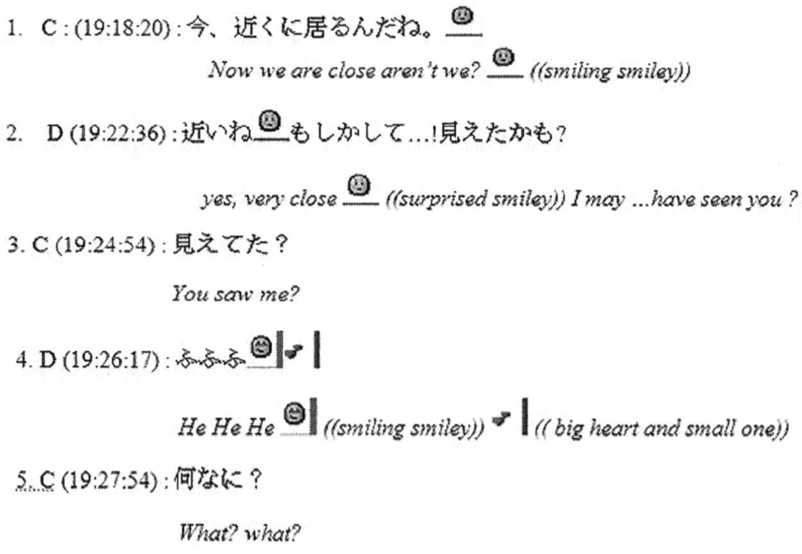

1. C : (19:18:20) : 今、近くに居るんだね。 🔘

    Now we are close aren't we? ___ 🔘 *((smiling smiley))*

2. D (19:22:36) : 近いね🔘もしかして…!見えたかも?

    yes, very close 🔘 *((surprised smiley)) I may …have seen you ?*

3. C (19:24:54) : 見えてた?

    You saw me?

4. D (19:26:17) : ふふふ🔘💙❘

    He He He 🔘 *((smiling smiley))* 💙❘ *((big heart and small one))*

5. C (19:27:54) : 何なに?

    What? what?

Figure 3.1 Transcription of empirical work in image format created by author

Mobile 'Pseudonymous Strangers' 45

taken from our early study of the location-aware game Mogi, in which players have geolocated maps figuring their location and that of virtual objects to be collected in the city (Licoppe and Inada 2006), one female player, C, initiates contact with another player on the basis of their mutual proximity, as perceived on screen (message 1).

In his reply (message 2), the second player, D, acknowledges their proximity and hints that he might be seeing the first player. C's next message makes it clear that she has not seen him. This makes salient a visual asymmetry in the situation, the realization and treatment of which rests on its seamfulness (they can exchange text messages independently of face-to-face interaction) and raises a potential issue from her perspective, with respect to the unity and coherence of her situation. She sees D on screen and they have acknowledged their mutual proximity, but she cannot reconcile this mediated representation with her co-present experience in which she cannot make him. This is a characteristic issue which may often arise in 'folded' settings, which involve a parallel orientation to two different modes of perceiving the 'here and now' and possible disjunctions between on-screen and co-present experiences. Such concerns are brought to the fore when D first hints at the power such an asymmetry might be giving him (the 'superior' laughter in message 4), thus breaking the normative expectations of equal rights in encounters between strangers in public places, and then evokes the potential disquiet and emotions such a situation might elicit in her.

His final proposal to meet, eventually declined, can be seen in this sequential context as an offer to resolve the fold-related tension by finally realigning their co-present and online awareness and interactional statuses and making them coincide (Figure 3.2).

In another telling example from the Mogi field studies, one female player at home expresses her worry to other players with whom she is familiar about a player who often appears on screen near her home and who, although they are spatially close and mutually aware of the proximity, does not try to initiate contact with her (Licoppe and Inada 2010). Because of such a pregnant 'silence,' he cuts an equivocal figure. Because he keeps silent, he behaves as a stranger would. However, because he is in the game, he is expected to behave as a player (i.e. to acknowledge on-screen proximity by initiating a text message contact), for whom civil inattention is not an option when very close on screen. Anthropology has shown us that things which cross categorical boundaries are often perceived as dangerous (Douglas 1966), and this categorical ambiguity makes this player's conduct equivocal and transgressive in her view, and leads her to perceive him as potentially dangerous, as a possible 'stalker' (a category redefined in this context to describe a player who appears repeatedly close on screen while remaining 'silent'), and to seek the help of her player friends. Playing Goffman's silent stranger within the location-aware game world may occasion disquiet in a way that is understandable by all players. The particular form of seamfulness which characterizes the above situation, and which makes relevant different

46   *Christian Licoppe*

6. D (19:29:00) : おっ😲

Oh 😲 ((astonished smiley))

7. C (19:32:30) : どうしたの？

What is happening to you?

8. D (19:34:23) : ドキドキしてる……?

Is your heart beating?

9. C (19:34:54) : うん！

Yes!

10. D (19:36:18) : 会う?

Do you want us to meet?

11. C (19:37:46) : ううん。今仕事中だもん！駄目だよ。😉

No I am at work we cannot 😉 ((winking smiley))

Figure 3.2 Transcription of empirical work in image format created by author

categorizations and types of related conduct at the same time, shapes the way pseudonymous encounters may become the locus of forms of behavior perceivable as transgressive or threatening.

Conclusion

I have shown how a crucial feature of location- and proximity-sensitive technologies with respect to urban sociality is to make possible the repeated, unplanned discovery of other users in one's vicinity on screen, the visibility of whom is usually supplemented with profiles and electronic communication resources. Because they can be thus known digitally, such 'discoverable' passersby are not just the anonymous strangers which were populating Goffman's metropolis but 'pseudonymous strangers.' The proliferation of chance encounters with pseudonymous strangers is therefore a consequence of the development of the use of locative media in highly networked urban environments, and part of what makes such an experience distinctive. Their organization, the kind of social conduct that is expected, and the way they might develop in a creative or transgressive way, all build on the seamfulness of the situation (separate mediations for action and communication, 'evidential boundaries' separating on-screen and off-screen activities, the relevance of different categorization devices and category-bound conduct, such as passerby/civil inattention and mobile application user/mobile-based conversation) and on the form of the situation which is made relevant (which makes some configurations recognizable as mismatches with respect to the 'direct' and screen-mediated access to the surrounding world, and the management of such mismatches-relevant issues). Some of the behaviors I have described, such as 'timid encounters,' also rest on the fact that there is usually only a minority of locative media users who move along the streets with mobile terminals sensitive to one another's proximity and digital aura.

Today, because the uses of locative media are not widespread, chance encounters with pseudonymous strangers may remain rarer than the kind of encounters between (unconnected) anonymous strangers, the interaction order of which Goffman and more generally urban studies have analyzed in detail. However, if we imagine a future in which the use of locative media become so commonplace that all urban denizens would be digitally connected and location-aware, then the city becomes less a 'place of strangers' than a place of discoverable 'pseudonymous strangers' with retrievable profiles. With respect to the organization of sociality in urban public places, a fully smart city would be one in which the default expectation would be that the stranger one meets on the street is a pseudonymous stranger, accessible off screen and on screen, thus deeply affecting the management of interactions in public, or rather in augmented public places. For instance, 'civil inattention' might still be somewhat relevant, for noticing every on-screen proximity or consulting the profiles of all discovered passersby might prove tedious, but it would be a different sort of civil inattention, involving both the minimal gaze management of embodied proximities, but also refraining from checking online available information about passersby and acting upon it.

References

Benford, S., Anastasi, R., Flintham, M., Drozd, A., Crabtree, A., Greenhalgh, C., Tandavanitj, N., Adams, M. and Row-Farr, J. 2003. "Coping with uncertainty in a location-based game". *Pervasive Computing*, 3, 34–41.

Blackwell, C., Birnholtz, J. and Abbott, C. 2014. "Seeing and being seen: Co-situation and impression formation using Grindr, a location-aware gay dating app". *New Media and Society*, 17(7), 1117–36.

Brown, B. and Laurier, E. 2012. "The normal natural troubles of driving with GPS". In *Proceedings of the SIGCHI Conference on Human Factors in Computing Systems*. 1620–30 New York: ACM Press.

48 *Christian Licoppe*

Brubaker, J., Ananny, M. and Campbell, K. 2014. "Departing glances: A sociotechnical account of 'leaving' Grindr". *New Media & Society*, 18(3), 373–90.

Cocks, H. G. 2009. *Classified: The History of the Personal Column*. London: Random House.

De Souza e Silva, A. and Sheller, M. 2014. *Local and Mobile: Linking Mobilities, Mobile Communication and Locative Media*. London: Routledge.

De Souza e Silva, A. and Sutko, D. 2009. *Digital Cityscapes*. New York: Peter Lang.

Douglas, M. 1966. *Purity & Danger*. London: Routledge.

Farman, J. 2013. *The Mobile Story: Narrative Practices with Locative Technologies*. New York: Routledge.

Frith, J. 2013. "Turning life into a game: Foursquare, gamification and personal mobility". *Mobile Media and Communication*, 1(2), 248–62.

Frith, J. 2014. "Communicating through Location: The understood meaning of the Foursquare Check-in". *Journal of Computer-Mediated Communication*, 19(4), 890–905.

Goffman, E. 1971. *Relations in Public: Microstructure of the Public Order*. New York: Harper and Row.

Goffman, E. 1974. *Frame Analysis: An Essay on the Organization of Experience*. New York: Harper and Row.

Hjorth, L. and Richardson, I. 2014. *Gaming in Social, Locative & Mobile Media*. Basingstoke: Palgrave Macmillan.

Humphreys, L. 2007. "Mobile social networks and social practice: A case study of Dodgeball". *Journal of Computer-Mediated-Communication*, 13(1), 341–60.

Humphreys, L. 2010. "Mobile social networks and urban public space". *New Media & Society*, 12(5), 763–78.

Licoppe, C. 2016. "Mobilities and urban encounters in public places in the age of locative media. Seams, folds and encounters with 'pseudonymous strangers'". *Mobilities*, 11(1), 99–116.

Licoppe, C. and Inada, Y. 2006. "Emergent uses of a location aware multiplayer game: The interactional consequences of mediated encounters". *Mobilities*, 1(1), 39–61.

Licoppe, C. and Inada, Y. 2010. "Locative media and cultures of mediated proximity: The case of the Mogi game location-aware community". *Environment and Planning D: Society and Space*, 28(4), 691–709.

Licoppe, C. and Inada, Y. 2016. "Mobility and sociality in proximity-sensitive digital urban ecologies: 'Timid encounters' and 'seam-sensitive walks'". *Mobilities*, 11(2), 264–83.

Licoppe, C. and Legout, M.-C. 2014. "Living inside location-aware mobile social information: The pragmatics of Foursquare notifications". In *Living inside Mobile Social Information*, edited by Katz, J., 109–30. Dayton, OH: Greyden Press.

Licoppe, C., Rivière, C.-A. and Morel, J. 2015. "Grindr casual hook-ups as interactional achievements". *New Media and Society*, 18(11), 2540–58.

Lofland, L. 1998. The Public Realm: Exploring the City's Quintessential Social Territory. New York: Aldine de Gruyter.

Milgram, S. 1972. "The familiar stranger: An aspect of urban anonymity". In *The Individual in a Social World: Essays and Experiments*, edited by Sabini, J. and Silver, M., 51–3. New York: McGraw-Hill.

Morel, J. 2014. "Ingress. Mobilités et sociabilités dans un jeu de réalité augmentée". *Interfaces numériques*, 3(3), 447–72.

Race, K. 2015. "Speculative pragmatism and intimate arrangements: Online hook-up devices in gay life". *Culture, Health & Sexuality: An International Journal for Research, Intervention and Care*, 17(4), 496–511.

Simmel, G. 1971. *On Individuality and Other Social Forms*. Chicago: Chicago University Press, 143–9.

Whyte, W. H. 1980. *The Social Life of Small Urban Spaces*. Ann Arbor: Edwards Brothers Publishers.

Wilken, R. and Goggin, G. 2012. *Mobile Technology and Place*. New York: Routledge.

4 The Worlds of Offshoring

John Urry

The fate of what is held in common has never appeared as problematic as today with climate change, population growth, food and water shortages, and competition for energy threatening the global commons of planet earth, as well as many smaller-scale commons (for more detail see Urry 2014). Much that has been thought of as 'public' has been in various ways privatized, enclosed, or commercialized. Even research and knowledge relating to the commons is often commercially confidential and less subject to public visibility and scrutiny. This privatizing has not of course occurred without many struggles and imaginaries of collective ownership, wellbeing, and use.

There are material, discursive, and ideological processes through which different kinds of entities are held, managed, and imagined as in some manner 'common.' This chapter examines under-explored elements of this terrain of struggle around the public. It especially explores the significance of offshore worlds for holding, managing, and imagining 'in common.' Brittain-Catlin describes "the negative, dark spirit . . . today pervades the offshore world and its network of secret paraphernalia and hidden practices that are so closely bound into the global economy" (2005, 118).

In some cases it seems that offshore worlds were strategically developed to facilitate the privatizing of various commons. New physical, economic, and virtual borders or boundaries have been generated through struggles especially by the 'rich class.' Warren Buffett recently maintained: "There is class warfare, all right, but it's my class, the rich class, that's making war, and we're winning" (quoted in Farrell 2013). Part of that war has been waged through generating many new offshore worlds.

The 1980s onwards saw the striking emergence of many interdependent global processes. It was argued that the global movement of money, people, ideas, images, information, and objects was broadly beneficial. Most aspects of contemporary societies were thought to be positively transformed through an increased borderlessness and forming of many new kinds of commons. Writing in 1990, Ohmae described this borderless world as

> the free flow of ideas, individuals, investments and industries . . . the emergence of the interlinked economy brings with it an erosion of

The Worlds of Offshoring   51

national sovereignty as the power of information directly touches local communities; academic, professional, and social institutions; corporations; and individuals.

(1990, 269)

Borderlessness generated a new sense of a shared planet with the appearance of the first IPCC Report (1990), novel businesses, cosmopolitan polities, international friendship, family lives, international understanding, and a greater openness of information and communications. Many believed that societies would be invigorated through these flows of ideas, information, and people, making societies more 'cosmopolitan.' Especially significant was the Web, which led to very many virtual worlds which transformed economic and social life. The development of various 'virtual commons' contributed to a 1990s 'global optimism' as to a progressive open 'common' future.

But this 1990s decade did not turn out to be the harbinger of a long-term, optimistic, and borderless future. It turned out that there are many dark sides to all this movement. Migrating across borders are not just consumer goods and services, and a more open commons. Also moving across borders are environmental risks, trafficked women, drug runners, terrorists, asylum seekers, international criminals, outsourced work, slave traders, property speculators, smuggled workers, waste, financial risks, and untaxed income. All these flows across borders made the achievement of common interests more problematic as multiple borders and boundaries developed and multiplied.

Indeed *Offshoring* shows that there has been a striking proliferation of various 'secret worlds.' Globalization did not generate openness and multiple commons but their very antithesis. Specifically offshoring involves moving resources, practices, peoples, and monies from one national territory to another but hiding them within secrecy jurisdictions. It involves evading rules, laws, taxes, regulations, or norms. It is all about rule-breaking, getting around rules in ways that are illegal, or going against the spirit of the law, or using laws in one jurisdiction to undermine laws in another. Offshore worlds, we might say, depend upon secrets and lies.

These worlds were made possible by new mobility systems. These include container-based cargo shipping; aeromobility; the Internet and new virtual worlds; car and lorry traffic; new electronic money-transfer systems; taxation and legal and financial expertise oriented to avoiding national regulations; and 'mobile lives' with frequent legal and illegal movement across borders.

This offshoring world is dynamic, reorganizing economic, social, political, and material relations between societies and within them. Populations and states find more and more resources, practices, peoples, and monies that are made or kept secret and unrealizable. The global order is the opposite of an open world—it is one of concealment, of secret gardens orchestrated in and for the rich class. And *Offshoring* shows that there are many offshored

52 *John Urry*

worlds: of manufacturing work, waste, energy, torture, surveillance, pleasure, CO_2 emissions, property ownership, and especially untaxed income and wealth.

Central to most of these offshored worlds are virtual environments enabling information, money, trades, images, connections, and objects to move digitally along routeways lying in the shadows especially in the deep or dark web. Virtual environments are part and parcel of contemporary offshoring and the de-localizing of production, consumption, and sociability that characterized the past few decades.

The processes of 'offshoring' range from those where there is a mere dependence upon overseas resources, to those which are onshore but which enjoy offshore status and may be concealed, to those which are literally out to sea, over the horizon, secret, and often illegal. Offshoring has become a generic principle of contemporary societies, and it is impossible to draw a clear divide between what is onshore and what is offshore.

Centrally significant here is that of water which has often been presumed to be a key common resource. The seven billion humans are crowded onto just one-quarter of the earth's surface. Oceans provide ways to assemble as secret what would otherwise be onshore and visible. Almost all the ocean world is out of sight, an 'outlaw sea' (Langewiesche 2004). The oceans contain many unregulated 'treasure islands' of low tax and much pleasure; there are ships flying flags of convenience with conditions of work driven to the bottom; oceans are places where many poor migrants lose their lives; oceans are a global rubbish dump with the Great Pacific Garbage Patch said to be twice the size of France; and there are unregulated climates as the outlaw sea subjects humans to its heightened unruliness, as more intense storms, hurricanes, storm surges, rising sea levels, and flooding boomerang back onto land. The sea is a neoliberal paradise for the rich class, a vision of a world almost without government, taxes, laws, and where only powerful ships and their companies survive, with the rest often literally sinking to the bottom. It is an unruly space not really owned and governed by states; it is mostly risky, free, and unregulated. Contemporary oceans demonstrate the tragedy of the commons.

There are many offshoring practices: offshoring production to cheaper sites; systematically reducing tax liabilities and hence heightening inequalities; creating many secret offshore companies; engendering new forms of financialization; developing expertise in novel ways of marginalizing workforces; new places of pleasure away from observation by friends/family; extracting infrastructural investment from states; externalizing the costs of waste and emissions; using moments of crisis to force through neoliberal restructuring; mobilizing various discourses promoting marketization; and creating astonishing new products based upon new 'needs,' including for security. These all derive from the global freedom to move monies, income, wealth, people, waste, and loyalties from pillar to post. This dizzying 'mobile' world, bright and dark, open and secret, free and destructive, is difficult to regulate in 'common' interests and that of course is often their point.

The Worlds of Offshoring   53

This was no accident. In various secret societies and meetings the post-war capitalist class plotted the development of offshore worlds during the long period of post-war Keynesianism. In particular, in 1947 in Switzerland, the country that was and still is the world's premier tax haven, a senior bank official brought together scholars to a secret meeting at Mont Pèlerin, near Geneva. This was organized to revive liberalism under the direction of Friedrich Hayek. This meeting, and the subsequent development of the Mont Pèlerin Society funded by Swiss banks, was central in commencing the global fightback against dominant Keynesianism. Such a Keynesianism involved support for many kinds of state interventionism, for the idea that the national economy is in a way a commons, as opposed to the specific interest of separate corporations and rich individuals. In promoting offshore worlds during the post-war period the rich class succeeded beyond its wildest dreams.

In particular, since the 1980s there has been an astonishing growth in the movement of finance and wealth to and through the world's 60 to 70 tax havens, representing more than one-quarter of contemporary societies including not only Switzerland but also Jersey, Cyprus, Macao, Cayman Islands, Monaco, Panama, Dubai, Liechtenstein, Singapore, Hong Kong, Dubai, Gibraltar, City of London, and Delaware (Shaxson 2011). These 'secrecy jurisdictions' are core to neoliberalizing the world economy from around 1980 with the ending of many exchange controls. To be offshore is to be in paradise, by contrast with the high-state-high-tax life experienced onshore. Tax havens are places of escape and freedom, a paradise of low taxes, wealth management, deregulation, secrecy, and often nice beaches.

Almost all major companies have offshore accounts/subsidiaries, often running into the hundreds (Goldman Sachs is said to have 4000); more than half of world trade passes through them; almost all high net worth individuals possess offshore accounts enabling tax 'planning'; and 99 of Europe's hundred largest companies use offshore subsidiaries. Offshored money has grown from US$11 billion in 1968 to US$21 trillion in 2010 (equivalent to about one-third of the annual world income). Fewer than ten million people currently own this US$21 trillion offshore fortune, a sum equivalent to the combined GDPs of the United States and Japan (Tax Justice Network 2012). This is the source of the power and wealth of the super-rich; almost all owe their fortunes to the rapid and secret moving of money and ownership 'offshore.'

Shaxson shows that offshore is how the world of power now works. Money staying onshore is almost the exception, suitable only for the 'little people' still paying taxes. Most big money is offshored. The United States is by a mile the world's most important secrecy jurisdiction. In the little state of Delaware there is a single building which houses 217,000 companies, the largest and most unethical building in the world, we might conclude (Shaxson 2011, 146). More than one million business entities are incorporated in Delaware, including over 50% of all publicly traded US companies.

54 *John Urry*

A successful offshore tax haven normally includes the following features: it should not tax income, profits, or inheritance; its banks should offer various currencies and operate online and not require personal visits; new accounts in banks require minimal documentation; there is bank secrecy with no Tax Information Exchange Agreements with other countries (about 40 havens have no such agreements); and bank accounts can be opened using an 'anonymous bearer share corporation' so that people's names do not appear in any public registry or database. A tax haven seeks to deliver secrecy and discretion: 'ask no questions, tell no lies.' Most big money is thus offshored, although offshore includes most mainstream banks and financial institutions. The annual loss of taxation from this offshoring world is hundreds of billions of US dollars. Offshore worlds also make it hard for small and medium-sized companies to compete.

Contemporary companies are built rather like Russian dolls, with multiple layers of secrecy and concealment (Urry 2014, 2). There is a company called Goldman Sachs Structured Products (Asia) Limited based in the tax haven of Hong Kong. It is controlled by another company called Goldman Sachs (Asia) Finance registered in another tax haven, Mauritius. That is administered by a further company in Hong Kong, which in turn is directed by a company located in New York. This is controlled by another company in Delaware, a major tax haven, and that company is administered by yet another company that is also in Delaware, GS Holdings (Delaware) L.L.C. II. This is in turn a subsidiary of the Goldman Sachs Group which generated a worldwide turnover of around US$34 billion and employed nearly 30,000 staff. This chain of ownership is one of hundreds of such chains within the single company Goldman Sachs (see www.goldmansachs.com/who-we-are/index.html).

One commentator thus reports that in the case of billionaires, "you don't live anywhere, and neither does your money. Or rather you live everywhere, and so does your money" (quoted in Urry 2014, 85). This world involves rapid movement across the oceans, with homes dotted around the world, endless business travel, private schools, family life structured around occasional get-togethers, private leisure clubs, luxury ground transport, airport lounges, private jets, luxury destinations, and places of distinction and luxury for encountering other super-rich. Place, property, and power are intertwined so forming and sustaining such a networked and often hidden rich class avoiding the commons and generating complex private routeways.

Inequality has engendered powerful interests to protect and further extend the bases of such unequally distributed global income and wealth. Offshoring is part and parcel of the realizing of such unequal interests. And such inequalities matter a great deal, since access to 'services' increasingly depends upon each person's income and wealth; the more unequal these are, the less chance there is that people will be regarded as in any way equal. The rampant marketization of almost everything crowds out many other reasons

The Worlds of Offshoring 55

why people may act towards each other, such as fairness, service, duty, and sociability.

Offshoring involves getting around rules. Most offshoring practices are not incidental but systemically engineered and legally reinforced to avoid regulations, to be kept secret, and to 'escape' offshore, helping to form and sustain multiple intersecting offshore worlds. Elites can escape many kinds of formal and informal sanctions and set up conditions for further extending their income and wealth. This inaccessibility makes elites less responsible for their actions, especially in the societies where their actions appear to occur. They are literally irresponsible. Such elites meet as secret societies, such as the offshored annual meetings of the Bilderberg Group (Urry 2014, 20). As elites circulated spatially, with meetings often in places of offshore leisure and pleasure, so they developed connections to extend further offshored worlds and its discourses. Private meetings and more public thinktanks helped to orchestrate this offshore world and its corporate, individual, and policy world beneficiaries.

But since around 2000, issues of tax evasion by the rich and powerful and the role of tax havens have become central to the emerging counter-politics of taxation. From the turn of the millennium a new array of taxation politics emerged. There are many critical reports (by Oxfam on how tax havens contribute to global poverty); campaigning NGOs (such as Offshore Watch); interventions by the World Social Forum (establishing a global campaign against tax havens); media stories (even in the pro-business *Wall Street Journal* or *The Economist*); new kinds of research capability (such as the International Consortium of Investigative Journalists). There is also a greater role for the OECD and EU (to curb 'unfair tax competition'); an increased rate of leakage of financial data to the media; and the raised public identification and critique of corporations 'scandalously' involved in aggressive tax avoidance/evasion (Google being the latest, as of early 2016). Tax has unambiguously moved from a private to a major public issue.

This taxation counter-politics, this assertion of the interests of the 'commons,' is now a torrent; no longer is tax a private matter just for oneself and one's accountant. Much direct action, NGO activities, official government reports, and a new activism exposed and denigrated many different forms and aspects of 'tax dodging.' Such dodging is seen as reducing the capacity to tax revenues where income and wealth are generated and as undermining a level playing field, since local companies normally pay full taxes while transnational corporations do not.

Tax shaming is a major political issue which is rapidly developing into a global movement. This was strikingly shown in early 2013 when the International Consortium of Investigative Journalists received in their mail a computer hard drive packed with corporate data and personal information and e-mails. This totaled more than 260 gigabytes of data and originated from ten offshore jurisdictions and included details of more than 122,000 offshore companies, nearly 12,000 intermediaries (agents or 'introducers'), and

56 John Urry

about 130,000 records relating to those who run, own, benefit from, or hide behind offshore companies. It showed that those setting up offshore entities often lived in China, Hong Kong, Russia, and former Soviet republics. Many positions are held by so-called nominee directors, whose names appear in hundreds of companies. Nominee directors are people who, for a fee, lend their names as office holders of companies that they know little about.

Other authors have begun to generalize this issue of tax. Large corporations and rich individuals are increasingly forced to defend their tax position, often seeking a 'taxwash' to keep the scandal-hungry media and protestors at bay. This issue of taxation as a kind of commons increasingly threatens the world's major brands, critiqued for their aggressive tax avoidance and deliberate evading of transparency and public scrutiny. The widespread development of 'tax shaming' reveals the power of the commons especially within certain cities to fight back. And many other aspects of offshoring, such as waste, CO_2 emissions, and tortured bodies, have also been subject to increasing protest.

The social sciences neglect these offshore worlds at their peril. Such offshoring and lack of transparency is bad for democracy and for societies ever being able to move back to a low-carbon future. Moreover, offshore does not have to be literally offshore from centers of economic power. Offshore, we might say, is everywhere. One company's onshore is another's offshore. And this powerful world is, in a way, located nowhere as such. Richard Murphy powerfully writes how

> illicit financial flows . . . do not flow through locations as such, but do instead flow through the secrecy space that secrecy jurisdictions create. . . . They float over and around the locations which are used to facilitate their existence as if in an unregulated ether.
>
> (2009, 7)

As a consequence, much of this overlapping 'secrecy world,' this unregulated ether,' cannot be regulated by single national states and, indeed, may not be regulatable at all. A world of multiple secrets has developed on such a scale and through an 'unregulated ether' that is almost impossible to tame.

Much has been moved offshore—hidden from view, legally protected, and not subject to potential democratic oversight, control, and regulation. This offshore world is detrimental to democracy. Indeed many of the quintessential 'offshore societies' are highly undemocratic, often established by a host power to benefit its elites (Britain and the Cayman Islands, China and Macao, France and Monaco, and so on). Such offshoring involves the most sustained of attacks upon governance orchestrated through national states and especially efforts to regulate and legislate on the basis of democratic control.

Neoliberal capitalism has brought about a systemic disorganization of potential democratic structures. The offshored flows of money, finance, manufacturing, services, security, waste, and emissions are catastrophic for

The Worlds of Offshoring 57

transparent governance. Such transparency necessitates debate and dialogue being able to determine and implement policies through citizens being aware of, and having control over, a clear set of onshored resources. The absolute requirement for good governance is transparency, and that is what secrecy jurisdictions preclude, as Keynes (1933) warned about in the 1930s.

There is what can be described as an offshoring of democracy, since money and many other resources are rendered invisible and unaccountable. Democracy requires money and resources being subject to clear, transparent, and accountable contestation between the members of a given society. It needs activities to be brought back 'home' and the interests of *its* citizens to be regarded as primary. Much needs to be reshored so as to re-establish potential democratic control by the members of a given society over activities and resources that are specific to them. This is of course a formidably difficult requirement in a global order.

One interesting policy is that proposed by the Tax Justice Network (and the EU). This is that the taxation of corporations should be based upon treating such a corporation as a single entity around the world. Companies would have to submit one set of consolidated accounts and apportion activities to countries according to their actual 'economic' presence within each country. This presence would be formula-based, relating to the number of staff employed, the geographical location of the company's fixed assets, and the value of its sales. Corporation-type tax would then be levied in each country according to this 'country-by-country' reporting for taxation.

Offshoring is also problematic for developing effective policies to deal with rising CO_2 emissions. Powering down to a low-carbon future requires a strong mutual indebtedness of people within societies and around the globe, especially of current generations towards future generations, including those not yet born. The need for this public or social indebtedness is powerfully expressed in many global documents (the 1997 UNESCO Declaration on the Responsibilities of the Present Generations Towards Future Generations). However, this is a massive challenge which offshoring has made far more intractable. Such indebtedness between people has been overwhelmed in much of the world through financial indebtedness. Without sufficient tax revenues post-carbon futures are unlikely, since both public money and a strong notion of public interest are necessary to plan and orchestrate low carbonism. Offshoring and enhanced inequalities renders unlikely the effective powering down of economies and societies.

This new order is one of multiple concealments, of many secrets and some lies. Offshoring erodes 'democracy' and notions of fairness within and between societies. It can generate a kind of regime-shopping as well as precluding the slowing down of the rate of growth of CO_2 emissions, which presupposes shared and open global agreements between responsible states, corporations, and publics.

Thus we see that offshoring has become a generic principle of contemporary societies, and it is impossible to draw a clear divide between what is

58 *John Urry*

onshore and what is offshore. This has many consequences for urban relations, housing supply and prices, and the nature of work.

There is here a major terrain of struggle between offshore worlds and various kinds of democratic and global organizations. The stakes are high indeed as to how these struggles will play themselves out. And it is possible, as various dystopian futures remind us, that we may not have seen anything yet and the twenty-first century could be a century of 'extreme offshoring' with many further dark consequences for democracy and the possibilities of developing a post-carbon future.

References

Brittain-Catlin, W. 2005. *Offshore: The Dark Side of Globalisation.* New York: Picador.
Farrell, P. 2013. "Rich class fighting 99%, winning big-time". *MarketWatch,* November 1, 2011, at www.marketwatch.com/story/rich-class-beating-99-to-a-pulp-2011-11-01 (accessed September 7, 2016).
Keynes, J. M. 1933. "National self-sufficiency". *Yale Review*, 22, 755–69.
Langewiesche, W. 2004. *The Outlaw Sea.* London: Granta.
Murphy, R. 2009. *Defining the Secrecy World.* London: Tax Justice Network.
Ohmae, K. 1990. *The Borderless World.* London: Collins.
Shaxson, N. 2011. *Treasure Islands.* London: Bodley Head.
Tax Justice Network. 2012. 'Revealed: Global super-rich has at least $21 trillion hidden in secret tax havens', 22 July 2012, www.taxjustice.net/cms/upload/pdf/The_Price_of_Offshore_Revisited_Presser_120722.pdf.
Urry, J. 2014. *Offshoring.* Cambridge: Polity.

5 Networked Urbanism and Disaster

Monika Büscher, Xaroula Kerasidou,
Katrina Petersen, and Rachel Oliphant

In a world of networked urbanism, where people affected by disaster connect intensively with each other, the media, and emergency agencies, why do warnings go amiss? Why does knowledge of risk not translate into preparedness? Why are the mobilities of information so poorly understood? In this chapter, we build on a synthesis of insights from disaster management, policy, mobilities, and design research, and science and technology studies (STS) to study how these disaster-related networked mobilities create complex landscapes of communication, interdependence, and responsibility that are difficult to translate into preparedness. Our analysis informs, and is informed by, research collaborations with emergency responders, engineers, and technology designers with the aim of understanding and developing social and digital technologies for collaboration (Petersen et al. 2014).[1] By bringing attention to new networked partnerships, we aim to provide a set of critical tools with which to consider practices of risk governance as an example of networked urbanism.

In the decade 2005–2014, 1.7 billion people were affected by disasters. Around 90% of these disasters are climate-related floods, storms, and heat waves, which are, with some degree of precision, predictable. Yet, even though some risks can be anticipated, residents of affected areas often do not take appropriate precautions even if they are given notice of a danger which is on top of the list of those disasters citizens fear the most. For example, a key action point in the latest report by the United Nations Office for Disaster Risk Reduction is to study why residents do not evacuate in time (UNISDR 2015). Similarly, despite the well-known calamity of 6.47 million internally displaced people in Syria and Afghanistan in 2014 (OCHA 2015), Europe and the world were unprepared for the refugee crisis in 2015. Information that could enhance preparedness is often not noticed or acted upon on individual and organizational levels. At the same time, information can also be too freely shared. For example, when involved in crises, the media and bystanders frequently publicize information that can compromise the safety of victims or emergency services (e.g. BBC 2015; Oh, Agrawal, and Rao 2010).

A closer look at key dimensions of networked urbanism in disaster can help us map out some answers as to why information flows are disorganized (Figure 5.1). In a recent study 69% of respondents expect emergency agencies

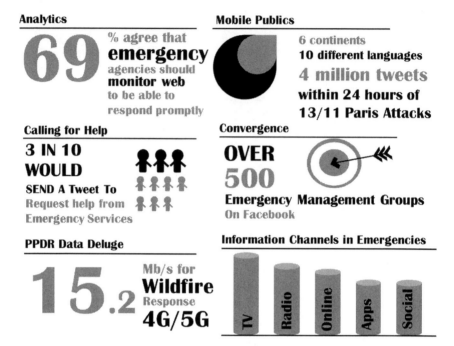

Figure 5.1 Networked communications
Sources: Mashable (2011), Ferrãos and Sallent (2015), and Goel and Ember (2015).

to monitor the web for crisis-relevant information. Three in ten citizens now expect to receive help after sending an emergency tweet, even though emergency agencies strongly discourage this because they do not have the capacity to monitor social media for emergency calls (Hughes, St. Denis, Palen, and Anderson 2014). Such posts might include reports from people involved in an emergency, such as images from the Paris attacks on 13 November 2015 or self-organized response initiatives like #porteouverte, where Parisians offered people affected shelter. The amount of information to monitor is vast, with four million tweets sent from six continents in the first 24 hours after the Paris attacks. And, overall, there are over 500 emergency groups on Facebook, evidence that the well-known phenomenon of convergence—people gathering at the sites of emergencies—now has a significant virtual and global dimension (Hughes, Palen, Sutton, Liu, and Vieweg 2008). The motivations behind these acts may be the same as they have always been: to help, to find friends and relatives, and to witness exceptional events. But the practices and expectations are changing.

Part of the reason for these transformations is that online, digital apps and social media have become established emergency information channels. Unlike traditional TV and radio, digital media afford many-to-many communications, live documentation, and direct dialogue, raising expectations for more immediate and interactive emergency communications. This informationalization of citizens' experiences, practices, and expectations in relation to disaster is accompanied by an informationalization of Public Protection and Disaster Response (PPDR) organizations (Büscher, Perng, and Liegl 2015). Accelerating this transformation are pivotal decisions about the use of technology, such as the move to Long-Term Evolution (LTE) wireless high-speed data and big data analytics for Public Protection and Disaster Relief taken at the end of 2015 (Ferrãos and Sallent 2015, 79; Lund 2015).

This chapter explores what it means to have networked urbanism in disasters as it draws on a range of discussions around the constitution of publics in relation to risks, resilience, and new forms of socio-technical interactions that lead to challenges to traditional forms of disaster management. We assemble conceptual resources, including 'technologies of humility' (Jasanoff 2003), 'communities of risk' (Beck 1999), and 'networks of trust' (Mosley 2009), to think beyond top-down or bottom-up solutions to risk, instead asking questions about what it means to engage in new partnerships of risk governance.

Networked Partnerships

As the risk society has unfolded into a century of disasters (eScience 2012), it has engendered a shift in organizational and public practices around risk. Disastrous socio-technological accidents (Chernobyl, Bhopal), natural-technical disasters (Fukushima), and socio-environmental threats of the Anthropocene like climate change have increased awareness of humanity's vulnerability and responsibility for risk. Modern science has lost its monopoly on knowledge and truth (Beck 1992), and diverse new publics are demanding a voice in decisions about risk. Society's relationship with experts has become ambivalent, blaming science and technology yet still seeing it as the (only) solution.

This has reassembled the relationship between science, governance, the media, and the public. Publics frequently constitute in relation to disaster risk. They may take shape as groupings of the directly affected (the inhabitants of New Orleans after Hurricane Katrina) or as wider groups connected to those affected (the global Haitian diaspora, who played a major role in mobilizing help after the 2010 earthquake (Munro 2013)). The formation of publics around disaster risk also includes the international community, such as those bound together as media publics (who, for example, mobilized a record $14 billion in donations after the 2004 South Asian tsunami (Older 2014)) or as activists (like the Bhopal Group for Information and Action, who have campaigned for justice for over 30 years (Fortun 2011)). A study of 22 European countries found that how these groups are involved in emergency response varies significantly (Bossong and Hegemann 2015).

62   *Monika Büscher et al.*

The question now emerges: How *should* these diverse stakeholders interact? This is a focus for intense debate in disaster management, and policy and social science disciplines, where difficulties in dealing with the unpredictability of disasters have undermined confidence in the more top-down approaches known as command and control. These approaches function on hierarchical divisions of responsibility and vertical lines of communication. Strategic decision makers who are not directly active at a scene make decisions about goals and tasks that coordinate the actions of others more directly involved. Responsibility for risk analysis, preparedness, and response rests "almost exclusively on organisational shoulders and the public is perceived as passive receivers of technical information" (Scolobig, Prior, Schröter, Jörin, and Patt 2015, 2). This hampers locally flexible management and diminishes the emergency services' capability to activate community resilience (Birkland 2009, 430). This is because command and control approaches operate on a deficit model; a model that assumes that the public does not have the capacity to understand or adequately respond to disasters, echoing Lippman's distrust in the public (Plantin 2011).

Research shows that the one-way risk communication model that flows from these assumptions actively generates failures of preparedness, such as the reluctance to evacuate that concerns the UNISDR, as we mentioned at the beginning of this chapter. Warnings, in a command and control system, do not acknowledge the complex relationality of decisions about evacuating with family, neighbors, friends, livestock, or pets and leaving property behind (White et al. 2014). Moreover, reliance on command and control approaches often produces a narrow focus on specific risks and ignores their systemic nature (Jasanoff 2010). In response to this, one of the key principles in the United Nations *Sendai Framework for Disaster Risk Reduction 2015–2030* states: "Disaster risk reduction requires an all-of-society engagement and partnership" (UNISDR 2015, 13). Without considering how publics form in relation to risks, it becomes difficult to simply protect and serve the public from outside and above.

Policy analysts like Scolobig and Birkland, and international institutions like the UNISDR with their *Sendai Framework*, assume that people-centered approaches can counteract these weaknesses because they leverage local knowledge, and enable a more democratic, broad-based understanding of the complexities of risks and thereby foster more effective preparedness and response. However, such approaches are also developed for economic and political reasons. The year 2011 has been characterized as the costliest year on record by Munich RE, one of the world's leading reinsurance companies (Chen et al. 2013), and there is increasing pressure to distribute some of the responsibility for risk management to individuals and communities. An example is the wildfire triage approach taken in Tasmania to manage the high unpredictability and uncertainty of wildfires and scarce public resources. Depending on the specific unfolding patterns of a wildfire, residents may be told by emergency services in real time (not in advance) that their property cannot be defended. It is their choice to prepare for this possibility in advance themselves. The authorities see such sharing of responsibility for risk management as "an appropriate form of response due to the lack of resources that might be drawn on to guarantee a fair and equal level of protection to all citizens in a dynamic risk environment" (Scolobig et al. 2015, 6). At this juncture, contradictory ideological energies come together. On the one hand, the deepening 'institutionalized individualism' (Beck 1999, 9) indexes a loss of control over risk. The 'manufactured uncertainties' of Beck's 'world risk society' are beyond insurance and beyond top-down governance, and by devolving responsibility to individuals and communities, a highly unequal distribution of despair becomes, paradoxically, simultaneously structural and a matter of individual choice and responsibility. On the other hand, there is 'hope embedded in despair,' as dialogue and deeper engagement with residents and their local knowledge and practices creates democratic momentum for the constitution of 'communities of risk' (Beck 1999). These are non-territorial, potentially post-national communities that share risks, responsibilities, and burdens. They are political communities, often of those who have to "live with the risks that others take" (Beck 1999, 16), but with the potential to make the links between those who produce and profit from risks and those who suffer the consequences more visible and amenable to debate.

On the waves created by these ideological frictions, networked approaches are emerging, particularly in urban contexts. Principles of 'netcentric' work have been developed in the Public Protection and Disaster Relief domain to "improve the exchange of information between heterogeneous actors" (Boersma, Wolbers, and Wagenaar 2010, 1). In the Netherlands, where Boersma and his colleagues study this approach, it is based on a break with "established patterns of command and control . . . [and] supposed to enable new networks of communication" (Boersma et al. 2010, 1). Providing better means of navigating the choppy waters of the organizational and technological transformations involved in this is not just a matter for new networked infrastructures, but also a matter of developing new practices of noticing and collaborating with diverse, dynamically assembled, relevant actors, a design avenue we develop in the SecInCoRe project.

In their review of international public-private partnerships, Chen et al. (2013) identify eight different types of collaborations, three of which involve publics. Firstly, *government-community collaborative resilience building* seeks to utilize informal social networks. One example is the US Federal Emergency Management Agency's 'Whole Community Approach to Emergency Management' (FEMA 2011), which follows three core principles: "Understanding and meeting the actual needs of the whole community, engaging and empowering all parts of the community, and strengthening what works well in communities" (FEMA 2011, 23). However, the approach misconceives community as well defined, sedentary and local when especially urban communities are mobile, fluid, and globally networked (Büscher, Liegl, and Thomas 2014).

64 *Monika Büscher et al.*

Chen et al. contrast FEMA's whole community approach with a second model of *government-civil society partnerships*, drawing an example from Cuba, where high-level political commitment to resilience has informed institution of an annual hurricane exercise that involves the whole population. Integral to the Cuban 'culture of preparedness' is a 'fish-scale role structure' that assigns clear, permanent civil protection roles to local community members like health workers and teachers (Kapucu et al. 2013). They are responsible for local resilience planning and serve as coordinators during the exercise and in real emergencies. This creates flexible overlaps, like the scales of fish, between a local neighborhood or community-based resilience system and the formal command and control model, which are "integrated virtually through the minds of individual responders who operate in dual capacities" (Chen et al. 2013, 135). Other *government-civil society partnerships* rely on Memoranda of Agreement (MOA) or long-term arrangements, such as between the Buddhist organization Tzu Chi and the Taiwanese government. Less effective are ad-hoc coordination attempts, such as those between NGOs and the Chinese government after the Wenchuan earthquake, which led to delayed distribution of resources.

Chen et al.'s third public partnership category, *many-to-many network partnerships*, also aims to bridge distances between different parties. Apart from official agencies and NGOs, it also enrolls more ephemeral mobile publics, where communities temporarily converge around issues of concern, often via digital and mobile technologies used every day. These are of particular interest with a view to networked urbanism, as we will discuss. However, before we move into considerations of emergent mobile publics, the premises of concepts of new networked partnerships warrant closer inspection.

Teething Problems?

Some analysts describe difficulties in distributing responsibilities for risk definition and management as 'teething problems' because it requires "individuals and communities to know the risks, face up to them, safeguard their rights, make informed choices and take an active part in decision making processes" (Scolobig et al. 2015, 4). But the question runs deeper, as experiences raise doubts over whether communities actually want to be more involved. Scolobig et al. (2015) find that, in fact, many do not. And when the different actors proceed on the basis of different (often unspoken) expectations, responsibilities can become unclear, placing communities who wrongly assume that official agencies will provide protection at greater risk, while also placing agencies who expect 'their' communities to be well prepared on treacherous ground. Through a series of case studies, Scolobig et al. reveal further difficulties of conflicting interests. When residents of an Italian town faced with the risk of landslides openly discussed resilience measures, it became clear that communal and individual land-owners' interests did not

Networked Urbanism and Disaster 65

align and investments in preparedness measures were difficult to agree upon. This example is also indicative of a more general problem: Official agencies and expert advisors often struggle to provide fit-for-purpose-information tailored to the highly differentiated interests and levels of knowledge amongst the publics that should be involved. Scolobig et al. conclude that

> if official authorities are to implement effective people-centred disaster risk management, they need to become more attentive observers of social dynamics and more competent communicators, understand the implications of different reciprocal responsibility expectations, and engage in a long term relationship and dialogue with people at risk.
>
> (2015, 8)

These are insightful recommendations. However, by framing conflicts of interest and communication troubles as teething problems, they enter the stage as irritants. It suggests that they should be eliminated before fruitful engagement can proceed. However, there are deeper dynamics at work that show that these 'problems' are actually inevitable, important constitutive components of the lived cooperation in networked communities of risk.

Technologies of Humility

We can use Jasanoff's STS concept of 'technologies of humility' to explore these depths of dealing with risk further. She argues that command and control attempts at "disciplining the incalculable through sophisticated forms of calculation" enact ill-advised hubris (2010, 19). To counteract it, she argues, a shift from disaster risk management to democratic risk governance is necessary. This does *not* mean abandoning command and control. Like the policy scholars above, Jasanoff envisages public engagement as complementary to formal efforts. But there is more to a shift to risk governance than networking. In resonance with Beck's argument of a world risk society, Jasanoff shows that risk governance requires not only expert professionalism and broad-based engagement with local knowledge, but also an understanding of how vulnerability and resilience reflect and enact political choices that affect individuals and communities unequally. In her analysis, the conflicts of interest and difficulties in the recipient design of information that Scolobig et al. observe are not problems that must be overcome before partnerships can function. Indeed, the idea that agreement requires erasure of conflict and difference is misleading. STS research shows that science and politics often misunderstand the public (and thus itself, as Wynne (2007) states). The public (however constituted) are often in a better position to understand risks and be reflexive, because the institutions within which experts practice build upon assumptions about structures, social relations, and local conditions that often do not reflect reality (see also Beck 1999, 10). Plantin (2011) and Kuchinskaya (2012) explore this concretely

66 Monika Büscher et al.

with reference to the Fukushima disaster in Japan and Chernobyl, as we discuss further in relation to 'networks of trust.' Important to note here is that gaining a richer and more broadly shared awareness of risks is not a matter of giving the public the same information the experts use and expecting the same interpretations, understandings, and decisions. Different kinds of information, knowledge, and decisions arise from different perspectives, and risks themselves are not objective facts but arise from within society, despite their often being treated as independent of situation and context (Wynne 1996). Neither scientific nor local experts can provide a single truth or full picture; each provides an incomplete basis for good decisions without the other (Wynne 2007). Risk governance requires new ways of dealing with the inevitable reality disjunctures. There are multiple interpretations of risk, conflicts of interest, and difficulties in communication that arise here, and approaches that address the diversity of risk perceptions as an integral feature of dealing with risks could be constructively leveraged for networked partnerships. Multiple interpretations are not irritants that must be eliminated before such partnerships can work. In resonance with such debates, participatory design scholars and practitioners explore how to shape socio-technical design processes and technologies that can enable agonist pluralism in ways that engage with, rather than erase, these practices (Storni 2013). Jasanoff's epistemological technologies of humility provide four particularly valuable conceptual resources, and we outline these briefly below to develop a deeper understanding of how more pluralist dialogues and controversies around risk and capacities for building communities of risk might be developed.

Firstly, framing risks more widely and seeking insight into multi-causal complexities instill humility. It also fosters reflection and iterative revision. Fortun's (2011) study of the mismanagement of risk in the city of Bhopal illustrates the value of this epistemological and moral technology: In the aftermath of the disaster at the Union Carbide India Limited company, it was not enough to consider the risk of harmful chemicals on the basis of individual substances affecting individual human bodies at a particular point in time. Interactions between multiple substances and long-term interdependencies must be taken into account, and the evaluation of risk and damage may change over time. But while framing brings out the systemic nature of risk, such enhanced circumspection does not address the relational quality of risks. Jasanoff's second technology of humility is a participatory focus on vulnerability, which develops new analytical sensitivities by contrasting practices of risk management with risk governance, echoing Beck's (1999) critique. Risk management often narrowly defines categories of vulnerability on the basis of expert analysis. Risk governance, in contrast, seeks to understand vulnerability in collaboration with those who find themselves or are deemed vulnerable. This approach not only reveals a diversity of vulnerabilities, but also draws out capabilities that otherwise often go unnoticed. In the 2004 South Asian tsunami, for example, different communities coped very differently with the destruction. A focus on vulnerabilities and capacities shows that factors such as history, place, and social connectedness "play crucial roles in determining the resilience of human societies" (Jasanoff 2010, 32). Thirdly, Jasanoff shows how concentrating attention on the distribution of risk can be an effective technology of humility, because it makes clear how risks and damages follow established faultlines of inequality. Klinenberg's (2002) study of the 1995 Chicago heat wave and Hartman and Squires' (2006) research on New Orleans after hurricane Katrina show in distressing detail how these faultlines can deal death in one neighborhood, while sustaining life in the one across the road. Together with a fourth technology of humility, deliberative learning, a focus on the unequal distribution of risk enables collective reflection and evaluation of explanations and approaches (Jasanoff 2003, 242). Deliberative learning brings to the table a form of "social learning where the knowledge of the expert (based on formal experimentum) and that of the concerned laypeople (based on experentia) do not mutually exclude one another," a framework for interaction that resonates with the debates about knowledge in STS outlined briefly above and participatory design (Storni 2013, 52ff.).

When in 2014 the number of people displaced by conflict and persecution increased by 8.3 million, reaching a total of 59.5 million worldwide (OCHA 2015), risk management perspectives failed to raise appropriate awareness of an unfolding crisis. Technologies of humility could have helped frame these figures more circumspectly in relation to their complex causes and potential consequences, heightening awareness of vulnerabilities and capacities for response, and fostering consideration of the distribution of risks. Moreover, by highlighting faultlines of injustice *before* disaster strikes, risk governance raises hopes for the development of communities of risk (Beck 1999). A more relational ethics of risk (Büscher, Kerasidou, Liegl, and Petersen 2016), where "it would not take a hurricane to make visible the plight of the poor" (Jasanoff 2010, 33) or a refugee crisis to highlight a need for integrated European and global responses to displacement, would enable planning for futures where risks are addressed in more richly informed and—if not more just—more richly and broadly understood and contested ways.

These observational and normative arguments are not naive. They recognize that increased participation and transparency in risk governance can "exacerbate rather than quell controversy" (Jasanoff 2003, 237), and they suggest a "reasoned combination and integration of the strengths of both the techno-centric [command and control] and people-centred approaches, rather than . . . complete rejection of one or the other" (Scolobig et al. 2015, 9). Moreover, concepts like communities of risk, agonist pluralism, and technologies of humility are not just normative. They also describe empirical facts of new socio-technical practices of convergence, where mobile publics

68 *Monika Büscher et al.*

drive social, organizational, and socio-technical innovation at the intersection of networked urbanism and disaster risk governance.

Mobile Publics

'Mobile publics' have been a defining feature of networked urbanism for a long time (Bruns 2008; Sheller 2004). They appropriate digital and mobile technologies that have become integral to social life, allowing distributed individuals to converge locally and sometimes globally around issues of concern. These new 'mobile' or 'issue publics' temporarily 'gel' together and disband when interest wanes. In response to disasters, the last decade has seen unprecedented innovation leading to a multiplicity of culturally and politically important, yet often fleeting, mobile publics.

Digital humanitarians form one of these publics. In a news interview, Sharon Reader, beneficiary communications delegate for the Red Cross, captures how the 2010 Haiti earthquake was a landmark moment in networked humanitarian disaster response. She said, what was

> unique about Haiti was how much of an urban disaster [it] was. . . . It hit Port au Prince and Leogane very heavily . . . so you were dealing with a fairly, you know, dense population who do have access to different technologies—Internet, mobile phone . . . even [in] countries like Haiti and right across Africa, this is technology that we can't afford to ignore as humanitarians.[2]

After the earthquake 60–80% of Haitians had access to a mobile phone after the earthquake, and within 48 hours a number of people came together to launch 'Mission 4636,' building on a local freephone weather reporting system. The initiative allowed thousands of people to contribute reports via SMS and developed into a network of over 2000 volunteers to address calls for help where possible and to structure and translate the messages (Munro 2013). It also leveraged the fact that a globally distributed diaspora and concerned individuals converged on social media sites, using Twitter hashtags #haiti and #haitiquake to organize collective efforts. These 'digital humanitarians' (Meier 2015) and 'voluntweeters' (Starbird and Palen 2011) translated messages written in Kreyol, often containing slang terms for locations. Their work facilitated self-organized spontaneous volunteer efforts of mobilizing self-help and resources. They also 'tagged' messages in ways that could be computationally parsed and mapped. Meier and a group of students in Boston set up the Ushahidi Haiti Project (UHP), the first global 'crisis mapping' project, training hundreds of volunteers within the first 100 hours after the earthquake (Meier 2015). And over 600 remote volunteers, mostly members of the Open Street Map community, produced a detailed map of Port au Prince and affected areas, including the location of shelters and available hospitals (Soden and Palen 2014). Together, these collaborations also produced a map of needs that was used by the Department of State analysts for the US government interagency task force and US marines to enhance situation awareness and identify centers of gravity for the deployment of field teams (Morrow, Mock, Papendieck, and Kocmich 2011, Figure 5.2).

What happened in Haiti and its capital Port au Prince "marked the start of something new" (Meier 2015, 16). Digital humanitarianism and crisis mapping have spiraled in significance in a way that now irreversibly embeds social media in disaster management. This increasingly bridges between digital and on the ground practices and globally distributed and local participants, providing approaches that are neither purely top-down nor bottom-up.

Recent networked humanitarian efforts include collaborations in Kathmandu, Nepal, where communities added local knowledge "about the location of debris, temporary shelters, drinking water" to crowd-sourced 3D crisis mapping models of the 2015 earthquake damage via paper printouts (Meier 2015; Figure 5.3) and Facebook's implementation of a 'Safety Check' feature, which had initially been designed and used for natural disasters. In response to the Paris attacks over 4.1 million people checked in as safe—for their family and friends to see—within 24 hours (Breeden 2015).

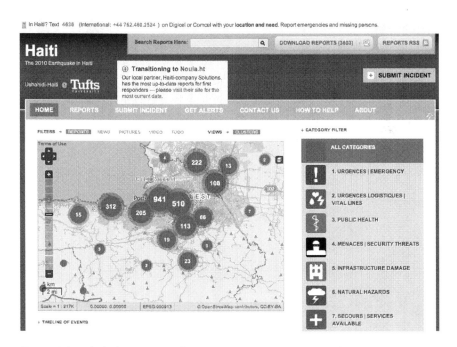

Figure 5.2 Ushahidi Haiti map for Port au Prince, January 2010
Source: www.ushahidi.com/blog/2010/04/15/crisis-mapping-haiti-some-finalreflections

Figure 5.3 Local experts map local knowledge in collaboration with crisis mappers in Kathmandu

Source: http://irevolution.net/2015/11/04/crisis-mapping-nepal-aerial-robotics/

Difficulties and Contradictions

But these new publics and new ways of approaching risk are not without friction and discord. There are some fundamental changes happening. For example:

> What 'Web 2.0' platforms do is shift the primary means of coordination away from hierarchical forms of organization to a network-based coordination structure, where the government is just one of the many nodes within the network.
>
> (Chen et al. 2013, 137)

However, the integration of many-to-many communications into more broad-based risk governance partnerships is by no means smooth. For example, while the digital humanitarian efforts in Haiti clearly made a difference, some professional responders called it a "shadow operation that was not part of the emergency response plan" (Morrow et al. 2011, 16), and some practitioners see serious problems with 'spontaneous volunteers' and digital humanitarians, whereas others see a lack of social, organizational, and digital technolo-

Networked Urbanism and Disaster 71

gies that can support communication, cooperation, and coordination. The challenges in interoperability on all of these layers are amongst the motivations for the SecInCoRe project's concept of a common information space (Pottebaum et al. 2016).

The exchange below, between senior emergency services practitioners at a recent SecInCoRe project workshop, provides a glimpse of such disagreements:

GREEK FIRE SERVICE COMMANDER: The crucial point is that if they are directed through our structures they live under our public liability insurance. . . . If people just turn up digging, [they are] at risk themselves let alone putting other people at risk. Problem [is, they] don't want to be organised but [they've] got to be organised. It's very difficult.

GERMAN RED CROSS OFFICER: I cannot agree on the discussion about spontaneous volunteers . . . that they may be doing dangerous things themselves. The question is exactly the other way around. Why are we not able at the moment to manage that and there an information platform may be helpful cause to be honest from a Red Cross perspective we don't know . . . I don't know what offers they are making, especially really special offers, what skills do we need, when do we need them and how to organise them.

They point out how responsibility and resilience are bound to broader social infrastructures, such as the legal regulations that turn decisions into issues of liability or the institutional foundations that build not just on internal rules but also on feelings and practices of trust beyond 'safe' organizational boundaries and established professional networks.

Moreover, accounts of digital humanitarianism often neglect wider dynamics. Mimi Sheller (2013) highlights how asymmetries of power were re-enacted through the activities of the crisis mappers in Haiti. She shows that the physical and digital influx of highly mobile international responders, from the World Bank to the crisis mappers with their birds-eye maps, coincided with a local population who mostly had neither the means nor the right to move outside the danger zone. In a similar manner, Facebook's decision to open 'Safety Check' to people affected by the Paris attacks, while not offering the same service to those affected by the Beirut bombings, which had killed over 40 people the day before, enacts asymmetries of power and ideology (Breeden 2015). Moreover, if the Facebook service were extended, it could continuously alert millions of people to who might have been (but was not) affected by disasters, stoking a culture of fear (Breeden 2015; Furedi 2006). Another question is how effective the new communication practices are. Many Haitians were unaware of the digital humanitarian effort or did not have a voice in evaluating its usefulness, and many of their calls for help could not be met either by spontaneous volunteers or official agencies (Clémenzo 2011). This highlights an element of 'communicative capitalism' where a concern with the circulation of messages eclipses commitment to dialogue and (political) action (Dean 2005), as well as drawing attention to socio-economic, political,

72   Monika Büscher et al.

and organizational limits of disaster relief. Innumerable post-disaster reports from across the world, from Port au Prince to New Orleans, from Kathmandu to Lancaster, UK, show that all too often there simply is not sufficient capacity made available to address the needs arising in disaster. Voicing and mapping needs more effectively and democratically does not change this. The fact that today over 60,000 Haitians are still in camps, the political system "remains fragile, sustainable jobs are scarce, and the environment is still as vulnerable now as it was" (UNDP 2015), while many of the digital humanitarians and formal relief agencies have moved on to new crises, illustrates this difficulty.

Networks of Trust and Technologies of Articulation

However, crisis mapping activists, members of mobile publics, scholars, and technology developers have developed a range of conceptual, social, organizational, and digital technologies for communication and coordinating and sustaining engagement in ways that begin to work with these concerns and broader frames. Attempts at structuring digital volunteer work and crisis mapping through the UN co-founded Digital Humanitarian Network (Meier 2015) and Virtual Operations Support Teams or VOST (St. Denis, Hughes, and Palen 2012) have begun to create bridges between crisis mappers and formal emergency agencies (Kaminska et al. 2015). They establish networks of trust, that is, mechanisms that combine standardization, training, and agreed channels of communication in ways that mirror historical and sociological examples of successful public engagement in risk governance. These include engagements around air pollution in the nineteenth and early twentieth century (Mosley 2009) and radiation risks from Chernobyl where 'descriptive standards,' 'alignment,' 'unblackboxing,' and 'mobile measuring' proved central to prevent risks from becoming 'twice invisible' (Kuchinskaya 2012). Experiences with such networks of trust show that, for example, accuracy of information is less important than standardized formats enabling comparison across different cities and contexts (Plantin 2011; Mosley 2009). These networks thus inevitably frame risks more broadly and, because they take measure of risks and effects *in situ*, they involve locals without dislodging them from their global connections. They encounter vulnerabilities and capacities for resilience at faultlines of inequality and can thereby effectively gather momentum to inject their insights and concerns into official response efforts and facilitate mutual and deliberative learning. The communities of risk that emerge are less territorial and more distributed, complexly interconnected, diverse, and mobile than the communities currently considered by frameworks like FEMA's 'Whole Community Approach to Emergency Management.'

For example, in the aftermath of the Fukushima nuclear disaster—which was characterized by an absence of information from public authorities—private individuals, companies, and voluntary bodies initiated multiple

Networked Urbanism and Disaster 73

projects of 'critical mapping' of radiation (Plantin 2011). Individuals bought or built their own Geiger counters, learned to measure and map results, and, as their activities coalesced, they shaped official information strategies:

> official information were [*sic*] not the only available anymore as parallel sensor-networks were created; when the official data were published online, they could not be confined to non-readable formats but were harvested to be shared and remix[ed]; finally, official data could be verified by comparing them with other sources of data, as aggregation prevailed over selection.
>
> (Plantin 2011)

Because of a lack of official efforts to inform the public and enable public engagement, the public created an alternative set of information that challenged the authority of the official sources and practices, creating distrust in the official response and forcing them to make their practices more visible and thus able to be debated and aligned to. Networks of trust are emerging as a social 'technology' that allows communities of risk to bring those who live with risk to the same table as those who produce and profit from taking them, necessitating and enabling agonistic pluralist consideration of risks. This puts an additional spin on Beck's 'boomerang effect,' where those who produce certain risks (such as water or air pollution) will eventually also be affected by them (Beck 1992).[3] But to practically support this, technologies of articulation are needed.

In an ethnographic study, Starbird and Palen (2013) illustrate in detail how the emergent VOST organization 'Humanity Road' (HR) coordinates collaboration between a globally distributed, highly fluid group of episodic volunteers. They identify how practices of information stewardship are central to establishing trust and coordinating information exchange. For the HR volunteers and activists this involves orchestrating reflexive, deliberative learning of best practices for producing relevant and reliable information on the fly, by doing. New volunteers are supported by leaders, who lead by virtue of the fact that they are being followed as demonstrably experienced crisis mappers, not due to some pre-assigned status of authority. Instruction proceeds through example and through tools that support articulation work, that is, the externalization of knowledge required to competently accomplish and coordinate the work. Checklists are an example, as the one below, formulated by participants in a 20-person HR Skype chat that evolved in response to an earthquake in Peru in 2011 (from Starbird and Palen 2013, 498):

HR Chris (2:16:40 pm): Checklist
HR Chris (2:16:48 pm): What happened, did it really happen, where, when, details
If yes—share information on texting

74   *Monika Büscher et al.*

If no—share information on verifying before tweeting
Who is the Event Official Source
Examples: Hurrican [*sic*], Tornado, Flood, Earthquake, Wildfire, Health [*sic*]
What is the potential impact to the population
Examples: collapsed buildings, approaching fire, tornado, storm

Starbird and Palen (2013, 498) explain:

> The Checklist is a dynamic document, built through members' media monitoring experiences as digital volunteers, and continuously evolving as members incorporate lessons learned and leaders seek to clarify and streamline the inscribed work process . . . the Checklist is a resource that leaders and experienced volunteers use referentially in their own work practice and prescriptively when training others. In both capacities, the Checklist, . . . structure[s] the organization and its work.

The checklist is a technology of articulation in two senses. Firstly, it supports 'articulation work' (Schmidt and Bannon 1992) by putting into words the work that needs to be done to produce relevant, reliable, and actionable information that will allow formal and informal responders to mobilize appropriate response measures. Secondly, as Latour (2004) shows, it links discursive and material components. Like the pivoting joint that allows an articulated vehicle to turn more sharply, the checklist joins a new volunteer into the organization, it joins the many activities and actors together as an articulated organization, and it offers interfaces for joining digital humanitarian efforts into more widely articulated communities of risk and pluralist forms of disaster risk governance that can be more agile and more constructively agonistic and accommodating of different perspectives.

Discussion: Agile, Articulated, and Constructively Agonistic?

Networks of trust and technologies of articulation are made in engagement with the affordances of new technologies, new partners, new publics, and the complexities of risk. They are ambiguous: simultaneously sites of new forms of community and humanity, and new forms of risk and conflict. In our synthesis, the characterization of the checklist as a technology that articulates the organization, the work, and the emergent communities of risk is important. An example may serve to highlight how the development of new techniques for articulation is, at least in part, driven by difficulties of understanding today's complex mobilities of information and the resulting informational topographies and, simultaneously, a constructive, innovative response to these difficulties. During the search for suspects in the days after the 2015 Paris attacks, Brussels' police imposed a lockdown of the city, engendering lively social media coverage of the events. Then "authorities asked residents not to tweet the whereabouts of raids fearing the suspects would likely monitor police movements," and citizens responded by tweeting cats instead (Vale 2015).

Trivializing and sarcastic perhaps, but attuned to the need for more sensitive situation awareness, citizens learned how their communications can affect and support, as well as challenge and shift, risk governance in practice. More generally, the practices we have discussed in this chapter constitute a particular form of networked urbanism, characterized by interconnected infrastructures, netcentric organizations, and self-organized mobile publics. There are still many more dimensions than we have been able to discuss, such as the 'data deluge' generated as Public Protection and Disaster Relief organizations appropriate this networked urbanism, new modes of exclusion and surveillance (Graham and Marvin 2001) as well as new forms of collective intelligence and action (Büscher et al. 2014; Lévy 1997). Still our analysis provides insights into the need for and the type of work necessary to forge new partnerships and publics. There is a need to understand communities of risk not as static communities of those affected by risks, located physically and permanently in a specific place and in need of protecting, but as socio-technical, dynamic, fleeting, distributed, and mobile collectives that coalesce around risks, that interpret and contest them. The quality of new partnerships does not depend on resolving conflicts of interests and difficulties in defining and communicating about risk. Instead, they require support for communities of risk to form dynamically to express and explore the diversity of interests and interpretations, to practice agonist pluralism, connecting those who produce and assess risks with those who live with and coproduce them, finding ways of leveraging technologies of humility to frame risks, vulnerabilities, and capacities in ways that seek fairness and justice, and to critically consider the distribution of risk. Developing common information spaces, networks of trust, and technologies of articulation can support such practices and the mutual learning needed.

Acknowledgements

The research is part of research funded by the European Union 7th Framework Programme in the SecInCoRe project (Grant no.: 261817) and BRIDGE project (Grant no.: 261817). We thank our colleagues for their inspiration, generous comments and suggestions, especially Paul Hirst, Maike Kuhnert, Michael Liegl, Jens Pottebaum, and Christina Schäfer. The anonymous reviewers of this chapter also provided deeply insightful encouragement to engage more widely with debates of the risk society and we greatly appreciate their comments.

Notes

1. Two recent projects include SecInCoRe (www.secincore.eu) and BRIDGE (www.bridgeproject.eu/en).

76 *Monika Büscher et al.*

2. Transcribed from www.cbc.ca/dispatches/episode/2012/01/26/jan-26-29-from-haiti---kingston-jamaica---butare-rwanda---nicaragua/.
3. We are grateful to the editors for drawing our attention to this connection.

References

BBC News. 2015. "Paris shootings survivor sues French media". *BBC News*, August 18, at www.bbc.co.uk/news/world-europe-33983599 (accessed September 7, 2016).

Beck, U. 1992. *Risk Society*. Sage: London.

Beck, U. 1999. *World Risk Society*. Cambridge: Polity.

Birkland, T. 2009. "Disasters, catastrophes, and policy failure in the homeland security era". *Review of Policy Research*, 26(4), 423–38.

Boersma, K., Wolbers, J. and Wagenaar, P. 2010. "Organizing emergent safety organizations: The travelling of the concept 'Netcentric Work' in the Dutch safety sector". In *Proceedings of the 7th International Conference on Information Systems for Crisis Response and Management Conference*, May, Seattle, USA.

Bossong, R. and Hegemann, H., eds. 2015. *European Civil Security Governance: Diversity and Cooperation in Crisis and Disaster Management*. Basingstoke, UK: Palgrave Macmillan.

Breeden, J. 2015. "Are you safe?" *Disaster Research* 652, November 20, at https://hazards.colorado.edu/article/are-you-safe-social-media-safety-checks-are-useful-maybe (accessed September 7, 2016).

Bruns, A. 2008. "Life beyond the public sphere: Towards a networked model for political deliberation". *Information Polity*, 13(1–2), 71–85.

Büscher, M., Kerasidou, X., Liegl, M. and Petersen, K. 2016. "Digital urbanism in crises". In *Code in the City*, edited by Kitchin, R. and Perng, S.-Y., 163–77. London: Routledge.

Büscher, M., Liegl, M. and Thomas, V. 2014. "Collective intelligence in crises". In *Social Collective Intelligence: Combining the Powers of Humans and Machines to Build a Smarter Society*, edited by Miorandi, D., Maltese, V., Rovatsos, M., Nijholt, A. and Stewart, J., 243–65. Computational Social Sciences Series. Cham and Heidelberg: Springer.

Büscher, M., Perng, S.-Y. and Liegl, M. 2015. "Privacy, security, liberty: ICT in crises". *International Journal of Information Systems for Crisis Response and Management (IJISCRAM)*, 6(4), 76–92.

Chen, J., Chen, T. H. Y., Vertinsky, I., Yumagulova, L., & Park, C. (2013). Public-private partnerships for the development of disaster resilient communities. *Journal of Contingencies and Crisis Management*, 21(3), 130–43. http://doi.org/10.1111/1468-5973.12021.

CBC News. 2015. "Dramatic video and photos from Paris attacks shared on social media". *CBC News Trending*, November 13, at www.cbc.ca/news/trending/paris-attacks-video-photos-social-media-1.3318626 (accessed September 7, 2016).

Clémenzo, J.-Y. 2011. *Ushahidi Project and Mission 4636 in Haiti: Participation, Representation and Political Economy*. MA Thesis, London School of Economics, London.

Dean, J. 2005. "Communicative capitalism: Circulation and the foreclosure of politics". *Cultural Politics*, 1(1), 51–74.

eScience. 2012. "Earth faces a century of disasters, report warns". *(e)Science News*, at http://esciencenews.com/sources/the.guardian.science/2012/04/26/earth.faces.a.century.disasters.report.warns (accessed January 4, 2016).

Networked Urbanism and Disaster   77

Federal Emergency Management Agency (FEMA). 2011. "A whole community app-roach to emergency management: Principles, themes, and pathways for action". *FDOC 104–008–1*, at www.fema.gov/media-library-data/20130726-1813-25045-0649/whole_community_dec2011__2_.pdf (accessed September 7, 2016).

Ferrãos, R. and Sallent, O. 2015. *Mobile Broadband Communications for Public Safety: The Road Ahead Through LTE Technology*. London: Wiley.

Fortun, K. 2011. "Remembering Bhopal, re-figuring liability". *Interventions: International Journal of Postcolonial Studies*, 2(2), 187–98.

Furedi, F. 2006. *Culture of Fear Revisited*. London: Continuum.

Graham, S. and Marvin, S. 2001. *Splintering Urbanism: Networked Infrastructures, Technological Mobilities and the Urban Condition*. London: Routledge.

Hartman, C. and Squires, G. 2006. *There Is No Such Thing as a Natural Disaster: Race, Class, and Katrina*. New York: Routledge.

Hughes, A., Palen, L., Sutton, J., Liu, S. B. and Vieweg, S. 2008. "'Site-seeing' in disas-ter: An examination of on-line social convergence (pp. 324–333)". In *Proceedings of the 5th International ISCRAM Conference*, May 5–7, Washington, DC.

Hughes, A., St. Denis, L. A., Palen, L. and Anderson, K. 2014. "Online public com-munications by police & fire services during the 2012 Hurricane Sandy". In *Proceedings of the 32nd Annual ACM Conference on Human Factors in Computing Systems CHI '14*, 1505–14. New York: ACM Press.

Jasanoff, S. 2003. "Technologies of humility: Citizen participation in governing sci-ence". *Minerva*, 41(3), 223–44.

Jasanoff, S. 2010. "Beyond calculation: A democratic response to risk". In *Disaster and the Politics of Intervention*, edited by Lakoff, G., 14–41. New York: Columbia University Press.

Kaminska, K., Dawe, P., Forbes, K., Duncan, D., Becking, I., Rutten, B. and O'Donnell, D. 2015. "Digital volunteer supported recovery operations experiment". *Defence Research and Development Canada, Scientific Report DRDC-RDDC-2015-R035*, April, at http://pubs.drdc-rddc.gc.ca/BASIS/pcandid/www/engpub/DDW?W%3D KEYWORDS+PH+WORDS+%27Digital+Volunteer+Supported+Recovery+Oper ations+Experiment%27+ORDER+BY+Repdate/Descend%26M%3D1%26K%3 D801344%26U%3D1 (accessed September 7, 2016).

Kapucu, N., Hawkins, C. and Rivera, F. 2013. *Disaster Resiliency: Interdisciplinary Perspectives*. London: Routledge.

Klinenberg, E. 2002. *Heat Wave: A Social Autopsy of Disaster in Chicago*. Chicago: University of Chicago Press.

Kuchinskaya, O. 2012. "Twice invisible: Formal representations of radiation dan-ger". *Social Studies of Science*, 43(1), 78–96.

Latour, B. 2004. "How to talk about the body? The normative dimension of science studies". *Body Society*, 10(2–3), 205–29.

Lévy, P. 1997. *Collective Intelligence: Mankind's Emerging World in Cyberspace*, translated by Bononno, R., Cambridge, MA: Perseus Books.

Lund, D. 2015. "European public-safety stakeholders debate broadband chal-lenges, spectrum at PSCE forum". *Mission Critical Communications*, Monday, December 14, at www.radioresourcemag.com/Features/FeaturesDetails/FID/624 (accessed September 7, 2016).

Mashable. 2011. *Via Red Cross Pinterest Board*, at https://uk.pinterest.com/pin/508977195356660231/ (accessed September 7, 2016).

Meier, P. 2015. *Digital Humanitarians: How Big Data Is Changing the Face of Humanitarian Response*. Boca Raton, FL: CRC Press.

78 Monika Büscher et al.

Morrow, N., Mock, N., Papendieck, A. and Kocmich, N. 2011. "Independent evaluation of the Ushahidi Haiti project". *Development Information systems International*, at www.alnap.org/pool/files/1282.pdf (accessed September 7, 2016).

Mosley, S. 2009. "'A network of trust': Measuring and monitoring air pollution in British cities, 1912–1960". *Environment and History*, 15(3), 273–302.

Munro, R. 2013. "Crowdsourcing and the crisis-affected community: Lessons learned and looking forward from mission 4636". *Information Retrieval*, 16(2), 210–66.

OCHA. 2015. "World humanitarian data and trends 2015". *Policy Development and Studies Branch, United Nations Office for the Coordination of Humanitarian Affairs*, at https://docs.unocha.org/sites/dms/Documents/WHDT2015_2Dec.pdf (accessed September 7, 2016).

Oh, O., Agrawal, M. and Rao, H. R. 2010. "Information control and terrorism: Tracking the Mumbai terrorist attack through twitter". *Information Systems Frontiers*, 13(1), 1–11.

Older, M. 2014. "When is too much money worse than too little? Giving, aid, and impact after the Indian Ocean Tsunami of 2004". In *Recovery from the Indian Ocean Tsunami*, edited by Shaw, R., 121–37. Tokyo: Springer Japan.

Petersen, K., Büscher, M., Becklake, S., Thomas, V., Easton, C., Liegl, M., Leventakis, G., Tsoulkas, V., Daniilidis, I., Malliaros, S., Kavallieros, D., Hirst, P., Schneider, S., Ferrara, F. and Firus, K. 2014. "Overview of disaster events, crisis management models and stakeholders". *SecInCoRe Deliverable D2.1*, at www.secincore.eu/wp-content/uploads/2015/09/D2.1_Overview-of-Inventory_20150831_v2.pdf (accessed September 7, 2016).

Plantin, J.-C. 2011. "The map is the debate: Radiation webmapping and public involvement during the Fukushima issue". Paper presented at the Oxford Internet Institute, *A Decade in Internet Time: Symposium on the Dynamics of the Internet and Society*, at SSRN: http://ssrn.com/abstract=1926276 or http://dx.doi.org/10.2139/ssrn.1926276 (accessed May 8, 2016).

Pottebaum, J., Kuhnert, M., Schäfer, C., Behnke, D., Büscher, M., Petersen, K. and Wietfeld, C. 2016. "Common information space for collaborative emergency management". In *Proceedings of the IEEE International Symposium on Technologies for Homeland Security 2016*, Boston.

Red Cross Pinterest board. At https://uk.pinterest.com/pin/380624605978546110/?from_navigate=true (accessed September 7, 2016).

Schmidt, K. and Bannon, L. 1992. "Taking CSCW seriously: Supporting articulation work". *Computer Supported Cooperative Work Journal*, 1(1), 7–40.

Scolobig, A., Prior, T., Schröter, D., Jörin, J. and Patt, A. 2015. "Towards people-centred approaches for effective disaster risk management: Balancing rhetoric with reality". *International Journal of Disaster Risk Reduction*, 12, 202–12.

Sheller, M. 2004. "Mobile publics: Beyond the network perspective". *Environment and Planning D: Society and Space*, 22(1), 39–52.

Sheller, M. 2013. "The islanding effect: Post-disaster mobility systems and humanitarian logistics in Haiti". *Cultural Geographies*, 20(2), 185–204.

Soden, R. and Palen, L. 2014. "From crowdsourced mapping to community mapping: The post-earthquake work of OpenStreetMap Haiti. In *COOP 2014—Proceedings of the 11th International Conference on the Design of Cooperative Systems, 27–30 May 2014, Nice (France)*, edited by Rossitto C., Ciolfi L., Martin, D. and Conein, B. Cham: Springer.

St. Denis, L.-A., Hughes, A. and Palen, L. 2012. "Trial by fire: The deployment of trusted digital volunteers in the 2011 Shadow Lake fire". In *Proceedings of the 9th International ISCRAM Conference*, April 1–10, Vancouver, Canada.

Starbird, K. and Palen, L. 2011. "'Voluntweeters': Self-Organizing by Digital Volunteers in Times of Crisis". In *Proceedings of the ACM 2011 Conference on Human Factors in Computing Systems (CHI 2011)*, Vancouver, CA. Honorable Mention Award.

Starbird, K. and Palen, L. 2013. "Working and sustaining the virtual 'Disaster Desk'". In *Proceedings of the 2013 Conference on Computer Supported Cooperative Work—CSCW '13*, 491–502. New York: ACM Press.

Storni, C. 2013. "Design for future uses: Pluralism, fetishism and ignorance". *Nordes*, 5, 50–9.

UNDP. 2015. "'Rebuilding Haiti.' Our projects and initiatives". *United Nations Development Program*, at www.undp.org/content/undp/en/home/ourwork/our-projects-and-initiatives/crisis_in_haiti.html (accessed December 28, 2016).

UNISDR. 2015. "Sendai framework for disaster risk reduction". *United Nations Office for Disaster Risk Reduction*, at www.unisdr.org/we/coordinate/sendai-framework (accessed September 7, 2016).

Vale, P. 2015. "Brussels lockdown sparks residents to flood Twitter with cat pictures as police search for Paris suspects". *Huffington Post*, November 23, 2015, at www.huffingtonpost.co.uk/2015/11/22/brussels-lockdown-cat-pictures_n_8624456.html (accessed September 7, 2016).

White, J., Palen, L. and Anderson, K. 2014. "Digital mobilization in disaster response". In *Proceedings of the 17th ACM Conference on Computer Supported Cooperative Work & Social Computing—CSCW '14*, 866–76. New York: ACM Press.

Wynne, B. 1996. "Misunderstood misunderstandings: Social identities and public uptake of science". In *Misunderstanding Science? The Public Reconstruction of Science and Technology*, edited by Irwin, A. and Wynne, B., 19–45. Cambridge: Cambridge University Press.

Wynne, B. 2007. "Risk as globalizing 'democratic' discourse? Framing subjects and citizens". In *Science and Citizens: Globalization and the Challenge of Engagement*, edited by Leach, M., Scoones, I. and Wynne, B., 66–82. London: Zed Books.

6 Vertical Mobilities

Confronting the Politics of Elevators in Tall Buildings and Ultra-Deep Mining

Stephen Graham

Looming high above the Japanese city of Fuchu, a dense suburb 20 kilometers to the west of central Tokyo, a 213-meter building dominates the low suburban skyline. Seemingly too thin to be of any commercial use, the 'G1 Tower' sits, surrounded by a glade of trees, rather incongruously, at the heart of a huge research campus of the giant Hitachi Corporation.

Opened in 2010, the purpose of the tower is not to whisk affluent urbanites above the smog, noise, and traffic. Nor is it some material embodiment of hubris and ego in the material 'race' upward that is so evident in the global spread of super-tall skyscrapers. It is, rather, a vertical test-track: the world's highest elevator research tower, a living testament to the central role of Japanese engineers in, as Ryan Sayre (n.d.) so pithily puts it, "technologically reworking the innards of 'up'."

Tasked with developing ultra-high-capacity and ultra-high-speed elevators now demanded by the world's vertically sprawling megacities, the tower—the world's tallest lift research structure—is basically a series of lift shafts unadorned with surrounding residential or commercial space. It is a perfect monument to the skyward reach of the world's cities and, more particularly, to the crucial but often ignored roles of new vertical transportation technologies in facilitating this reach. Hitachi is using the $61 million tower to design and develop a new generation of elevators that will be like the Shinkansen of the urban skies: super-fast, high-capacity elevators that will exceed 1 kilometer a minute in speed. "If you worked at the Hitachi G1 Tower," gushes Meghan Young of the *Trendhunter* blog in 2010, "I'm sure one day will be enough to satisfy your need for speed. Roller coasters? Easy as pie. A formula 1 race car ride? You could do it sleeping. The world's fastest elevator? Now that's a ride!"

Hitachi, like other big elevator manufacturers, is also using the tower to design a whole new array of high-tech elevator technologies. There are new design, power, and materials technologies to design lighter, smaller lift shafts and elevator cars; double decker lift cars (in effect, elevators stacked one on top of the other); 'destination dispatch' elevators which assess the preferred destinations of potential riders in advance of their entering the elevator and use algorithms to assign them to specific cars to reduce overall movement;

and even pressurization systems that automatically compensate riders' ears for the reducing pressure of ascent.

The first of these is especially important as 'super-tall' skyscrapers of over 100 stories proliferate across the world because elevator shafts consume a higher proportion of overall space as the floor-plate of buildings reduce in size as they reach greater heights (from 7% to 20% as towers shift from 70 to 100 stories, for example; see Simmen 2009, 17).

The weight of steel ropes and lifting systems, meanwhile, has limited vertical ascents to around 500 meters in one go. Elevators have thus "become the bottleneck of the super high-rise building," as Johannes de Jong, of the Kone elevator company, points out to *Business Week* in 2013 (quoted in Catts 2013). Echoing the long coevolution of skyscraper and mine elevators, Kone's 350-meter research elevators, built to research the same challenges as Hitachi's tower, are placed in a disused mine in the Helsinki suburb of Lohja. Capturing this coevolution perfectly, the shaft is called the 'High-Rise Laboratory.'

Kone executives are especially hopeful that their new carbon-fiber rope technology, which they claim is the 'holy grail' in skyscraper engineering, will allow elevators to safely ascend 1000 meters in one go (double the current limit). This would allow the widespread construction of skyscrapers way beyond 1 kilometer tall. "Today most engineers will tell you that the limit of vertical height in buildings has more to do with the steel cable in elevator shafts than any other factor" (Rosen 2013).

Startlingly, beyond a few technical articles in the trade presses of the 'vertical transportation' industry (see Strakosch and Caporale 2010), structures like the G1 Tower, and the elevators that they shape, remain almost invisible within social scientific debates on cities, urbanism, and the burgeoning 'mobilities turn.' Indeed, such is the absence of the elevator from the new social science literature on mobilities that it is easy to forget that elevators are complex systems of mobility (albeit ones that travel vertical space).

Similarly, beyond its appearance within certain genres of cinematic film, and periods when elevators were carefully designed as ornamental spaces in their own right, elevator urbanism has received little of the wider poetic celebration of, say, airplane urbanism, auto-urbanism, or railroad urbanism. "While anthems have been written to jet travel, locomotives, and the lure of the open road, the poetry of vertical transportation is scant" (Paumgarten 2008).

Entire libraries can be filled with volumes exploring the cultures, politics, and geographies of the largely *horizontal* mobilities and transportation infrastructures that are intrinsic to urban modernity (highways, railways, subways, public transit, and so on). Indeed, a highly important 'mobilities turn,' linked closely to the cultural analysis of speed (Virilio 2006), has been underway in the last two decades within the social sciences and humanities aimed at excavating the cultural politics of such embodied flows within contemporary societies (see Urry 2007). By contrast, the cultural geographies and politics of *vertical* transportation within and between the buildings of

82 *Stephen Graham*

vertically structured cityscapes have been largely ignored by social scientists and humanities scholars (although see Cwerner (2006) on elite helicopter verticalities). The social scientific literature on lifts, elevators, and vertical people movers thus remains both minuscule and esoteric (see Goetz 2003; Simmen 2009).

The lift or elevator, then, remains a preeminent example of what sociologists of mobility and technology call a 'black box': a complex socio-technical system or assemblage relied upon to sustain the routine processes of urban life, but where that routine dependence—and the internal operation of the artifact—is only very rarely examined or exposed (see Winner 1993).

All of this means that the elevator, I would argue, needs to be brought centrally into social scientific discussions of the cultural politics of urban space. With this in mind, what follows is an attempt to offer a preliminary cultural politics of elevator urbanism. As an attempt to encourage a critical social science of elevator urbanism, my discussions are deliberately very broad in scope (they, for example, connect elevator urbanism to the even more neglected worlds of ultra-deep subterranean mining using new elevator systems). The paper discusses, in turn: the historical emergence of elevator urbanism; the cultural significance of the elevator as spectacle; the global 'race' in elevator speed; shifts towards the 'splintering' of elevator experiences; experiments with new mobility systems which blend elevators and automobiles; problems of vertical abandonment; and, finally, the neglected politics of elevators which, rather than ascending upwards within buildings, descend deep into the earth to sustain 'ultra-deep' mining.

Beyond some work indirectly discussing the crucial roles of elevators in the emergence of skyscrapers (Gottman 1966), or in modernist housing programs (Jacobs and Cairns 2013), I am aware of not a single academic paper explicitly addressing the detailed geographies of elevators within my own particular sub-discipline of urban geography—an academic discourse that, one would have thought, might have a great deal to say on the subject. (It is paradoxical, indeed, that the world's geographers gather in their thousands every year in a major corporate hotel in a US city for the American Association of Geographers conference. During this they perform complex vertical choreographies using elevators to move between multiple sessions on 'mobilities,' 'time-space compression,' 'logistical urbanism,' 'transport geographies,' and so on, where the ubiquitous and crucial power of this taken-for-granted device remains utterly absent.)

This particular neglect, no doubt, is one legacy of the largely flat constructions of geographic space in geography that has come with a widespread reliance on the 'Bird's Eye' views of the cartographic gaze that Eyal Weizman diagnosed in his critique of conventionally 'flat' geopolitical discourses (see Weizman 2002).

Reflecting its own origins in the traditions of top-down cartography, the sub-discipline of transport geography, too, has tended to treat cities and regions merely as flat surfaces rather than volumes. As part of a broader 'vertical turn' in urban studies (see Graham and Hewitt 2013), however, transport geographers and planners are finally starting to realize that the politics of accessibility in vertically stacked and vertically sprawling cities, laced together by assemblages combining multiple vertical and horizontal transportation systems, requires urgent attention.

"The comprehension of the very nature and complexity of spatial and functional relationships between these spaces," write Jean Claude Thill and colleagues (2011, 405), "framed by the indoor and outdoor infrastructures supporting human movement (hallways, elevator shafts, walkways, and others) is enhanced once it is recognized that the city is not flat." Some residents in that most verticalized of contemporary cities—Hong Kong—now apparently travel almost as far vertically using elevators as they do horizontally by foot, bus, or subway.

The 'Colonization of the Up'

> The elevator is a special prop for the imagination. . . . [But] of all the imaginings associated with the elevator [in film, futurism, and science fiction], one extreme vision has already become reality. Elevators, as the 'germs' or technological imperatives that can determine a skyscraper's height and footprint, have travelled through urban fields with the speed of an epidemic, making, in less than half a century, cities grow in block after block of towers.
>
> (Simmen 2009, 18)

The elevator has a history of at least 2000 years: Rome's Colosseum even had a system of 12 winch-powered elevators operated by slaves to lift wild animals and gladiators straight into the bloody action of the arena. Without a means of drawing power from more than human muscle, however, such systems were inevitably highly limited.

It was Elisha Otis' invention of a safe, automatically braking elevator in Yonkers, New York, in the 1850s that created a technology for the vertical movement of people as well as goods that has been central to the rapid colonization of vertical space through urban growth. (However, as Andreas Bernard (2014) demonstrates, the origins of the elevator are complex and multifaceted; Otis merely added the crucial innovation safe breaking to well-established hoisting systems.)

"This small innovation," writes Ryan Sayre (n.d.), "opened an entirely new kind of space; a space we might call the 'up'." "'Up' had of course always existed," he writes, "but not until the late 19th century had it become a place to work and live. Up as a habitable territory had to be made, sometimes forcefully but always without precedent."

When combined with electric or hydraulic power and cable drum innovations adopted from the mining industry—of which more, later—safely-braked or 'safety' elevators released cities from the millennia-old constraints

84 Stephen Graham

created by the human ascent of stairs; the overcoming of gravity for the movement upward of human inhabitants was able to match the overcoming of gravity through innovations in skyscraper construction. By 1916, the Woolworth Building in Manhattan—the world's highest 'skyscraper' at the time—boasted 29 elevators that ascended at 3.5 meters per second to an altitude of 207 meters (Simmen 2009, 20).

Faster, bigger, and more reliable elevators have been fundamental to the skyward shift in architecture and engineering ever since. Hitachi's research elevators are now running at speeds that are 300 times as fast as those in New York a hundred years ago. Whilst geographers talk widely of a 'time-space compression' (Harvey 1989) effect caused by the widespread diffusion of new transport and communications technologies over the past century and a half—telegraphs, telephones, the Internet, air travel, global shipping, automobiles, and railways—a similar, albeit neglected, effect of vertical time-space compression has occurred through the dramatic speeding up of elevator cars.

Elevators also played less obvious roles in the iconic growth upwards of the skyscrapers of corporate America—especially in Chicago and New York—during the late nineteenth and early twentieth centuries. Social historian of technology Ithiel de Sola Pool (1977) stressed that the history of the skyscraper has, in fact, been inseparable from the history of both the elevator—which allowed ingress and egress of required office workers—and of the horizontally stretched networks of electronic communication (telegraphs and then telephones) that allowed those people both to commute to work and to attempt to exercise control at a distance over dispersed sites once there. Without telephones to allow the central power of the modern metropolis to concentrate and pile high into the sky, so many lift shafts would have been necessary to carry the multitudes of messenger-boys to the destination of the message (factories, warehouses, shipping centers, and the like) that there would have been far too little office space left for the buildings to be viable.

Elevator travel has long been a central component of cultural notions of urban modernity. This relationship is complex, however. In one sense, the experience of being crammed in a box with strangers moving rapidly upward, pulled by a suite of hidden motors and cables, can induce powerful, almost primeval, anxieties. Indeed, psychologists recognize fear of elevators as a serious and widespread phobia. Such anxieties are rapidly compounded with unexpected delay and malfunctions—hence the introduction of 'elevator music' in 1928. The shift away from staffed elevators to automated ones added to the sense of dissocialized vulnerability and was paralleled by a shift from ornate to utilitarian styles of design of elevator interiors (Hall 2003).

Elevators are by far the safest form of powered transport: only 61 people dying within them in the US whilst at work between 1992–2001 (Wilk 2006). However, the becalmed normality and hushed voices of habitual vertical ascent merges into the purest horror with the prospect of being trapped completely, the (extraordinarily rare) breakage of a cable, or, rarer still, the collapse of the overall building. (In the World Trade Center disaster

Vertical Mobilities 85

in September, 2001, when an estimated 200 people died in elevators in free-falls, smoke, fire, or eventual structural collapse, "the elevator shafts . . . became chimneys of accelerating fire" (Simmen 2009, 24)).

More prosaically—as we shall see later—unreliable, vandalized, and poorly maintained elevators have long been the Achilles' heel of modernist dreams of mass social housing housed in vertical towers, especially in North American and European cities. Without functioning elevators, these Corbusian blocks, rather than emancipating 'machines for living' or modern spaces projected into the light and air of vertical space, quickly reduce to dystopian nightmares of extreme isolation and enforced withdrawal, especially for those with children or the less mobile. J.G. Ballard's (1975) novel *High-Rise* is a superb evocation of such a breakdown.

"The elevator is an utterly essential technology for high-rise housing" (Jacobs and Cairns 2013, 84). Recognizing this, the better managers of mass vertical housing systems—such as the Singaporean Housing Development Board—maintain an emergency 24-hour response team to allay residents' concerns about vertical isolation caused by elevator failure.

Vertical (Post)Modernities

> This small room, so commonplace and so compressed . . . this elevator contains them all: space, time, cause, motion, magnitude, class.
>
> (Coover 1969, 4; cited in Garfinkel 2003, 173)

Elevator ascent, surrounded as it is by primeval anxieties, is also profoundly modern. It has been likened to a rather banal form of vertical teleportation. "Unlike ship, air or rail travel," Jeannot Simmen argues, it "does not entail journeying from place to place and offers nothing to see. Instead of passage over time, the relevant parameter is the time wasted while ascending" (2009, 28).

And yet the elevator remains extraordinary: Human enclosure within them is a fascinating exercise in urban anthropology. As density increases, imperceptible adjustments are made by inhabitants as to their location, demeanor, and eye position. This maximizes personal space and minimizes the risk of unwanted intimacy. "Passengers seem to know instinctively how to arrange themselves in an elevator," writes Nick Paumgarten (2008):

> Two strangers will gravitate to the back corners, a third will stand by the door, at an isosceles remove, until a fourth comes in, at which point passengers three and four will spread toward the front corners, making room, in the center, for a fifth, and so on, like the dots on a die.

The experience of elevator travel is also over coded with a rich history of fictional, filmic, poetic, and science-fictional imagination. From the mysterious and secret seven-and-a-half floor in the 1999 film *Being John Malkovich*,

86   Stephen Graham

to a whole chapter of urban folklore, or a myriad of unfortunate and filmic deaths and catastrophes, the elevator stalks the interface being the banal and the fearful or unknown within the vertical and technological cultures of the contemporary metropolis.

"Public yet private, enclosing yet permeable, separate from but integral to the architectural spaces that surround them," elevators, Susan Garfinkel (2003, 176) writes, "invite us to expect the unexpected in certain predictable ways." In film, she shows how elevators have variously been used to symbolize the 'corporate ladder'; aspirations of social or economic advancement or sexual liaison (or sexual predation); the democratization of "public space; anxieties of technological collapse; the monotony of corporate life; and anxieties of urban anomie. In Depression-era American cinema physical proximity and the elevator's rapid upward thrust are meant to augur the heterosexual liaisons that follow" (Schleier 2009, 68). Sometimes, as in Woody Allen's 1997 film *Deconstructing Harry*, elevators are used to symbolize anxieties about the how vertical connections might operate as thresholds to Heaven or Hell.

Importantly, the relatively standardized and enclosed experience of the modern elevator is increasingly shifting—at least amongst high-end office buildings or the celebrated and spectacular vertical structures visited by tourists. Since transparent 'rocket-ship' style elevators were installed along the interior atrium of John Portman's influential Hyatt Regency Hotel in Atlanta in 1967 (Figure 6.1), exterior, glass, or 'panorama' elevators on the inside or outside of buildings are increasingly common.

Connected with long-standing tropes of science fiction and space-age futurism, from H.G. Wells' 1936 film *Things to Come* or Charlie's journey skyward in Roald Dahl's *Charlie and the Great Glass Elevator*, here the vertical journey itself is increasingly exposed, commodified, and celebrated. Within some systems—most obviously at Seattle's Space Needle, built in 1972—the vertical journey also became packaged to directly ape the Apollo astronauts' vertical elevator ride up an Apollo gantry to be strapped into a Saturn V rocket for a moon launch.

As with other celebrated postmodern architectural icons, such as Los Angeles' Bonaventure hotel or Detroit's Renaissance Center, Portman's transparent elevators in Atlanta were crucial in creating the sense of a mini, self-contained city—a pure space of consumption and spectacle, powerfully removed from the world beyond the curtilage. "The elevator really established the dynamics of the whole space," Portman recalled. "To pull the elevators out of the wall made them like moving seats in a theatre" (cited in Patton 2003, 110–111). In turn, they quickly became icons of Atlanta's rapid growth in the 1970s and symbols of a much broader geographic rebalancing of US urban growth towards the South. After the opening of Portman's hotel, Phil Patton recalls that

> visitors from the rural hinterlands around Atlanta made special trips to the city to see the elevators. The multiple cars, rising as others fell,

Figure 6.1 The atrium elevators in Atlanta's Hyatt Regency Hotel

Source: Photographed by Rick, Attribution License. www.everystockphoto.com/photo.php?imageId=2118096&searchId=df5c185d11d7b7c09b6f8085f14d18e8&npos=3

were tapered at the ends like candies in twist wrappers and lit like miniature riverboats. . . . The elevator ride was worth the whole trip: a rocket launch take off, then the passage through the building's roof to the Polaris rotating restaurant.

(2003, 106)

Notably high or fast vertical journeys within iconic towers, meanwhile, are increasingly fetishized as part of wider fantasy landscapes of urban tourism and consumption. The elevator ride increasingly becomes a commodified destination and spectacle in and of itself. Elevators in glitzy new towers on Australia's Gold Coast, for example, now have video screens on the ceilings depicting the image of the receding lift shaft above—along with indicators of speed and location—so that occupants can be more exposed to the nature of the journey (Figure 6.2). (Predictably, they don't show the view *below* when descending; presumably this might be a source of occupants' fear.)

Whether or not such reminders of the vertical mobility underway beyond the (usually) opaque box are always appreciated, though, is a moot point.

Figure 6.2 'One of Australia's fastest elevators': The real-time video screen on the cab roof of the tower to the sky lobby on the Skypoint Tower on Australia's Gold Coast

Source: Photograph by Stephen Graham.

The Otis Company recently conducted research to assess whether elevator passengers would appreciate screens emphasizing the fact that they were hurtling vertically up and down deep vertical shafts. They found "that people would rather be distracted from that fact" (cited in Paumgarten 2008).

"Where Are the Fastest Elevators?"

The spread of vertical cities, not surprisingly, is linked to a global boom in the industries of vertical transportation. In 2012 there were roughly 11 million elevators and escalators in service across the world. Around 700,000 were being sold a year and the global market was expected to grow at 6% per year to be worth $90 billion a year by 2016, up from $56 billion in 2008 (Bodimeade 2012). Not surprisingly, Asia, and especially China, totally dominates this growing market: Half of all investment was in China in 2010 (Koncept Analytics 2010).

Rapid advances in lift/elevator technology are as fundamental to the global proliferation of super-tall skyscrapers as are innovations in materials science and civil engineering. In Japan, new elevator technology has been central to relatively recent moves beyond long-standing earthquake-limited height controls—30-meter limits were in place until 1968—that have spawned a series of multi-use 'city within city' vertical complexes. In some ways, these resemble scaled-up and vertically stretched versions of John Portman's 1970s and 1980s North American designs. (Examples include the Sunshine 60 building—which had the world's fastest elevators between 1978 and 1993—and Roppongi Hills.)

These "vascular shafts" (Sayre 2011, 11), encompassing super-thin malls, elite condominiums, multistory parking garages, corporate HQs, and expensive hotels and restaurants, are serviced by some of the world's fastest elevators. These are marketed publicly as icons of national modernity, every bit as symbolic of radical time-space compression or kinetic elitism as the more familiar Shinkansen bullet train networks that lace the country's cities horizontally. "With four of the world's five fastest elevators today produced by Japanese companies," writes Ryan Sayre, "Japan has actively promoted velocity as a worthy rival to altitude in the colonization of 'up'" (Sayre, n.d.).

Indeed, super-fast elevators are now being lauded by the world's business press as proxy indicators of what's really going on in the fast-changing economic geographies of globalization, urban growth, and real estate speculation. "If you want to know where the world's hottest economies are," *Forbes* magazine gushes, "skip the GDP reports, employment statistics and consumer spending trends. All you need to do is answer one question: Where are the fastest elevators?" (Van Riper and Malone 2007, quoted in Sayre 2011, 10). The world's fastest elevators currently—installed by Toshiba in the Taipei Financial Center, Taiwan—currently peak at a vertical speed of 60 km/hour and are pressurized to avoid ear damage amongst riders (Figure 6.3).

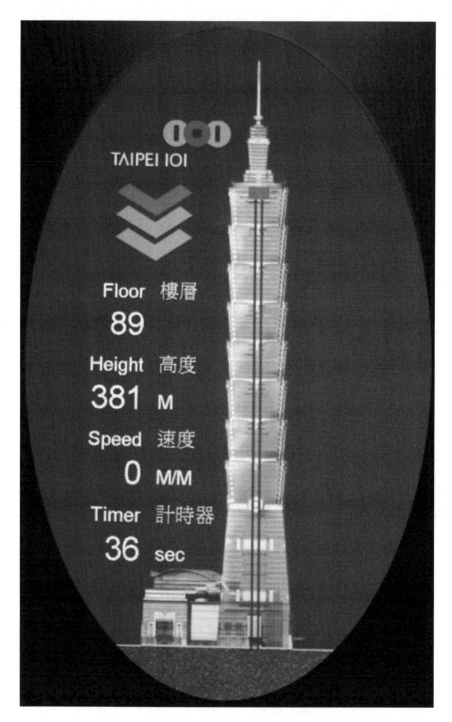

Figure 6.3 Vertical Shinkansen: The video screen and accompanying data graphics for the world's fastest elevator—made by Toshiba—which serves the 508-meter Taipei 101 tower in Taiwan. When the building opened in 2004 it was the world's tallest skyscraper. Floor, height, speed, and position in the building are all displayed as part of the spectacle of ascent

Source: Erik Charlton, Attribution License. www.everystockphoto.com/photo.php?imageId= 2487517&searchId=4c2d42fe0e4e397a8fcfddc39815bb06&npos=20

In April 2013, Hitachi excitedly announced that they were taking over the vertical speed record with the construction of even faster elevators—developed in the G1 Tower already discussed—in a new 530-meter tower in Guangzhou, China. These will climb 95 floors in a mere 43 seconds, a maximum speed of 72 km/hour.

Much higher super-tall towers served by unprecedented vertical transportation systems have long featured in modernist architectural imaginaries. In 1956, for example, Frank Lloyd Wright designed a mile-high tower—a 528-story city-tower for Chicago. This was replete with 66 atomic-powered quintuple-decker elevators traveling at 60 miles an hour. Ever since, architectural fantasy has centered on constructing ever-higher and more grandiose vertical visions. (Currently, Dubai's Burj Khalifa is being trumped by the 1-kilometer Kingdom Tower rising to the sky in Jeddah.)

Elsewhere, automated elevators have been incorporated into radically vertical structures for stacking everything from containers to cars within broader systems of logistics, warehousing, and transportation. The 'Car Tower' operated by Volkswagen in Wolfsburg, Germany, is perhaps the most iconic example here (Figure 6.4).

Way beyond even the gigantic scale of projected architecture, the dream of a functioning elevator linking the earth's surface to a geostationary satellite—or even the moon—has long gripped science fiction writers. The International Academy of Astronautics even argued in 2014 that a 100,000-kilometer 'space elevator' will be feasible by 2035 by applying emerging research into super-strength carbon nanotube materials. A means of radically reducing the costs of launching satellites, such a project, built as a 'tether' to winch loads vertically into space, would also, they argue, be a crucial step to much more intensive extra-planetary exploration and colonization (Swan 2013).

Street People, Air People

> There were the Street People and there were the Air People. Air people levitated like fakirs. . . . Access to the elevator was proof that your life had the buoyancy that was needed to stay afloat in a city where the ground was seen as the realm of failure and menace.
>
> (Raban 1991, 80)

As such vertical megaprojects are imagined, marketed, and constructed, whether as putative responses to sustainability challenges, demographic and urban growth, the changing possibilities of speculation and construction technology, or sheer megalomania, so the uneven social geographies surrounding vertical mobility are likely to become more and more stark. Social inequalities in access to vertical transportation are already starting to mimic the increasingly 'splintered' geographies which have long surrounded horizontal systems (with 'premium' services like airport trains and TGVs 'bypassing' poorer geographical areas; see Graham and Marvin 2001).

Figure 6.4 VW's Car Tower in Wolfsburg, Germany, a system of vertically moving and storing customers' new cars via an elevator which is part of a large car-themed theme park

Source: I Love Butter, Attribution License. www.everystockphoto.com/photo.php?imageId= 6243169&searchId=81e1664fbd4d22263b41462d67220fd4&npos=2

Vertical Mobilities 93

Ascension of the super-tall towers of the 1930s, limited by elevator technology of the time, involved several time-consuming changes between elevators that were vertically staggered in sequence up the structure. These elevators were able to stop at every floor. "Experience of these repeated journeys in the Empire State building, Mark Kingwell (2006, 192) writes, served to remind the upward traveller of his [*sic*] constant and continued suspension." "There is nothing," he continues, "like having to change elevators three times that shows that cable does not stretch indefinitely far."

The design of stronger cables, though, allowed single-leap elevators to reach the tops of super-tall towers. Such a shift both allowed the super-fast and super-tall elevator experience to be sedimented into urban culture as the ultimate socio-technical 'black box'—a miraculous teletransportor involving merely the act of walking into and walking out of a room at startlingly different heights. "I enter a small room," Kingwell observes, "the doors close; when they open again, I am somewhere else. The taken-for-granted elevator is perhaps the closest thing we have to the *Star Trek* transporter device, and it is so ordinary we hardly even think to think about it" (2006, 192).

Such new technologies also facilitated the engineering of 'unbundled' and 'splintered' elevator experiences: radically diversified elevator speeds and leaps, organized to allow elite or premium users to experience intensified processes of vertical time-space compression whilst 'bypassing' less valued users who were removed into more prosaic and slower elevators (Graham and Marvin 2001). Since the architects of New York's World Trade Center introduced the idea of the 'sky lobby' in 1973—a lobby halfway up super-tall towers where 'express' and 'local' elevators can exchange traffic—super-high towers, mimicking the pattern of subway trains on the New York subway, have increasingly been built with fast, long-distance, or 'shuttle' elevators and 'local' slower ones which stop on every floor. Such approaches are starting to allow designers and architects to carefully customize different elevator speeds and experiences to different classes of residents or visitors.

In effect, such transformations work to diversify experiences of vertical mobilities, replacing single public passage-points up and down with a spectrum of vertical mobility systems organized using the latest card and radio-chip-based access-control technologies familiar in many hotels. Compounding widening fears about the vertical secession of elites in the world's cities (see Cwerner 2006), express and VIP elevators can bring elite users occupying the prestigious penthouse spaces of towers radically 'closer' to the ground whilst conveniently bypassing the mass crowds confined to the shuttles that stop at every floor below.

Already, a variety of lifts provide highly segmented vertical topologies through which to ascend the world's tallest building, the Burj Khalifa in Dubai. Those lucky enough to access the 'VIP' lift to the luxury restaurants and viewing platforms on the 123rd floor (Figure 6.5) ride upwards in a

Figure 6.5 View from the viewing platform on top of the Burj Khalifa in Dubai

Source: Le Grand portage, Attribution License. www.everystockphoto.com/photo.php?imageId= 8744614&searchId=aa64abcf0aca61fb01fc7c07d204db11&npos=32

luxurious lift car in around a minute beneath a sign that reads "the stars come out to play" (and hence extolls both the status of the selected passengers and their velocity upwards).

Meanwhile, super-luxury hotel towers like the Waldorf Astoria in Ras Al Khaimah, also in the UAE, are keen to extend the capsular geographies that their clients demand: They now advertise that their penthouse suites are now equipped with entirely private VIP lifts (see De Cauter 2005). Many corporate office towers are now also now being equipped with VIP lifts that whisk CEOs and top executives straight to their offices at the apex of buildings without having to stop at intervening floors or rub shoulders with the company's workforce from the 'lower' tiers of corporate hierarchies.

The extreme vertical urbanism embodied in possible future projects like the 2.4-kilometer, 400-story 'vertical city' projected for Dubai is an example of the projected use of a range of elevator systems to deliver different levels of time-space compression to different users on the vertical plane. It has been deliberately designed with "internal elevator layout[s] splitting the working populations from the residents and providing high speed VIP express services to designated areas" (*Khaleej Times* 2008).

Trapped: Vertical Transport Crises

> Good high-rises rely on good elevators.
>
> (Cizek 2011a)

Beyond the glitz of the VIP elevators serving super-tall residential towers, with their modernist imagery of serene and frictionless ascent in incredibly fast capsules, the vertical mobilities sustained by elevators remain starkly contested. On the one hand, the complete dependence of occupants in tall towers on vertical transport means that elevator access to the world beyond can become the ultimate 'ransom strip'—a means to extort higher and higher service charges from dependent tenants (Figure 6.6).

Many residential tenants renting out some of the 1000 apartments in the Burj Khalifa, for example, have recently found themselves to be electronically locked out of some of the luxurious spas, gyms, and other facilities that they assumed their £40,000 annual rent allowed them to access. Such communal services have been withdrawn because the tenants' landlords have been failing to pay the building's owners the high maintenance and service charges stipulated in their contracts. In 2013, typically, these amount to around £155,000 for owners of a £1 million apartment. Increases have gone way beyond rates of inflation: In 2012 they rose 27%. When property owners can't or won't pay, building owners resort to locking tenants out of key communal facilities or posting 'name-and-shame' lists of non-paying tenants next to elevator doors (Armitage 2014).

In social or low-income housing towers, meanwhile, the costs and problems of maintaining elevators is a perennial problem. Often, vertical transport crises caused by decrepit and unreliable elevators lead to social isolation in cities just as powerfully as the more visible and reported horizontal crises of failed rail, auto, or air travel systems.

Whilst attention in Canadian cities has centered on the rise of private condo towers, many of low incomes are often marooned in the sky by the failure to maintain continuous elevator services in the cities' stock of increasingly decrepit high-rise rented towers that are populated by low-income communities. The United Way (2011) lobby group warns that Toronto, for one, is becoming a city of 'vertical poverty' where the physical renewal of these towers' elevators—as well as the rest of the buildings—is necessary to prevent a major infrastructural crisis which systematically isolates the population's most vulnerable members high in the sky. Growing up in a decrepit tower in an inner city in Toronto, Jamal, a participant in the study, recalls that

> the elevator would skip floors, jumping and jolting, moving up and down. I used to wonder if we would survive if the elevator dropped from the 13th floor to B2. I was so terrified when my family went in there. I

Figure 6.6 A broken elevator in Chicago

Source: The Dark Thing, Attribution License. www.everystockphoto.com/photo.php?imageId=10805698&searchId=63ccd1baa824e17f8456520cc2befac4&npos=13

Vertical Mobilities   97

had disturbing thoughts that they wouldn't come out. To this day, I'm scared of the elevator.

(quoted in Cizek 2011b, 3)

In France, meanwhile, the plight of immigrant communities in high-rise banlieues where elevator services have become ever more perilous has become a widespread symbol of the troubled politics of assimilation in the post-colonial Republic since the 2005 riots. Clichy-sous-bois, a largely African neighborhood on Paris' Eastern periphery where the 2005 riots started, has become a symbol of processes of vertical as well as social and horizontal abandonment. Since the riots, the physical spaces of high-rises have deteriorated, anyone who could afford it has moved out, and crime levels have escalated. Elevators maintenance has collapsed (especially in private rented blocks). Many families have found themselves to be isolated in the sky for long periods.

In 2013, Margareth, a Congolese immigrant living near the top of a high tower, was interviewed by Paris' *LesinRocks* magazine. The elevators in Margareth's block are now "mere ornaments," the magazine reported (Doucet and Sudry-le-Dû 2013). Repairs, at best, take several months. When interviewed, it had been over a week since Margareth had been to ground level to shop. "With the kids, just the trip, it would take me almost an hour" she says (quoted in Doucet and Sudry-le-Dû 2013). When she does shop, she minimizes weight to make the ascent of the stairs easier. "I have techniques. I take the syrup to avoid packs of juice." "A woman ascends slowly and silently up the stairs, bent double under the weight of a full cart, she pulls with a strap from the front," the local mayor, Claude Dilain, writes scathingly in *Le Monde*. "She lives on the 8th floor. We are 15 km from Paris, is this possible?" (quoted in Doucet and Sudry-le-Dû 2013).

A complex support and barter system amongst neighbors, along with an improvised pulley system to raise shopping bags to higher floors, is the only thing keeping the less mobile tenants from real hunger. In 2013, as tenants waited for elevator repairs, Dilain intervened and organized a system of 'live elevators': volunteers to help residents ascend the stairs. (The name of one of the towers so served—Tour Victor Hugo—inadvertently reminds us of another scene in the complex history of Paris' vertical politics.)

The reliance of modern elevators on electricity adds a further twist to the vulnerability of high-rise occupants. Whilst power outages never featured in the imaginings of the modernist architects who postulated life in vertical towers, thrust up into the 'light and air' and away from the urban ground, the fragilities of contemporary power grids can quickly turn vertical living into vertical isolation. This was powerfully demonstrated in October 2012 as Hurricane Sandy tore into New York City. "With Hurricane Sandy knocking out power to much of Lower Manhattan, the downside of living near the top of a glittering new skyscraper was made clear" (Cameron 2012). Residents were forced to discover the stairwells of buildings that they had not seen in years (if at all).

98 Stephen Graham

The 400,000 residents in public housing 'projects' were particularly badly hit with over 430 elevators shut down due to power outages. These also stopped water and sewage pumping, forcing often vulnerable, disabled, and frail residents and children to try to improvise the carrying of water—as well as food—up long stairways. Ill residents had to be manhandled down stairways; nearby fire hydrants were opened to obtain water; dark stairwells became fearful and exhausting structures that had to be rediscovered and negotiated (often painfully). Widespread calls ensued for emergency back-up power to be installed into towers in the event of future outages, calls that were rejected because of inadequate funds.

Going Down: Elevators and 'Ultra-Deep' Mining

> As gold prices reach near-record highs, South Africa's mining companies are keeping up by drilling to record depths.
>
> (Wadhams 2007)

Discussions of the cultural politics of the elevator, where they happen at all, suggest that these stop entirely at ground level. And yet, as suggested above, the subterranean worlds of elevator travel—subsumed within the crucial but usually invisible worlds of mining—are even more startling than those above ground (Figure 6.7). As with the world's largest bunkers, the most enormous subterranean mining complexes are like cities underground that exist far from—and yet operate to sustain—the world's rapidly expanding surface-level metropolises.

Indeed, whilst the language changes—with an 'elevator' relabeled a 'cage'— the technologies of building massive vertical mining structures deeper and deeper into the ground have fundamentally coevolved with those for building the growing forests of taller and taller skyscrapers into the sky. Whilst the latter, located at the cores of the North's global cities, house the corporate executives, stock markets, and super-rich financiers that draw vast wealth from deep, neo-colonial excavation of scarce and valuable metals and ores in the Global South, the former provide the sources of some of the key materials used to construct vertical urban towers. And yet the popular graphs showing the rising heights of skyscrapers over the last century are never accompanied by graphs showing the parallel, but much more extraordinary and dangerous, excavations down.

"When one tries to clarify the role played by mining in the early history of the elevator," Andreas Bernard (2014, 28) writes, "one finds an interesting simultaneity under and above ground." This is grasped visually when the familiar pattern of the historic growth of tall buildings is juxtaposed with the much more neglected, but far more spectacular, excavation of elevator-mobilities into deeper and deeper mines (Figure 6.8).

Gray Brechin (1999), in his pioneering work on the imperial ecological politics that surrounded the growth of San Francisco, also stresses deep

Figure 6.7 Belgian coal miners ascending to the surface in a mining elevator or 'cage,' 1920s

Source: Public domain.

connections between mining and skyscrapers and the complex coevolution of their elevator systems. He shows how many other elements that were key to the corporate skyscrapers in North American downtowns from the late nineteenth century onwards actually emerged first in deep mines. California

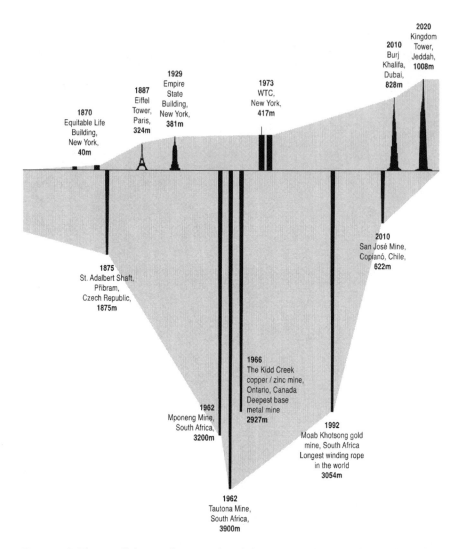

Figure 6.8 The parallel growth upward and downward of the world's highest skyscrapers and its deepest mines between 1850 and the contemporary period

Source: Modified and updated from Koolhaas (2014, 12–13).

gold mines provided the sites where the ventilators, multilevel telephones, early electric lighting, and high-speed safety elevators that would be crucial to skyscraper construction were first used systematically. "All were demanded and paid for by the prodigious output and prospects of the gold mines of California" (Brechin 1999, 70). In addition, the use of square supports to

Vertical Mobilities   101

build large multistory structures within mines to provide support as material was removed provided the basis for the famous steel girder structures of corporate towers.

The parallel processes of using these suites of technology to dig down, to provide the raw materials to construct raised-up skyscrapers, were not lost on contemporary commentators. "Imagine [the mine] hoisted out of the ground and left standing on the surface," wrote reporter Dan De Quille. The viewer

> would then see before him [*sic*] an immense structure, four or five times as large as the biggest hotel in America, about twice or three times as wide and over two thousand feet high. In a grand hotel communication between these floors would be by means of an elevator; in the mine would be in use the same contrivances, but instead of an elevator it would be called a 'cage.'
>
> (quoted in Brechin 1999, 67)

Influenced by Lewis Mumford's (1934) ideas of the capitalist 'mega machine'—where financial industries constitute an economic apex based ultimately on the exploitative and dangerous processes of mining—Brechin stresses that De Quille's vision is even more evident in the contemporary context of super-tall 1-kilometer towers and 4- to 5-kilometer ultra-deep mines. Indeed, he even suggests that the clusters of finance towers that commonly signify the centers of 'global' cities should be seen as 'inverted minescapes' "reaching up from the staked claims of downtown real estate" (Brechin 1999, 70) and reliant ultimately on the speculative and commodified wealth sustained by the dangerous labor of mining at greater and greater depths (along with other primary or extractive industries).

Following the pioneering visions of De Quille, Mumford, and Brechin, much more attention needs to be paid to the neocolonial geographies of *vertical* resource grabs—and the wider 'resource curse' that often accompanies these processes for marginalized groups—as well as their more familiar horizontal counterparts.

One place to start doing this is with contemporary gold mining. Whilst deep mining is reaching further and further into earth's crust to reach remaining bodies of a wide range of scarce ores and metals in the context of burgeoning demand and high prices—at least until the recent crash in global commodities prices—it is the frenzy for gold that is driving the most extraordinary elevator descents deep into the earth's crust.

The Mponeng mine, 60 kilometers from Johannesburg—currently the world's deepest—is the poster child for so-called 'ultra-deep' gold mining where super-long elevators descend over 3.5 kilometers (2.2 miles) below the earth's crust. "New shallow deposits [of gold], aren't easily being discovered around the world," Ray Durrheim, a South African seismologist reported in 2007. "The resources are at greater depths" (quoted in Wadhams 2007).

102 *Stephen Graham*

Mponeng's huge vertical, three-deck elevators which descend down vast shafts into the earth—perhaps they should more properly be called 'depressivators' or 'lowervators'?—take 120 miners at a time. They descend downwards through the mine's 123 levels ten times further than the elevators to the viewing deck of the Empire State Building ascend. At such depths, the temperature of the rock, slightly closer to the radiation-based heat of the earth's core, reaches 60°C (140°F); the entire mine has to be refrigerated using 6000 tons of ice a day to stop the miners from baking alive.

Matthew Hart (2013), journeying to the depths of the Mponeng mine in 2013, reflects on the comparison of the mine's elevators with those of the world's tallest building. "In the . . . Burj Khalifa in Dubai," he writes,

> 57 elevators shuttle people up and down the tower, often in stages through upper-floor 'sky lobbies.' We had travelled five times the distance covered by the Burj Khalifa's system, and had done it in a single drop. We made our way to the cage that would take us deeper, to the active mining levels that lay far below. We stepped into the second cage and in two minutes dropped another mile into the furnace of the rock.
>
> (Hart 2013)

The mining galleries that reach away from the elevators would cover the areas of Manhattan between 59th and 110th Streets. And the tunnel systems built to allow miners to extract the ore are 30 miles longer than the New York City subway (Hart 2013).

But mines like Mponeng are more than interesting subjects for overexcited documentaries filled with endless lists of impressive statistics on the *Discovery Channel*. As the rescue of 33 miners from Copiapó copper mines in Chile in 2010 demonstrated very publicly, they are perilous places for extremely dangerous labor driven by the wild speculation of commodity processes that are a key feature of globalized neoliberalism. Matthew Hart (2013) calculates that the extraordinary price of gold in 2012—$1581 an ounce, a figure driven higher by declining confidence in other investments—meant that Mponeng alone produced $950 million worth of the metal that year.

Just as they are central to higher skyscrapers, faster and bigger elevator systems are crucial in opening up deeper and deeper layers of gold and other metals and minerals to systematic exploitation. "With improved winder and rope technologies," *Mining Weekly* reports, "cages can now be hoisted below 3000m in a single drop." This offers "great economic benefit in deep-level mines as it enables personnel to reach the rockface far sooner and thus have more productive time at the face" (Rebelo 2003).

Fueled by extraordinary levels of profitability caused by unprecedented gold process, gold mining corporations are already planning even deeper shafts to reach untapped, ultra-deep resources. The AngloGold corporation is planning to dig to 4.5 kilometers by 2018, tempted by the estimated

Vertical Mobilities   103

"100-million ounces of gold that cannot be mine conventionally" deep within South Africa's goldfields (Creamer 2013). As in skyscraper elevators, the weight of ropes is a key constraint. Back in 1997 mining engineer D.H. Diering admitted that "if someone asked the question 'what would stop us going to 5000m today, assuming there was an ore body worth going to and enough money to pay for it?,' the simplified answer would be 'ropes'" (1997, 250). Innovations like the carbon-fiber rope being launched for skyscraper elevators are thus likely to fuel the latest in a long line of technological crossovers over the next 20 years in the parallel pushes upwards for skyscrapers and downward for mines.

Whilst nowhere near as deadly as the thousands of illegal, informal, or artisanal mines that dot the mining regions of Latin America, Africa, and parts of Asia, the elevators in relatively high-tech deep mines remain extremely dangerous.

Like all major mines, Mponeng also reports regular deaths and injuries during normal operations. In South Africa, an average of five miners die each week (Bell 2000). At least six fatalities were reported in the mine by *Mining Weekly* during 2012/13; the killers involved seismic collapses, heavy machinery malfunctions, and electrocution. Scientists have also raised concerns that ultra-deep mines can trigger surface-level earthquakes.

In May, 1995, in the most notorious deep shaft disaster so far, the engine of an underground railcar in the Anglo-American Corporation's Vaal Reefs Mine near Orkney, South Africa, broke loose and fell down a 2-kilometer (7000 feet) elevator shaft. Crushing a two-deck cage completely flat, it instantly killed the 105 men within it.

"We would not generally oppose the idea of ultra-deep mining if our people were safe," Lesiba Sheshoka, of South Africa's National Union of Mineworkers (NUM), told *National Geographic* in 2007. "But we are opposing it on the basis that . . . we have already seen a significant rise of fatalities" (Wadhams 2007).

Such resistance to ultra-deep mining fails to even address the gold industry's catastrophic record of fatalities and debilitating illness through diseases like silicosis, nor its appalling track record in legal denials for liability. South Africa's NUM—currently taking UK-owned gold firms to court in London along with 3500 ex-miners to force recognition of the problem—calculates that there are at least 50,000 ex-goldminers in South Africa with silicosis (which is often fatal through reduced resistance to TB).

What is especially striking is that, whilst huge investments go in to deeper and deeper mines to keep miners alive whilst mining (and, of course, to secure and protect the all-important gold), very little is done about the air and ventilation problems that cause silicosis. "It was always possible through ventilation and proper clothing to protect people from silica dust in [gold] mines," NUM president Senzeni Zokwana said when interviewed about the case. "But in the past men were down [the mines] just to break rocks and make money" (cited in McVeigh 2014).

104 Stephen Graham

Conclusions

As the earth's surface becomes ever more densely settled and contested, so human structures are reaching upward and downward from the earth's surface with ever-greater reach and intensity. And yet, in their largely *horizontal* preoccupations with the geographies of globalization and urbanization, the 'mobilities' and 'infrastructural' turn in the social sciences and humanities remain startlingly blind to the pivotal importance of vertical mobility systems—and especially elevators—in facilitating such processes.

By adopting parallel perspectives to the histories, politics, sociologies, and geographies of vertical mobility systems extending both above and below the earth's surface, this chapter has hinted at a rich and important research frontier within these interdisciplinary bodies of research.

With some estimates in that most verticalized city of Hong Kong that some of the city's residents now travel vertically in elevators, escalators, and other conveyance devices as far as they travel horizontally on subways and sidewalks, it is time for the politics of elevator-based mobilities to be brought fully into the debates about the broader politics of infrastructure and mobility (for a fuller discussion of the politics of the vertical dimension, see Graham 2016).

Acknowledgements

This chapter draws on a previously published paper (*Theory, Culture & Society*, 31 (7/8), 2014). The author would like to gratefully acknowledge the crucial inputs of Lucy Hewitt into the research that shaped this article. He would also like to thank Newcastle University's Faculty of Arts, Humanities and Social Sciences for key financial support that allowed this research to be completed.

References

Armitage, J. 2014. "Trouble at the £1bn Burj Khalifa tower: Spiralling service costs see landlords falling behind on their bills". *The Independent*, February 13, at www.independent.co.uk/news/world/middle-east/trouble-at-the-1bn-burj-khalifa-tower-spiralling-service-costs-see-landlords-falling-behind-on-their-bills-9127085.html (accessed April 14, 2014).

Ballard, J. 1975. *High-Rise*. London: Harper.

Bell, T. 2000. "Miners who are doing dirty work deserve better". *Business Report*, October 6, at www.queensu.ca/samp/sampresources/migrationdocuments/commentaries/2000/better.htm (accessed March 14, 2014).

Bernard, A. 2014. *Lifted: A Cultural History of the Elevator*. New York: New York University Press.

Bodimeade, M. 2012. "Global elevator market led by Otis Elevator Company". *Companies and Markets*, at www.companiesandmarkets.com/News/Industrial/Global-elevator-market-led-by-Otis-Elevator-Company/NI5817 (accessed April 17, 2014).

Brechin, G. 1999. *Imperial San Francisco: Urban Power, Earthly Ruin*. Berkeley: University of California Press.

Cameron, C. 2012. "With elevators down, high-rise residents suffer". *The Real Deal Blog*,November 1,at http://therealdeal.com/blog/2012/11/01/with-elevators-down-high-rise-residents-suffer/ (accessed April 14, 2014).

Catts, T. 2013. 'Otis elevator vies for the ultratall skyscraper market". *Business Week*, January 31, at www.businessweek.com/articles/2013-01-31/otis-elevator-vies-for-the-ultratall-skyscraper-market (accessed April 14, 2014).

Cizek, K. 2011a. "Elevators—Highrises-cities". *Highrise Blog*, February 9, at http://highrise.nfb.ca/2011/02/elevators-highrises-cities/ (accessed April 14, 2014).

Cizek, K. 2011b. "Poverty is vertical—and the elevators are terrible". *Highrise Blog*, January 20,at http://highrise.nfb.ca/2011/01/poverty-is-vertical-and-the-elevators-are-terrible/ (accessed April 14, 2014).

Coover, R. 1969. *The Elevator, Pricksongs and Descants: Fictions*. New York: E. P. Dutton.

Creamer, M. 2013. "AngloGold Ashanti moving closer to ultradeep mining goal". *Mining Weekly*, March 2, at www.miningweekly.com/article/anglogold-ashanti-moving-closer-to-ultra-deep-mining-goal-2013-02-05 (accessed March 14, 2014).

Cwerner, S. 2006. "Vertical flight and urban mobilities: The promise and reality of helicopter travel". *Mobilities*, 1(2), 191–215.

De Cauter, L. 2005. *Capsular Civilization: On the City in the Age of Fear*. Rotterdam: NAI.

de Sola Pool, I. 1977. *The Social Impact of the Telephone*. Cambridge, MA: MIT Press.

Diering, D. H. 1997. "Ultra-deep level mining: Future requirements". *The Journal of The South African Institute of Mining and Metallurgy*, 97, 248–56.

Doucet, D. and Sudry-le-Dû, C. 2013. "Clichy-sous-Bois, entre abandon et solidarité". *LesinRocks*, January 28, at www.lesinrocks.com (accessed April 14, 2014).

Garfinkel, S. 2003. "Elevator stories: Vertical imagination and the spaces of possibility". In *Up, Down, Across: Elevators, Escalators, and Moving Sidewalks*, edited by Goetz, A., 173–95. Washington, DC: National Building Museum.

Goetz, A., ed. 2003. *Up, Down, Across: Elevators, Escalators, and Moving Sidewalks*. Washington, DC: National Building Museum.

Gottman, J. 1966. "Why the skyscraper?" *Geographical Review*, 56(2), 190–212.

Graham, S. 2016. *Vertical: The City from Satellites to Bunkers*. London and New York: Verso.

Graham, S. and Hewitt, L. 2013. "Getting off the ground: On the politics of urban verticality". *Progress in Human Geography*, 37(1), 72–92.

Graham, S. and Marvin, S. 2001. *Splintering Urbanism*. London: Routledge.

Hall, P. 2003. "Designing non-space: The evolution of the elevator interior". In *Up, Down, Across: Elevators, Escalators, and Moving Sidewalks*, edited by Goetz, A., 59–78. Washington, DC: National Building Museum.

Hart, M. 2013. "A journey into the world's deepest gold mine". *Wall Street Journal*, December 13, at http://online.wsj.com/news/articles/SB10001424052702304854804579236640793042718 (accessed April 14, 2014).

Harvey, D. 1989. *The Condition of Postmodernity*. Oxford: Blackwell.

Jacobs, J. and Cairns, S. 2013. "Ecologies of dwelling: Maintaining high-rise housing in Singapore". In *The New Blackwell Companion to the City*, edited by Bridge, G. and Watson, S., 79–95. Oxford: Blackwell.

106   Stephen Graham

Khaleej, T. 2008. *Dubai: Vertical City, 2.4 km (1.5 miles) Tall*, at http://al-burj.blogspot. dk/2008/09/dubai-vertical-city24km-15-miles-tall.html (accessed September 7, 2016).

Kingwell, M. 2006. *Nearest Thing to Heaven: The Empire State Building and American Dreams*. New Haven: Yale University Press.

Koncept Analytics. 2010. Global Escalator & Elevator Market Report: 2010 Edition. www.prlog.org/11007013-global-escalator-elevator-market-report-2010-edition-new-report-by-koncept-analytics.html.

Koolhaas, R. 2014. *Elevators*. Venice: Marsilio.

McVeigh, T. 2014. "South African miners take lung disease fight to London". *The Observer*, April 27, at www.theguardian.com/world/2014/apr/27/south-african-miners-lung-disease-fight-london (accessed April 29, 2014).

Mumford, L. 1934. *Technics and Civilization*. Chicago: Chicago University Press.

Patton, P. 2003. "Hovering vision". In *Up, Down, Across: Elevators, Escalators, and Moving Sidewalks*, edited by Goetz, A., 105–23. London and New York: Merrell [exhibition, National Building Museum, Washington, DC, September 12, 2003–April 18, 2004].

Paumgarten, N. 2008. "Up and then down: The lives of elevators". *The New Yorker*, April 21, at www.newyorker.com/reporting/2008/04/21/080421fa_fact_paumgarten?currentPage=all (accessed April 15, 2014).

Raban, J. 1991. *Hunting Mister Heartbreak: A Discovery of America*. London: Collins Harvill.

Rebelo, E. 2003. "World's deepest single-lift mine ever". *Mining Weekly*, September 29, at www.miningweekly.com/article/worlds-deepest-singlelift-mine-ever-2003-09-29 (accessed April 14, 2014).

Rosen, L. 2013. "Materials science update: New discovery may lead to mile-high buildings". *21st Century science*, June 21, at www.21stcentech.com/materials-science-update-discovery-lead-mile-high-buildings/ (accessed March 14, 2014).

Sayre, R. 2011. "The colonization of 'Up': Building up and to the right in postwar Japan". *Architectonic Tokyo*, at http://architectonictokyo.com/colonization_of_up.html (accessed April 15, 2014).

Schleier, M. 2009. *Skyscraper Cinema: Architecture and Gender in American Film*. Minneapolis: University of Minnesota Press.

Simmen, J. 2009. "Elevation: A cultural history of the elevator". In *Access for All: Approaches to the Built Environment*, edited by Christ, W., 15–30. Basel: Birkhäuser.

Strakosch, G. and Caporale, R., eds. 2010. *The Vertical Transportation Handbook*. London: Wiley.

Swan, P. 2013. *Space Elevators: An Assessment of the Technological Feasibility and the Way Forward*. London: Virginia Editions.

Thill, J., Dao, T. and Zhou, Y. 2011. "Traveling in the three-dimensional city: Applications in route planning, accessibility assessment, location analysis and beyond". *Journal of Transport Geography*, 19(3), 405–21.

United Way. 2011. *Poverty by Postal Code 2: Vertical Poverty*. Toronto: United Way.

Urry, J. 2007. *Mobilities*. London: Routledge.

Van Riper, T. and Malone, R. 2007. "The world's fastest elevators". *Forbes*, January 10, at www.forbes.com/2007/10/01/elevators-economics-construction-biz-logistics-cx_rm_tvr_1001elevators.html (accessed June 15, 2014).

Virilio, P. 2006. *Speed and Politics*, New edn. Los Angeles: Semiotext(e).

Wadhams, N. 2007. "World's deepest mines highlight risks of new gold rush". *National Geographic News*, November 6, at http://news.nationalgeographic.com/news/2007/11/071106-africa-mine.html (accessed April 14, 2014).

Weizman, E. 2002. "Introduction to the politics of verticality". *Open Democracy*, April 24, at www.opendemocracy.net/ecology-politicsverticality/article_801.jsp (accessed June 15, 2016).

Wilk, S. 2006. "Elevator safety: What to do if someone is trapped". *Elevator World*, September 2006, 129–32.

Winner, L. 1993. "Upon opening the black box and finding it empty: Social constructivism and the philosophy of technology". *Science, Technology, & Human Values*, 18(3), 362–78.

Young, M. 2010. "The Hitachi G1 tower will test world's fastest elevator". *Trendhunter*, February 25, at www.trendhunter.com/trends/hitachi-g1-tower (accessed April 15, 2014).

7 Mobilities Futures

Vincent Kaufmann

Mobility is at the heart of social dynamics, be it values, social stratification, or spaces. Mobility contributes to the ideological and structural foundations of a society. This happens via the territories it produces both in terms of geographical and social space, as well as defining models of social success (Harvey 2001). It also highlights what is changing through that which moves and how it moves.

Mobility is a powerful social analyzer, to the point of being regarded as a total social phenomenon, as defined by Marcel Mauss (Bassand and Brulhardt 1980). In other words, it "is never just a trip, but [rather is] always an action at the heart of social processes of function and change" (Bassand 1985, 25). Considering mobility as a total social phenomenon helps us use it as a reading lens for the whole of a society.

It is based on this idea that we wish to explore mobility in this article, by attempting to link its social and spatial dimensions. The fixed backdrops often reified in classic works on social mobility, space, and time now occupy a central place in sociological analysis from at least three standpoints.

- From the standpoint of movement in social space, there no longer exists a universal (i.e. imposed) model of social success but rather *numerous models*. As such, social mobility cannot merely be reduced to vertical movement between socio-professional positions, but must also include a spatial dimension. The very idea of vertical and horizontal movement is challenged as it is based on the existence of a single social ladder.
- From the standpoint of exchanges, societies are highly interconnected, and cannot be regarded as autonomous in terms of their structures. Their networking and cosmopolitanism require that they are no longer considered as autonomous entities, as per the canons of 'methodological nationalism' (Kalir 2013).
- From the standpoint of technical systems, telecommunications and transportation have become 'manipulators' of ever-shrinking time and space. Against this background, the social imperative to be mobile is becoming increasingly pressing, especially in the working world. Moving fast, far, and frequently has become an expectation for proving that one is

Mobilities Futures 109

dynamic, motivated, and ambitious. Knowing how to identify and bend the rules of this injunction has thus become an essential skill for social and professional integration in general, and for career ascension in particular.

Ultimately, what runs through debates in this research arena is the idea that the greater a person's or actor's mobility potential is, the greater their social mobility is. Luc Boltanski and Eve Chiapello (1999) summarize this position in *Le nouvel esprit du capitalisme*, asserting that social hierarchies are being challenged, and that social mobility is now expressed through the constant renewal of projects. The notion of a successful (i.e. vertical) career has changed; it is no longer first and foremost a question of conquering status in a hierarchical structure, but of being able to 'bounce back,' to move from one project to another in order to 'surf' from one enviable position to another in an ever-changing environment. As such, the issue of social critique has also changed: It is less a question of condemning inequalities linked to the reproduction of positions, than of addressing inequalities of access to the possibility of being socially mobile.

From its beginnings, industrial society has valued social mobility, as it allows for the creation of dynamics of collective development based on individuals' desire to improve their own socio-economic situation. Everyone participates in this endeavor, in the hopes of improving their living conditions and social status on a merit basis. This supposes two principles: personal freedom in the definition and realization of the statutory project and the principle of equality of individuals, so that personal background is no longer an obstacle to the desired social ascension. Paradoxically, this means maintaining egalitarian rhetoric in the competition for statuses that are inherently unequal. The paradox is usually raised by the implementation of processes that seek to ensure initial equality among actors. The contemporary valorization of mobility is built on the same logic. Fast and far embody the idea of freedom, through which individuals are free to establish whatever contacts they wish, without spatial or temporal obstacles—a logic that implies that those most likely to have enviable social statuses are also those who are the most flexible.

Thus, the particularity of the contemporary ideology of mobility is to assume, by a shift of meaning, that spatial mobility is therefore conducive to the equal distribution of individuals on the social ladder, and that simply facilitating access is enough to even the tables socially speaking. In this interpretation, the extensive development of rapid and long-distance mobility that societies throughout the world are experiencing is a strong indication of a shift towards a juster world. Questioning this equation seems essential as it is based on preconceptions. This will be the focus of my investigation in this article: Is increased spatial mobility a vector of social fluidification, in the sense of more equal social movement in the professional world?

To fully explore this issue, I must pay special attention to technical and territorial networks and the social changes that come with their development.

110 *Vincent Kaufmann*

The compression of time and space that has resulted from the development of transportation systems and telecommunications in the past 30 years, and the reduction of obstacles relative to the movement of people, goods, and capital are transforming societies and spaces by making them fairer, as they are based on meritocratic principles.

The mobility of the main factors of production has increased considerably. In terms of capital, mobility has developed simultaneously with the financial industry and increased yields. Liberalization, the development of ICT, and new services in the financial industry have created fast movement at the global scale. In daily life, these new opportunities have not only been adopted by populations, who use them intensively, but are also often used in ways that differ from those originally intended by their designers. Moreover, the spatial and temporal organization of cities and territories is now traversed by considerable differences of speed, from walking to the immediacy of telecommunications.

As such, a person's ability to move in geographical spaces has become a key resource of social mobility and social inclusion in general (Kaufmann 2011).

Actors are characterized by a more or less pronounced potential to be mobile in geographical, economic, and social space (Castells 1996). With the range of possibilities for moving in space, this potential can take very diverse forms. A person or a collective actor, such as a business, can uproot from one place and reroot in another. Another actor can be very good at maintaining long-distance social ties. In other words, mobility potential is localized and depends on actors' skills, aspirations, and constraints. We measure this potential through the notion of motility, which is defined as all the characteristics that allow an actor to move (Kaufmann et al. 2015; Kaufmann 2014). Motility therefore refers to the social conditions of access (to mobility services in a broad sense), the required skills, and mobility projects, that is, how the services are actually used to realize these projects. For example, with regard to transportation, motility is how people or groups use the travel options and networks offered by the transport provision in their mobility practices. Motility can remain in a potential state or be activated in the form of movement (De Witte et al. 2013; Kesselring 2006; Canzler et al. 2008).

The car has been the dominant means of transport for the past 50 years, due notably to its special resonance with advanced modernity. The individual autonomization of movement it allows for (private vehicle ownership and the fact that you can go anywhere anytime) is such that it has come to embody the concept of freedom. However, things have changed since the early 2010s; in many European cities with more than 500,000 inhabitants, car use is actually declining. This is more than a mere change in informal practices, which is more or less the natural consequence of the urban planning and transport policies of the past 20 years: It is a change that affects the way societies spatialize (Bauman 2000). For many who analyze such

Mobilities Futures 111

questions, we have entered a phase of mobility transition (Urry 2007; Cresswell 2006; Canzler and Knie 2016; Vincent-Geslin 2010).

For some analysts, the car as we know it today marked the beginning of an inexorable decline—a decline that now requires governments to invest heavily in alternative transport systems (public, active, and innovative modes). Their argument points to the fact that cars cause congestion that is becoming increasingly difficult to regulate. Moreover, cars less systematically epitomize freedom for young people between the ages of 18 and 20 in urban areas, who are increasingly less likely to obtain a driver's license. Several factors explain this: driver guilt, improvements in alternative transport systems in urban areas, the development of telecommunications, the Internet, and online gaming, and the high cost of acquiring a driver's license. In terms of transport modes, cycling can potentially replace car use in urban areas because it is an efficient and economical mode that lacks many of the constraints (i.e. parking) of driving.

Given these observations, some researchers on the contrary feel that we are at the dawn of a new automotive victory, and that public transport use, walking, and cycling as we know them may see a major decline in the future. In other words, governments would invest in infrastructure that accompany an increase in car use while abandoning certain costly public transport services. To support their argument, these actors insist on the fact that the quality of car mobility remains and will remain unrivaled, be it for the transport of objects, in terms of efficiency and comfort, or for the door-to-door service and autonomy it offers. In addition, they highlight the vast scalability of the car, whose uses are changing (i.e. different forms of vehicle sharing) and which, for the most part, are likely to be electrically propulsed and automated in the near future. Thus, the car as we know it today will be radically transformed. The automation of driving is crucial in this way because it would allow drivers to use their travel time constructively. In so doing, the driverless car will undoubtedly rival the train and public transport in general.

In this chapter we will explore the decline of car use in urban areas, and consider it in a context where mobility is becoming a key aspect of social and professional inclusion. Our investigation will be divided into three stages. First, we will explore the history of the modal shift from car use to other modes in daily life, followed by the reasons for the decline in car use, and will conclude by proposing three scenarios for daily urban mobility.

A Short History of the Modal Shift in Western Europe

A look back on urban transport policies in Western Europe since the 1960s helps us measure the shift in people's perception of the car and its impact on the use of this mode.

In the 1960s and 1970s, a dominant representation of the transport system—widely shared among people, policymakers, and experts alike—was

112 *Vincent Kaufmann*

built around the paradigm of technical progress (Dollinger 1972; Fichelet 1979). In this context, the individual car was seen as progress relative to public transport, as it freed users from the constraints of routes and schedules and allowed for independent travel in a private space (the passenger compartment). The idea that the car represented real progress compared to public transport was largely agreed upon, including by left-wing political parties (Maksim 2011). With growing awareness of the pollution linked to car traffic, this dominant representation nonetheless began to fragment, giving way to a wider variety of dispositions. In the 1980s, the modal shift from individual cars to modes that generate less negative externalities was a key controversial subject in urban transport policies throughout Europe (Banister 2005; Flamm 2004). Notably, it was supported by emerging social movements, environmental movements, and more generally those critical of consumerism advocating for a better quality of life. It was through the transformation of this reference of urban mobility that a modal shift gradually became a central objective of urban transport policies throughout Europe (Kaufmann 2003).

These policies resulted from the desire to address the consequences of car use in dense urban areas, and namely the congestion of public space and the environmental impact of traffic (Lefèvre and Offner 1990; Freudendal-Pedersen 2009).

The initial strategy of the modal shift in the 1980s and 1990s was to develop alternatives to the car that were efficient in terms of speed. This was the idea behind the concept of modal choice. Users choose their transport mode(s) based on a comparision of speeds and costs, and opt for the most advantageous solution (Goodwin 1985; Brög 1993). This led to a host of tram networks, light rail, tram-train, automatic subways small and large, the S-Bahn and other regional trains, whose efficiency was supposed to compete with that of the car (Metz 2008).

These projects failed in most cases to reduce the use of cars in cities. In all cases, an increase in the use of public transport was highlighted, with +20% to +50% five years after their entry into service (Gagnière 2012). However, vehicle traffic was only marginally affected. The new trams, subways, and the S-Bahn most notably gave rise to new trips and convinced former pedestrians to take public transport.

In a second stage, modal shift policies were analyzed as incoherent. Modal shift policies came to be regarded as comprehensive transport systems that incorporated walking and cycling in particular (Canzler and Knie 1998). The layout of public space thus became a key component of these policies (Apel and Pharoah 1995). It was at this time that coordination strategies between transport and development policy became the norm: It was necessary to link urban development to a walkable scale close to public transport hubs and stations (Gallez and Kaufmann 2010).

Until the mid-2000s, these policies did not greatly influence car use. While there were exceptions, overall the impact was modest. Car use was

Mobilities Futures   113

embedded in lifestyles whose pace and spatialities often implies changes in modal habits and spatial routines (Buhler 2012). Research shows that the latter are formed during specific life stages and correspond to periods of transition in the life course (Flamm 2004; Fouillé 2010).

Around 2005 marked a turning point: Car use in daily urban mobility actually began to decline in many urban agglomerations. Initially thought to be a cyclical effect due to a rise in oil prices, the trend that began slowly gradually became dense and widespread in northern and southern Europe, as shown by Anne Aguiléra's recent analyses (Aguiléra et al. 2014).[1] How to interpret this?

As is often the case in the emergence of new phenomena, a range of factors is the source, rather than a single cause.

To begin, there is the impact of investments and policies. This explains households' tendency to give up the car or multiple forms of motorized transport. However, this does not explain everything. Some facts are troubling, as the decline is widespread and affects both cities that have ambitious transport policies and cities that do not. This is the case in France, for example, where the decrease in the car market share for urban travel is as perceptible in Bordeaux—a city that has greatly developed its public transport system—as in cities like Toulon, where such development has not taken place (De Solère 2012; CERTU 2013). Since the late 2000s, the decline in car use has been comparable in these cities (roughly –5% of market share in the past decade).

What Other Factors Might Explain This Rapid Change?

Based on the scientific literature and the results of several studies I have conducted in recent years (Viry and Kaufmann 2015; Vincent-Geslin and Kaufmann 2012), I propose three new phenomena to explain this change. While others, such as the aging of the population and the impoverishing of the lower middle class (who less often can afford cars) can also be cited, I will focus on three relative to motility, and thus true indicators of profound social and societal changes.

Most notably, they indicate that the relationship between what is close, what is connected, and what is moving is changing, thus redefining the very meaning of being near, being connected, and moving. In a certain sense, this has the effect of disqualifying the car as the mode allowing for freedom of movement *par excellence*.

Polytopic Living

In the past 20 years, Europe has witnessed the development of several new forms of travel often referred to as high mobility (Meissonier 2001; Hofmeister 2005; Kellerman 2012; Gherardi 2010). This includes having two or more residences, whether following a divorce (children in joint

114 *Vincent Kaufmann*

custody arrangement), by choice for the dynamics of the couple (living apart together), because the couple's homes are far apart (distance- or time-wise), for work-related reasons (a pied-a-terre near the workplace when the main residence is several hundred miles away), or for leisure-related reasons (e.g. secondary residences where individuals spend part of the week or year) (Feldhaus and Schlegel 2015; Duncan and Phillips 2010). It also includes long-distance and long-duration commuting, which has resulted in an increasing number of people commuting hundreds of kilometers each day, or spending considerable time getting to and from work (Schneider and Collet 2010). Finally, it includes people who frequently spend the night away from home (overnighting), be it for work, leisure, or family reasons (Holmes 2014). Put together, these forms of travel—insignifiant just a few years ago—are now a social phenomenon that is impossible to ignore.

For work-related reasons alone, this phenomenon affects 13% to 16% of working people. Half of the population will be faced with it at some point in their career (Schneider and Collet 2010).

I also note that these practices are the result of changes in daily life. Our activities in general are much faster-paced. Moreover, private and professional spheres have become blurred. We work from home, check our email in the evening, receive personal calls at the office, and are in permanent contact with our partners via text messaging (Belton-Chevallier 2010).

What links these different lifestyles is that they indicate a polytopic habitat (Stock 2006). What is certain is that the people living in such contexts have daily existences that are scattered over a vast territory. This results in multiple loyalties and anchors. Car use is generally low among people who live in or frequent such polytopic habitats, especially when they commute between cities.

Zahavi 2.0, or the Increase in Daily Travel Time Budgets

In the 1970s, Yacov Zahavi demonstrated a constancy of travel time budgets in cities around the world. He formulated what is called the 'Zahavi Conjecture,' namely the fact that daily mobility is a function of transport speed for a time budget of approximately one hour (Zahavi 1979).

Zahavi's work highlights a key mechanism of urban development: The time saved by the speed potential of infrastructure is used to travel *further*, not to limit or reduce the time spent traveling (Zahavi and Talvitie 1980). This mechanism is particularly useful for modeling urban sprawl. Zahavi's work had an important impact on operational planning.

Since the 1990s, travel time budgets have been increasing throughout Europe. In Switzerland, for example, 10% of the working population works more than 50 kilometers from their principal residence. This trend is developing rapidly based on the use of the train: The further away from home people work, the more likely they are to take the train. A small portion of

Mobilities Futures 115

this increase is due to the saturation of infrastructures. Above all, however, it reflects the changing relationship to travel time.

In the past five years, time budgets have restabilized at around 1.5 hours. In a certain way, we have gone from Zahavi 1.0 and a 1-hour time budget, to Zahavi 2.0 and 1.5-hour time budget.

What has happened? Careful examination shows that the dispersion of time budgets has become more pronounced. It also shows that train users and walkers have the longest travel time budgets. This is due in particular to the possibility of being able to use one's time constructively (Lyons et al. 2007; Jain and Lyons 2008; Viry and Kaufmann 2015). With smartphones, tablets, and laptops, travel time is no longer dead or wasted time between activities. Rather, it is a time in its own right. Hence, individuals expect to spend more time doing it.

But in order for people to feel comfortable during their commutes, they do not only require personal aptitudes; their motility must also be met with the appropriate conditions in spaces of mobility. These affordances, in Gibson's sense, are essential for making use of this time. The latter can take very different forms, ranging from a comfortable seat on a train with Wi-Fi to renting a pied-a-terre closer to work.

The use of car travel time is limited to driving, which decreases the attractiveness of this mode of transport for more and more users.

Changing Desires Relative to the Car

Many surveys show that the car no longer is the great dream of young people. Automakers like Toyota and PSA Peugeot Citroën closely analyze this phenomenon, which is reflected not only in the use of transport modes, but also in car ownership and the acquisition of driver's licenses.

This is the result of several phenomena (Kuhnimhof et al. 2012; Newman and Kenworthy 2013; Graham--Rowe, Skippon, Gardner, and Abraham 2011):

- The disenchantment with the car linked to its environmental impact and competition with long-distance communication systems as an expression of freedom among young people (Lucas and Jones 2009). The resurgence of urban lifestyles aimed at proximity and frequent use of the Internet. This is reflected in particular by changes in the pace of life. For example, shopping tends to be done on a daily basis rather than a weekly one, with certain purchases often made online or via delivery (Kingsley and Urry 2009).
- The economic aspect plays also a central rule, which should not be underestimated. Money spent on telephones, computers, tablets, online games, and applications is no longer available to pay for a driver's license (which is becoming increasingly costly in many European countries), let alone a car. In other words, in the economic trade-offs of young urban

116 *Vincent Kaufmann*

households, the automobile tends to take a backseat (Graham-Rowe et al. 2011).

For all these reasons, the car has become an artifact that part of the population no longer knows what to do with. However, as cities and regions have been largely designed for cars, this change—if it continues—is likely to radically change the spatial organization of European societies.

Towards a Structural Decline of Car Use?

The emerging trends just described most importantly indicate changes in European society as a whole, thus confirming the importance of regarding mobility as a total social phenomenon:

- I noted a change in the pacing and scheduling of daily activities: By optimizing, doubling up, and resynchronizing our roles and activities, in some ways we have never been so mobile. Our daily schedules are increasingly diversified, and being present in a place embodied as a space—a closed time where everyone does a unique activity—is becoming rare. It is very common to do several things at once. We have gone from lifestyles where the activities and roles succeeded one another in time—a succession that usually involved traveling—to lifestyles with 'mixed' times, marked by rapid and numerous successions.
- I also noted the development of new forms of proximity. With polytopic living, it is not uncommon to have daily proximity practices in locations several dozen, even several hundred, kilometers apart. So-called familiar places thus become scattered, thereby leading to the development of spatial multi-belonging on a daily level.
- I likewise observed that daily travel time is gradually becoming a social time in its own right. Hence, people do not necessarily seek to minimize this time but rather to fully enjoy it.
- Finally, I observed an increase in reversible mobilities, meaning forms of mobility designed to avoid uprooting only to reroot somewhere else, through extensive travel between distant locations. The development of reversible mobilities is the joint result of the injunction to mobility that characterizes today's working world and the use of the speed potential of rapid transport and telecommunications systems.

Three Scenarios of the Mobility Transition

How do these emerging trends foreshadow future developments? To analyze this, I propose starting from the question of motility.

Identifying urban mobility of the future based on motility means considering the relationships between the three scales of sociological analysis—the individual level, the interpersonal level, and the collective level—along with

Mobilities Futures 117

three ways of dealing with space: being close, moving, or long-distance communicating. The metaphor of the 'hypertext society' dear to Francois Ascher (2000) is a good starting point for considering these relationships as the places produced by contemporary mobilities come in different layers that sometimes overlap and sometimes are laid out. They include what is close, what is connected, and that which moves.

The three scales of sociological analysis and three ways of dealing with distance are not new; thinking about it, they even seem as old as the world. What is changing, however, relates precisely to the hypertext dimension of society. Indeed, until recently, the relationship between the personal, interpersonal, and collective levels and between proximity, movement, and long-distance communication were largely spatialized like 'Russian dolls.' In other words, the boundaries between categories were clear and easily identifiable because they were nested. That is how it is, for instance, that daily life took place at the micro-local scale of the neighborhood or village.

This nesting was linked in particular to the fact that until the 1920s, travel and long-distance communication were slow-paced (walking, horses, and trolleys in cities), which resulted in an imperative to proximity in daily life. There was no way to work far from home when you had to get there by foot, and no way to communicate quickly when mail moved at the speed of a horse. With the development and democratization of transport speed and the development of remote communication, societies that were once organized by degrees according to the nesting logic of Russian dolls exploded spatially speaking. Nowadays, it is possible to work more than 100 kilometers from home and commute each day. It is also possible to maintain close social ties at a distance. In short, it is possible to overcome proximity. There is no longer a single boundary, and clashes of scale are becoming the norm (Neutens 2010). The way societies territorialize is changing and raising new issues, such as those of social cohesion, social and spatial anchors, and multiple identities.

In this light, the scenarios I will present in the following are based on 1) the many aspirations and constraints in terms of movement, as previously described, and 2) assumptions regarding the evolution of these developments and constraints/aspirations based on the emerging trends I have identified. De facto, these scenarios are built based on a dual logic: 1) the idea that, in order to be effective, political action must resonate with people's practices and aspirations, or will otherwise be ineffective or rejected, and 2) considering the relationship between supply and demand as a coproduction characterized by threshold effects. The concept of a threshold effect in the coproduction between mobility supply and demand notably helps account for modal shift phenomena from single occupancy vehicle use to public transport, including new and emerging forms like carpooling, car sharing, etc. (based in particular on the examples of Germany, Denmark, the Netherlands, and Switzerland and declining car use dynamics among urban households in those countries, in conjunction with practical, spatially/

118 *Vincent Kaufmann*

temporally available, comprehensive altermodal transport offers both locally and nationally).

Below are three highly contrasting baseline scenarios of urban mobility in the future in Europe, which correspond to very different levels of motility and ways of relating to space. These scenarios, conceived as ideal-types, may also be combined.

Scenario 1: Widespread High Mobility

This scenario is based on the idea that the increase in long-distance commuting continues, making Europe a giant metropolis of which cities are neighborhoods. In this first scenario, people travel the country for work and/or leisure activities each day, but co-presence remains the bedrock of social relations. At the same time, households are sedentary in the sense that they do not migrate from one region to another to be closer to their place of work. The basic frame of the city consists of a dense railway network offering highly developed transport capacities.

In this scenario, daily mobility is very intense and marked by the search for maximum spatial reversibility. The use of transport modes that allow for the use of travel time has increased considerably as the former are suited to the natural tendencies of the population. This includes the train most notably, but could also include automated control vehicles (should this technology develop) and urban public transport.

Investments in transport systems remains central. The main challenge is ensuring high-volume transport capacities while maintaining passenger comfort during travel.

This scenario reflects the spread of highly mobile lifestyles among the population, and the fact that travel time is integrated into the larger activities schedule (Viry and Kaufmann 2015). With regard to the literature, it echoes John Urry's Scenario 2 in *Post-Petroleum* (Urry 2014).

Scenario 2: The Age of Remote Communication and Mobile Goods

This scenario is based on the idea that the current trend towards increased high mobility is only a transitional phase before the overwhelming replacement of physical travel by telecommunications. Physical co-presence (people being in the same space together) will no longer be the bedrock of social relations.

Skype and videoconferencing will allow for co-presence. We will move less for work and leisure activities. Instead, the latter will come to us. Connected work from home will develop, as will online buying (furniture, books, films, etc.) and in-home services. Not only will restaurants deliver, but so will banks, public services, and so on. In this scenario, it is goods and commodities that will move. The development of 3D printers can be linked to this second scenario.

People's motility is strongly linked to their ability to use telecommunications systems. Daily mobility consists essentially of leisure travel. Other reasons (work, studies, and shopping in particular) have decreased substantially in volume as they have partially been replaced by distance communication. Only trips based on an obligation of physical presence, as defined by John Urry (2000), continue to be made.

In this second scenario, the challenge for transport will no longer be moving people but things, and the logistics involved in that. Rush hours will disappear, except those related to leisure travel (the beginning of school vacations, the end of long weekends, year-end festivities, etc.). Transport speed will no longer be as essential as it is now, as speed will be provided by the ubiquity of telecommunications.

This second scenario strongly echoes the proposal of the October 2013 'Now for the Long Term' Oxford Martin School Commission for Future Generations (Oxford Martin School Commission 2013). It is also very present in Anglo-Saxon literature on the development of home 3D printers. Regarding the trends highlighted in this article, it is in keeping with the observation of young people's disenchantment with the car.

Scenario 3: The Quality of Local Living

This scenario is based on the premise that proximity and 'local living' will become increasing valued, as will slowness. In view of current trends, this represents a double break with regard to the rapid growth of high mobility and telecommunications. Both practices are gradually rejected for their negative impact on social life. Immersion in other social and cultural realities replaces them for the sake of enrichment. Transport and telecommunication systems become secondary in the edification of lifestyles. Housing takes on greater importance, and vacation time becomes a key factor. Unlike the other scenarios, housing becomes more affordable and transport less expensive.

In this case, the population's motility is strongly oriented toward the capacity to migrate and therefore quickly adapt to new living situations. To facilitate this appropriation, people want offers who rules of use are stardardized, be it for transport or facilities.

In this third scenario, investment in transport systems also becomes secondary as local travel increases. In terms of daily mobility, while the structure of travel patterns and times has not greatly changed, the spatial range of this travel and daily travel-time budgets are decreasing.

The third scenario was directly inspired by German philosopher and sociologist Hartmut Rose's work on the exhaustion created by the acceleration of daily life, which also echoes John Urry's 'local life' scenario in *Post-Petroleum* (Urry 2014).

120 *Vincent Kaufmann*

Conclusions

The future is not written, of course. And yet, all the investigations presented in this article suggest, based on the accentuation of existing trends in the population's motility, that the car may no longer be the main mode of transport for daily mobility in European agglomerations in the future.

Is This, Indeed, Reason to Celebrate?

However, a cursory examination suggests that, if we look more closely, it is not certain that the prospect of declining car ownership and use is, socially speaking, good news.

No doubt a decrease in car use will help reduce energy consumption, air pollution, and disturbances from traffic (notably the street congestion, noise, and gasoline/diesel fumes that invade European cities). But what about jobs? But what about major road infrastructure? But what about spaces whose function was designed for the spatial and temporal metrics of the car?

A decrease in car use was never truly probable until quite recently. The development trends identified in this chapter show that it is now in the realm of the possible. In this context, it is likely that the mobility transition, regardless of the scenario or combination of scenarios, will be a difficult one if car use as we know it (i.e. single occupancy) does not change as well. Automated driving systems are a critical issue in the sense that they would free drivers from the *act* of driving, allowing them to use their travel time for other things and, in so doing, rival urban public transport (the demands of adhering to lines and schedules).

Fortunately, modal shift policies were slow in achieving the desired success, given that they did not think beyond the use of transport modes in daily life. While the trends I have identified become established, if car ownership and use continues to decline in keeping with one or the other of the scenarios outlined above, it is urgent to think about future Europe's urban areas and its spaces with generosity and creativity. Mobility is above all a societal affair.

The vision of desirable futures must be central in this endeavor, given that each of the three scenarios developed have limitations. By increasing distances, speeds, and the systematic use of time travel, the first scenario merely represents a new stage in the accentuating of the founding principles of modernity (i.e. the pursuit of increased productivity and the acceleration of everyday life). Yet, it is precisely based on the critique of this acceleration—which emanates from the population—that I developed the third scenario which, however, carries the seeds of communalism and withdrawal.

This leaves the second scenario, wherein it is by and large goods that travel, and wherein people living in urban areas are almost not obliged to leave their homes. Yet, this too seems to come at a price: that of solitude.

Mobilities Futures 121

It is undoubtedly by combining the three scenarios that we can forge a desirable future in terms of mobility. However, this involves political trade-offs based on genuine democratic debate.

Note

1. The decrease in car use is measurable by the market share of trips. This, however, does not mean that traffic flows are decreasing, as car users tend to make longer trips.

References

Aguiléra, A., Grébert, J. and Nandy Formentin, H. 2014. *Passengers Transport Modes Hierarchy and Trends in Cities: Results of a Worldwide Survey*. Paris: Transport Research Arena.

Apel, D. and Pharoah, T. 1995. *Transport Concepts in European Cities*. Avebury: Studies in Green Research.

Ascher, F. 2000. *Ces évènements nous dépassent, feignons d'en être les organisateurs*. La Tour d'Aigues: L'Aube.

Banister, D. 2005. *Unsustainable Transport*. London: Spon Press.

Bassand, M. 1985. *Les Suisses entre la mobilité et la sédentarité*. Lausanne: PPUR.

Bassand, M. and Brulhardt, M.-C. 1980. *Mobilité Spatiale*. St-Saphorin: Georgi.

Bauman, Z. 2000. *Liquid Modernity*. London: Polity.

Belton-Chevallier, L. 2010. "Mobile ICTs as tools of intensification of travel time use? Results of qualitative study based on French workers". In *12th World Conference on Transport Research*, Lisbon.

Boltanski, L. and Chiapello, E. 1999. *Le nouvel esprit du capitalisme*. Paris: Gallimard.

Brög, W. 1993. "Changer de comportement c'est d'abord changer d'état d'esprit, Marketing et qualité de service dans les transports en commun". In *Table ronde CEMT, 92. Conférence Européene des Ministres de Transport*, Paris.

Buhler, T. 2012. *Eléments pour la prise en compte de l'habitude dans les pratiques de déplacements urbains: le cas des résistances aux injonctions au changement de mode de déplacement dans l'agglomération lyonnaise*. Thèse en urbanisme et aménagement, INSA de Lyon, Lyon.

Canzler, W. and Knie, A. 1998. *Möglichkeitsräume—Grundrisse einer modernen Mobilitäts- und Verkehrspolitik*. Viena: Editions Böhlau.

Canzler, W. and Knie, A. 2016. "Mobility in the age of digital modernity: Why the private car is losing its significance, intermodal transport is winning and why digitalization is the key". *Applied Mobilities*, 1(1), 56–67.

Canzler, W., Kaufmann, V. and Kesselring, S., eds. 2008. *Tracing Mobilities: Towards a Cosmopolitan Perspective*. Aldershot: Ashgate.

Castells, M. 1996. *The Rise of the Network Society: The Information Age*. Oxford: Blackwell.

CERTU. 2013. *EMD standard CERTU*. Lyon: CERTU.

Cervero, R. and Radisch, C. 1996. "Travel choices in pedestrian versus automobile oriented neighborhoods". *Transport Policy*, 3(3), 127–41.

Cresswell, T. 2006. *On the Move: Mobility in the Modern Western World*. London: Routledge.

122 Vincent Kaufmann

De Solère, R. 2012. *La mobilité urbaine en France: Enseignements des années 2000–2010*. Lyon: Ed. du CERTU.

De Witte, A., Hollevoet, J., Dobruszkes, F., Hubert, M. and Macharis, C. 2013. "Linking modal choice to motility: A comprehensive review". *Transportation Research Part A*, 49, 329–41.

Dollinger, H. 1972. *Die Totale Autogesellschaft*. Munich: Carl Hanser Verlag.

Duncan, S. and Phillips, M. 2010. "People who live apart together (LATs): How different are they?" *The Sociological Review*, 58(1), 112–34.

Feldhaus, M. and Schlegel, M. 2015. "Living apart together and living together apart: Impacts of partnership-related and job-related circular mobility on partnership quality". In *Spatial Mobility, Migration and Living Arrangements*, edited by Aybek, C. M., Huinink, J. and Muttarak, R., 115–37. New York: Springer.

Fichelet, R. 1979. "Éléments pour une compréhension des pratiques de déplacement automobile'. In *Transport et société, actes du colloque de Royaumont*, edited by Direction Générale de la Recherche Scientifique et Technique. Paris: Economica.

Flamm, M. 2004. *Comprendre le choix modal: les déterminants des pratiques modales et des représentations individuelles des moyens de transport*. Thèse de doctorat, EPFL, Lausanne.

Fouillé, L. 2010. *L'attachement automobile mis à l'épreuve. Etude des dispositifs de détachement et de recomposition des mobilités*. Thèse de sociologie, Université de Rennes, Rennes.

Freudendal-Pedersen, M. 2009. *Mobility in Daily Life: Between Freedom and Unfreedom*. Farnham: Ashgate.

Gagnière, V. 2012. "Les effets du tramway sur la fréquentation du transport public. Un bilan des agglomérations françaises de province". *Revue Géographique de l'Est*, 52(1–2), at http://rge.revues.org/3508 (accessed September 7, 2016).

Gallez, C. and Kaufmann, V., eds. 2010. *Mythes et pratiques de la coordination urbanisme-transport, regards croisés sur les trajectoires de quatre agglomérations suisses et françaises*. Recherches INRETS 281. Paris: Lavoisier.

Gherardi, L. 2010. *La mobilité ambiguë: Espace, temps et pouvoir aux sommets de la société contemporaine*. Paris: Editions Universitaires Européennes.

Goodwin, P.-B. 1985. "Évolution de la motivation des usagers en matière de choix modal". In *Table ronde CEMT, 68. Conférence Européene des Ministres de Transport*, Paris.

Graham-Rowe, E., Skippon, S., Gardner, B. and Abraham, C. 2011. "Can we reduce and, if so, how? A review of available evidence". *Transportation Research Part A*, 45, 401–18.

Harvey, D. 2001. *Spaces of Capital: Towards a Critical Geography*. New York: Routledge.

Hofmeister, H. 2005. "Geographic mobility of couples in the United States: Relocation and commuting trends". *Zeitschrift für Familienforschung*, 2, 115–28.

Holmes, M. 2014. *Distance Relationships*. London: Palgrave Macmillan.

Jain, J. and Lyons, G. 2008. "The gift of travel time". *Transport Geography*, 16, 81–9.

Kalir, B. 2013. "Moving subjects, stagnant paradigms: Can the 'mobilities paradigm' transcend methodological nationalism?" *Journal of Ethnic and Migration Studies*, 39(2), 311–27.

Kaufmann, V. 2003. "Pratiques modales des déplacements de personnes en milieu urbain: des rationalités d'usage à la cohérence de l'action publique". *Revue d'Économie Régionale et Urbaine*, 1, 39–58.

Kaufmann, V. 2011. *Re-Thinking the City*. Lausanne and London: EPFL Press and Routledge.

Kaufmann, V. 2014. "Mobility as a tool for sociology". *Sociologica*, 1. doi:10.2383/77046.

Kaufmann, V., Ravalet, E. and Dupuit, E., eds. 2015. *Motilité et mobilité: mode d'emploi*. Neuchâtel: Alphil–Presses Universitaires Suisses.

Kellerman, A. 2012. "Potential mobilities". *Mobilities*, 7(1), 171–83.

Kesselring, S. 2006. "Pioneering mobilities: New patterns of movement and motility in a mobile world". *Environment and Planning A*, 38, 269–79.

Kingsley, D. and Urry, J. 2009. *After the Car*. Polity: London.

Kuhnimhof, T., Armoogum, J., Buehler, R., Dargay, J., Denstadli, J. M. and Yamamoto, T. 2012. "Men shape a downward trend in car use among young adults: Evidence from six industrialized countries". *Transport Reviews*, 33, 761–79.

Lefèvre, C. and Offner, J.-M. 1990. *Les transports urbains en question*. Paris: Celse.

Lucas, K. and Jones, P. 2009. *The Car in British Society*. London: RAC Foundation.

Lyons, G., Jain, J. and Holley, D. 2007. "The use of travel time by rail passengers in Great Britain". *Transportation Research Part A*, 41, 107–20.

Maksim, H. 2011. *Potentiels de mobilité et inégalités sociales: la matérialisation des politiques publiques dans quatre agglomérations en Suisse et en France*. Thèse de doctorat, EPFL, Lausanne.

Meissonier, J. 2001. *Provinciliens: les voyageurs du quotidian*. Paris: éditions de L'harmattan.

Metz, D. 2008. "The myth of travel time saving". *Transport Reviews*, 28(3), 321–36.

Neutens, T. 2010. *Space, Time and Accessibility: Analyzing Human Activities and Travel Possibilities from a Time-Geographic Perspective*. Thèse de Doctorat, University of Gent, Gent.

Newman, P. and Kenworthy, J. 2013. "Understanding the demise of automobile dependence". *World Transport Policy and Practice*, 17(2), 1–19.

Oxford Martin School Commission for Future Generations. 2013. *Now for the Long Term*. Oxford: Oxford Martin School.

Scheiner, J. 2010. "Interrelations between travel mode choice and trip distance: Trends in Germany 1976–2002". *Journal of Transport Geography*, 18(1), 75–84.

Schneider, N. F. and Collet, B., eds. 2010. *Mobile Living across Europe II*. Leverkusen and Opladen: Barbara Budrich.

Stock, M. 2006. "L'hypothèse de l'habiter poly-topique". *Espacestemps.net*, Textuel, February 26.

Urry, J. 2000. *Sociology Beyond Societies*. London: Routledge.

Urry, J. 2007. *Mobilities*. London: Polity.

Urry, J. 2014. *Post-Petroleum*. Paris: Loco éditions/Forum Vies Mobiles.

Vincent-Geslin, S. 2010. *Altermobilités, mode d'emploi. Déterminants et usages de mobilités alternatives au tout voiture*. Lyon: Editions du Certu.

Vincent-Geslin, S. and Kaufmann, V., eds. 2012. *Mobilité sans racines. Plus loin, plus vite . . . Plus mobiles?* Paris: Descartes & Cie.

Viry, G. and Kaufmann, V., eds. 2015. *Mobile Europe*. London: Palgrave McMillan.

Zahavi, Y. 1979. *The UMOT Project*. Washington: USDOT.

Zahavi, Y. and Talvitie, A. 1980. "Regularities in travel time and money expenditure". *Transportation Research Record*, 750, 13–19.

8 Performing or Deconstructing the Mobile Subject?
Linking Mobility Concepts, Research Designs, and Methods

Katharina Manderscheid

It is more than ten years ago that the 'mobility turn' (Sheller and Urry 2006; Hannam, Sheller, and Urry 2006) was officially and prominently declared and announced. In line with this claim of forming a new paradigm (Kuhn 1962), which typically entails the development of appropriate theories, terminologies, and methods, the key texts of mobilities research (e.g. Urry 2000; Cresswell 2006; Urry 2007; Sheller and Urry 2006; Paterson 2007) postulate the centrality of movement for social relations, highlighting the socio-cultural and material embedding of movement. On the methodological side, the last several years have witnessed a vivid debate on 'mobile methods' (Fincham, McGuinness and Murray 2010; Büscher, Urry, and Witchger 2011b; Merriman 2013; Büscher and Urry 2009) which are able to tune in to moving rather than static actors and socialities.

Yet, the construction of principally mobile rather than sedentary research units constitutes only one of the foundational breaks between mobile and sedentary metaphysics (Cresswell 2006, 26f.). Other elements that indicate the newness of mobilities research comprise the hybrid character of moving entities and shared agency, consisting of social networks of geographically stretched social ties, relations, and obligations as well as material networks of infrastructures of transport and communications. It is these aspects that are crucial to understand the complex interplay of networked socialities and materialities with practices and subjectivities.

In this paper I will try to bring this hybrid and networked character of mobile agency to the fore. I will elaborate this point by outlining some faultlines between the mobilities paradigm and 'traditional' social theory with regard to the understanding of agency and sociality. The focus of this analysis is placed on the scale of the research, the methods used, and the conceptualization of agency. In a second step I will outline some suggestions for alternative methodologies for mobilities research accounting for the hybrid network character of mobilities which is also seen as strengthening the critical stance of mobilities research.

Mobile Subjects and Networked Agency

The foundational faultline between the mobilities paradigm and 'traditional' social theory consists in focusing on movement and fluidity rather than on

The Mobile Subject? 125

territorially fixed social units (Sheller and Urry 2006; Hannam et al. 2006) which

> challenges the ways in which much social science research has been 'a-mobile'. Even while it has increasingly introduced spatial analysis the social sciences have still failed to examine how the spatialities of social life presuppose (and frequently involve conflict over) both the actual and the imagined movement of people from place to place, person to person, event to event.
>
> (Sheller and Urry 2006, 208)

In this view, people, objects, and symbols are understood as traveling virtually, physically, and imaginatively in multiple ways. *Mobility* encompasses a wide range of movements which can be seen as a quantitative continuum, ranging from the daily routine movements around the home at one end of the spectrum to long-distance migration and virtual mobility at the other end (Pooley et al. 2005, 5). Persons thus move physically on a frequent and regular basis in their everyday life and maybe once or twice a year for holidays; they relocate permanently or temporally their dwellings, and they move virtually by communicating and connecting using mobile devices and the Internet. These different forms of movement require a broad range of technical artifacts and infrastructures, norms, and regulations. Correspondingly, movement or mobility can only be understood *in relation to its material foundation*. Thus, movement as practice has to be contextualized within specific material, geographical, and broader spatial environments. As Urry (2000, 78) states,

> [t]he human and the material intersect in various combinations and networks, which in turn vary greatly in their degree of stabilisation over time and across space. . . . In such an account the human is highly decentred and is not to be seen as separate from the non-human.

The modern conceptualization of agency takes the figure of the autonomous subject as its (sole) author, framed discursively through the terminology of causality and rationality (Otto 2014, 17f.). The so-defined modern subject pervades social theory as well as social discourses and knowledge in general. In opposition to these concepts of subjects and agency, Büscher and Urry (2009, 100, emphasis K.M.) consider the analysis of mobilities as "an example of *post-human* analysis." More specifically, they presume "that the powers of 'humans' are co-constituted by various material agencies, of clothing, tools, objects, paths, buildings, machines, paper, and so on" (Büscher and Urry 2009, 100). Thus, the mobilities paradigm not only postulates a mobilized view on the social, but also an understanding of agency as constituted by hybrid socio-material networks.

On this token, the context within which humans are thought to act and are mobile needs closer attention in order to identify empowering and

126 *Katharina Manderscheid*

disempowering as well as mobilizing or even accelerating and decelerating or immobilizing social and material agents and forces within these networks. Without any claim to be exhaustive, I will discuss in the following locations and infrastructures (1) specific to socio-cultural settings and discursive formations as well as (2) personal social network embeddings and relationalities as (3) relevant contexts and co-agencies within the emergence of mobility practices.

The ideal of modern rational subjectivity and autonomous human agency disregards *location-specific*, especially *infrastructural*, unequal conditions of acting and being mobile. Yet, even walking rests on facilitating infrastructures such as paving and pathways, places to rest and to walk to, which enable walking to different places, at different speeds and in different styles (Urry 2007, 65). Similarly, commuting as the practices of bridging the distances between home and work location require either a private car plus access to a system of roads or the existences of as well as access to public transport infrastructures. These material mobility agents vary geographically with regard to their accessibility, extension, quality, and quantity.

In history, one element of modern nation building and territorial integration consisted in the attempt to even these disparities out. Subsumed under the concept of the *infrastructural ideal*, Stephen Graham and Simon Marvin (2001) illustrate spatial policies of Western states aiming at the production of equalizing options and chances across national territories. On this token, these policies produce the (hypothetically) equally motile subject and its spatial (and social) dis-embeddedness on which the legitimization of modern societies rests. The private car played a crucial role within these equalizing spatial policies (cf. Kuhm 1997). What is more, as Rajan (2006, 113f.) elaborates, the modern liberal promise of freedom of choice and individuality is paradigmatically materialized in the private automobile and the auto-mobilizing system of roads and highways—representing the liberation from local constraints. Yet, as Graham and Marvin (2001) exemplify in their book, this general equalization principle for spatial planning has been largely sacrificed in favor of processes of spatial and infrastructural differentiation and *splintering* neoliberal policy support for prosperous regions at the expense of the emergence of new peripheries on the global, national, regional, and urban scale (e.g. Sassen 2001; Peck and Tickell 2002).

Against this background of infrastructural and spatial disparities, researching and understanding movement practices implies not only to focus on the human agents but to identify their mobilizing or immobilizing locational context and available infrastructures. However, the infrastructural equipment of places should not be seen as meaningful or 'equalizing' per se, but its effect on people's lives depends (in addition to their physical capabilities and economic resources which allow the usage in the first place) on their individual life-geographies and the spatial extent of personal networks (cf. Urry 2003; Cass, Shove, and Urry, 2005; Larsen and Jacobsen 2009; Frei, Axhausen, and Ohnmacht 2009): Not everyone needs to move physically in order

The Mobile Subject? 127

to be socially integrated and not everyone's social network ties are at far distances. What is more, the degree to which people are able to compensate a lack of publicly provided access to services and infrastructures depends also on their economic, cultural, or social capital (Bourdieu 1986) or one's network capital (Urry 2007, 194ff.). Thus, the material-infrastructural context should be seen as potential mobility agents in connection with the *individual's networks* and *socio-spatial positionality* (Sheppard 2002).

Second, movements take place within a *spatially and historically defined socio-cultural context*. Mobility, infrastructures, and spaces are being constructed and made meaningful through a range of symbols, representations, and discourses. The collective meaning of mobility as well as the knowledge and representation of possible destinations and, more broadly speaking, of mobility practices, varies multidimensionally with the position in time, space, and society. What is regarded as desirable or detestable, legitimate or illegitimate mobility changes through history and with context. The following three quotes illustrate with regard to walking how the meaning of this seemingly natural human mobility changed from signifying the dangerous ones in the seventeenth century to constituting an elementary characteristic of (male) humans at present:

> Before the eighteenth century in Europe, walkers were the dangerous 'other', as vagrants or a potential mob. There were laws and systems designed to outlaw those who were walking about. . . . No one would go walking unless they could not avoid doing so.
>
> (Urry 2007, 63f.)

> [I]n Britain and Europe from around the 18th century onwards, the business of travel came to be distinguished from the activity of walking. . . . Walking was a mundane, everyday activity. . . . Walkers did not travel. But by the same token . . . travellers did not walk. Or rather, they walked as little as possible, preferring the horse or carriage even though neither was much faster, in those days, or any more comfortable. . . . So it was that the elites of Europe—at least from the 18th century—came to conduct and write about their travels as if they had no legs.
>
> (Ingold 2004, 321f.)

> Consider the act of walking once again. The disability theorist Michael Oliver has suggested that there is an ideology of walking that gives the fact of walking a set of meanings associated with being human and being masculine. Not being able to walk thus falls short of being fully human. Popular culture tells us that 'walking tall' is a sure sign of manhood.
>
> (Cresswell 2010, 21)

In the course of historical sedimentation and collective habitualization, the social origin of the spectrum and limitations of the realm of movement

128   Katharina Manderscheid

practices tends to become invisible, gradually being considered as a natural matter of course both by the human actors within these contexts and by scientific analysis. However, by making synchronic and syntopic or diachronic and diatopic comparisons, their 'giveness' or aura of naturalness gives way to the social construction and contestation of meanings. Against this background, individual and collective mobility choices, such as modes of transportations, destinations, speed, and their absence cannot be attributed sufficiently to conscious and informed individual decisions. Rather, mobilities as practices are inseparably linked with their social meaning. This means that mobility practices and choices are produced, shaped, and pervaded by preconscious and incorporated cultural discourses and knowledge (e.g. Freudendal-Pedersen 2007), infused with supra-subjective meanings and hierarchies. The moves and fixes think-able, choose-able, and 'do-able' by individuals, groups, and larger social networks are thus prescribed by discursive formations at a given space and time (cf. Foucault 1972). In this perspective, these discursive formations constitute further elements of networked mobility agency (cf. Frello 2008).

Third, movements take place not only embedded in material landscapes and specific discourse formations, but also on the micro level within specific *social contexts* within which these practices as broader mobility strategies involve further *rectified or alternative, dependent, and relational forms of movement, mooring, and stillness* (e.g. Schneider, Limmer, and Ruckdeschel 2002; Hannam et al. 2006). Thus, moves are rarely if at all decisions taken in complete social isolation by a socially and spatially independent subject. Rather, mobility decisions should be conceptualized as negotiated more or less directly within personal networks of relations, for example, residential mobility effects and matters within personal relationships, families, and other social networks (Schneider et al. 2002; Larsen, Urry, and Axhausen 2006, 74f.). Correspondingly, these relational others influence in one way or another residential choices. Furthermore, many forms of travel require and are the product of the immobility or the distanciation of significant others: Many forms of travel are undertaken in order to maintain relations with people at a distance, such as friends, family, or relatives. Even more general, at starting, resting, and end points of travel there are places with people attached to them—families, lovers, work colleagues and partners, services, maintenance—which form the immobile social prerequisite for travel. This focus points at mobility agency as distributed power within social networks. The relation between mobile and immobile people and bodies is inseparably tied up with power relations although it cannot be simply equalized to powerful and powerless subjectivities (e.g. Malkki 1992; Wolff 1993; Weiss 2005).

In this view on networked or relational mobility agency, movement practices emerge in specific social, cultural, material, and geographic settings within collectively and personally shaped spatial relations and social ties. Elsewhere (Manderscheid 2012, 2014b) I suggest referring to this trans-individual foundation of practices as 'mobility dispositif,' and other authors refer to it as "larger material and symbolic regimes" (D'Andrea, Ciolfi, and Gray 2011, 158) or "socio-technical systems" (Urry 2004). Yet, what is of interest here are the methodological consequences of these outlined axioms of mobilities research, especially the conceptualization and methodical operationalization of networked mobile agency.

Performing Mobilities—Missing Links Between Theory and Methods

Having outlined some central conceptual and ontological foundations of agency within mobilities literature, I will now turn to methodological issues of mobilities research. The key focus concerns the question of how core claims of mobilities as infrastructurally, socio-culturally, and individually embedded practices and networked agency are being translated into research designs.

Whereas commonly methods, scientific techniques, and methodologies are perceived as neutral instruments to be used and applied in order to observe pre-existing phenomena and entities, in an anti-positivist, performative, and holistic understanding of science, methods are seen as extending theoretical axioms into the empirical world (cf. Kuhn 1962; Diaz-Bone 2015). Methods such as scientific techniques of observation thus are understood as carriers of theoretical assumptions and trimmed models of the empirical world which, rather than simply illuminating an independently existing world, (co-)constitute their object of research. This performative view on research practices constitutes a prominent part of French Epistemology, which has roots in the works of Gaston Bachelard (2002) and can be found in the works of, amongst others, Roland Barthes, Georges Canguilhem, and Michel Foucault. The last states this holistic and performative role of knowledge and discourses in general, which he sees not "as groups of signs . . . signifying elements referring to concepts or representation . . . but as practices that systematically form the objects of which they speak" (Foucault 1972, 49). Or, as John Law and John Urry phrased it, social research practices are performative, "they enact realities and they can help to bring into being what they also discover" (2004, 393).

The emergence and establishing of the 'mobilities paradigm' was accompanied from its very beginning by a discussion of appropriate research methods (e.g. Büscher and Urry 2009; Ahas 2011; Fincham et al. 2010; Büscher, Urry, and Witchger 2011a; Merriman 2013). In a Kuhnian view (Kuhn 1962), the development of new theoretical approaches, terminologies, and methods marks the emergence of a new scientific paradigm, an idea which has been actively employed by mobility scholars in speaking of a 'mobilities paradigm' (e.g. Urry 2007, 39). On this token, in their foundational paper, Sheller and Urry argued that "[r]esearch methods will need to be 'on the move', in effect to simulate intermittent mobility" (2006, 217).

130   *Katharina Manderscheid*

The emphasis on the ability of methods to *follow* people, images, information, and objects constitutes an opposition to the assumption of fixity and sedentarism of 'traditional' social science research methods. The latter typically locate people through their residential address and assume more or less explicitly spatially fixed lives, social integration based on geographic proximity and spatial co-presence. These sedentary assumptions are reflected in multiple ways in the construction of social science data and the used classifications, as, amongst others, the discussion of analytical consequences of territorializing concepts of identity (Malkki 1992) or research on multi-local forms of dwelling (Hilti 2009) has been brought to the fore. Within conventional or sedentarist social research, the social is typically conceptualized as contained within territorial units—the neighborhood, the city, the region, the nation state—which then figure as sampling units for social science data collections. In opposition to these approaches, the aim of mobile methods consists in focusing on the multiple movements of people, information, and objects (Büscher and Urry 2009, 103ff.), thereby turning the spatialities and ongoing mobilities of the social themselves into an object of empirical research. The suggested methods within this strand of mobilities studies consist mainly of qualitative, partly technologically supported means of collecting data on moving people and systems (Büscher et al. 2011a, 7ff.; cf. Büscher et al. 2011b; Fincham et al. 2010).

Yet, the construction of principally mobile rather than sedentary research units through social science methods tackles only one of the issues raised by the mobilities paradigm. As outlined above, other elements indicating the newness of the paradigm comprise the *hybrid character of the moving entities*—consisting of human-technical networks—and thus their *embedding* into *geographical* and *infrastructural contexts*, into *networks of social ties and obligations* as well as their *position within a historically and culturally specific field of knowledge*. Although forming a prominent part of mobilities thinking, up until now these issues are not yet sufficiently addressed by the suggested mobile methods and methodologies for mobilities research (cf. Bissell 2010). In order to extend the theorem of hybrid socio-technical formations into mobilities research designs, we need to further develop methods "to examine the many ways in which objects and people are assembled and reassembled through time-space" (Urry 2007, 50).

In addition, there is the issue of contextualizing the mobile things and networked agency. As elaborated elsewhere (D'Andrea et al. 2011; Manderscheid 2014a), the empirical focus of most mobilities research tends to be either the micro level of experiences, practices, and motives or the macro level of flows and movements, their technological and material preconditions, past developments, political economies, and potential futures as well as links to specific constitutions of discourses and knowledge. Both methodological approaches have been without any doubt of high value for the development of mobilities studies. Yet, especially the focus on subjective representations of movement, studied through interview-generated textual

The Mobile Subject? 131

material, runs the risk of overstating the role of conscious reasoning by individuals. What slips from this empirical focus are other, less conscious, less active, and less reportable bodily experiences (Bissell 2010). Also, this de-contextualized research approach may eclipse incorporated knowledge and hierarchies and thereby pre- and unconscious habitual (cf. Bourdieu 2000) and structurally shaped factors.

Some of the stated problems and implicitly normative assumptions on *the good mobile subject* can be found in parts of research on children's mobility practices and usage of urban spaces. This strand of research tends to problematize the decrease of public spaces in towns and cities where children can play as well as the increase of car-transported children to places of leisure and activities spread all over the town or the city. The line of argumentation can be traced back through the history of urban studies and is found in the writings of Mumford, Jacobs, and also in the psychological writings of Piaget, Fromm, etc. The more or less explicit ideal of a child's socialization is seen in *independent mobility* (Zeiher 1990; Katz 1994; O'Brian et al. 2000; Shaw et al. 2013), which is defined as the "freedom [of children] to travel around their own neighbourhood or city without adult supervision" (Shaw et al. 2013, 35). The purpose of these travels may be leisure, school, or play. Researchers of children's mobilities as well as children's health and development policies agree on the mental and physical benefits of children's independent mobility, which, on the other side, is limited by traffic landscape designs as well as by parental judgments, restrictions, and 'licenses.' Yet, as Mikkelsen and Christensen (2009, 41, emphasis K.M.) state in their critical review of the concept,

> the idea of children's independent mobility reflects a cultural and adult-centred focus on individual agency seeing independent mobility as a natural step in children. . . . In this understanding childhood emerges as a phase in life in which children progressively grow up, and literally move out of the dependence of adults into independence. The cultural ideal is that children should be brought up to become an individual actor [*sic*] as opposed to a collective one.

Independence in this context is strongly biased to the absence of others, especially adults during journeys and outdoor movements. Other dependencies of children's mobile agency from economic, political, material, cultural, or other social network embeddings remain underexposed and thereby outside the common research focus. Thus, the enmeshment of children's mobility practices with networks of peer activities and their norms and rules (Mikkelsen and Christensen 2009; Goodman et al. 2013) is hidden behind this sole focus on accompanying adults. One may also question if it makes sense to talk about dependency or independency as a fixed status or if these concepts should be seen as part of social relations which are constituted through reciprocal actions (Mikkelsen and Christensen 2009). Furthermore,

132   *Katharina Manderscheid*

independent mobility is often equalized to walking and cycling as forms of *self-driven movements* (Goodman et al. 2013, 276) whereas procedures of *being moved*—by public transportation as well as car-passengering—are framed as inferior, less autonomous forms of movement. Taken together, these elements of the concept of independent children's mobility contain some major traits of the modern ideal of autonomous, independent mobility and personal mobile agency, which finds its prototypic mature form in the solitary car-driver. The process of learning "truly self-determined mobility," then, is seen as initially requiring "the company of peers" (Goodman et al. 2013, 288) as a necessary but immature stage within the process of becoming truly independently mobile. One could extrapolate an underlying idealization of adults' independent mobility, which finds its paradigmatic form in the automobile subject. Yet, at present the concept of children's independent mobility undergoes some critique (Goodman et al. 2013; Mikkelsen and Christensen 2009), which highlights the significance of social networks as part of children's mobility and thus broadens the focus on socially distributed mobile agency within situations of co-traveling peers. Further attention should be placed on material-infrastructural mobile agents such as accessible public transport or individual disposition of bicycles, the proximity of roads and pathways, etc.

Politics of Methods—Searching for Alternatives

The claim of forming a new paradigm entails the development of appropriate theories, terminologies, and methods. Furthermore, many central texts of mobilities research contain a more or less explicit critical stance on the social world by—to mention only a few critical topic examples—directing the focus on the socio-cultural embedding and governing of practices of movement and the increase of motorized mobilities. Thereby, these works constitute a critique of the one-dimensional approaches of transport studies and traffic policies which simply focus on an individual's behavior modeled as rational choices, abstracting from the social and the material world. Against this background, the claim for more coherence between concepts, terminologies, and methods can be seen as a political strategy within the contestation of hegemonic views of the world and within the critique of the present mobility order. In this light, to avoid unintended affirmations of the 'autonomous mobile subject,' it seems crucial to develop and discover methods and methodologies, which are not only co-mobile with their object of research, but which frame and perform the empirical object differently and in accordance to the outlined claims of its networked relational and hybrid character. Thereby, mobilities research would constitute and signify more coherently a new reality of empirical objects.

Turning the outlined points into points of departure for this search, I see some sources of inspiration which could form the basis for further elaborations. Firstly, the *decentering of the subject in relation to its material environment*, thus understanding agency as distributed amongst human and material agents, should be taken seriously, by working with *post-human methods*. Points of contact are the so called 'material turn' (e.g. Kazig and Weichhart 2009; Bennett and Joyce 2013) and, of course, Actor-Network Theory (ANT) (e.g. Law 2002; Latour 2005). Especially ANT focuses explicitly on the processual interaction between human and non-human actants, thereby representing a non-humanist perspective, decentering the human subject. As an ecological theory, ANT rejects the sociological approach to the non-human world as either the material condition of our existence or as no more than a set of symbols forming the ground for human activities (Murdoch 2001, 116f.). The approach is based on an understanding of practices as effecting change rather than as an intentional action of a human subject. Within a temporally stabilized network, human feelings, ideas, and intentions, as well as non-human entities like artifacts, machines, plants, animals, etc., are thus thought to have their own agency or practice potential. For example, transportation infrastructures, settlement structures, information and communication technology devices as well as legal documents (passports, driving licenses, rail cards) contain formative potential as a pre-scription, which can take the form of permissions and grants (cf. Akrich and Latour 1992). The extent of these actor-networks and thereby the research object cannot be defined ex ante but constitutes one result of the empirical analysis. Furthermore, the empirical contributions of the actors involved in a specific mobile practice constitute also objects of a 'de-scription.'

However, even ANT-research practice draws mainly on qualitative-ethnographic methods, thus privileging actors capable of speaking (humans) in regards to un-animated objects and thereby only insufficiently capturing the stated symmetry between human and material actors (Schad and Duchêne-Lacroix 2013, 269; Murdoch 2001). Recently, the methodological approach of 'technography' (cf. Rammert and Schubert 2006; Kien 2008; Jansen and Vellema 2011) has gained some attention within the STS and ANT related discussion on how to integrate technological and social aspects more symmetrically. Here, technology is understood in a broader sense as the use of skills, tools, knowledge, and techniques to accomplish certain ends (Jansen and Vellema 2011, 169). Rather than describing the elements of a network or array, the specific focus of technography is placed on the relationships themselves (Kien 2008). Or, as Vannini and Vannini (2008, 1299) phrased it, "technography is the study and the writing of technical structures of communication processes, both in their material and symbolic substance, and their potential for shaping social outcomes." The approach has been described as consisting of three steps: First, the study of 'performance' which consists of a description of the material and social circumstances of technological practices and their interrelationships, thus of the processual technology-in-use (Jansen and Vellema 2011, 170f.). The second step analyzes the task-related knowledge transmitted in a network, thus how

134 *Katharina Manderscheid*

the knowledge and skills of the different actors are mobilized and coordinated and how bearers of skills and knowledge are included or excluded from the performance or practice (Jansen and Vellema 2011, 171f.). Finally, the third step tries to excavate the rules, protocols, routines, and rituals that shape the specific practices, their organization, and the inclusion of actors (Jansen and Vellema 2011, 172f.). Ideally, the descriptions are empirically grounded mainly in observations rather than interviews with human actors, thus placing emphasis on the organization of the networks and practices rather than their human rationalization (Jansen and Vellema 2011, 174). Although up until now only a few technographic studies exist in relation to mobilities research (Schad and Duchêne-Lacroix 2013; Vannini and Vannini 2008), this approach seems to hold some potential for the performance of the post-human claim of mobilities research through empirical studies. For example, in relation to car mobility, it suggests an empirical take on the mobile body as an assemblage of social practices, embodied dispositions, and skills as well as technological potential and affordances which are commonly taken for granted and treated as unremarkable (Dant 2004, 74; Jensen, Sheller, and Wind 2015, 365). Another interesting approach consists in the concept of 'interactive metal fatigue' (Pel 2014). Methods and research designs accounting for the material side of the mobile social world would substantiate an alternative view on automobility and agency in regards to transportation and contribute to a more political understanding of technology and infrastructure policies.

The second challenge for mobilities research practice was seen in the need to contextualize the mobile agency and linking the micro level of individual or collective experiences and rationalities with the macro level of discourses, infrastructures, and social order. As D'Andrea et al. (2011, 155f.) stated, a "significant challenge for mobilities studies is the systematic unbundling and formalization of research protocols, methods and analyses that can integrate macro and micro components, rather than allowing these to continue developing separately." As one strategy, the qualitative data collected on the micro level may be contrasted with information on the contextual structures. Elsewhere (Manderscheid 2016; similarly: Taipale 2014), I suggested to use the statistical technique of multiple correspondence analysis in order to search for structuring dimensions underlying patterns of practices. Similarly, Huete, Mantecón, and Estévez (2013) argue that the subjective assessments of individuals may be skewed and are not sufficient as the sole analytical framework. Analyzing the research differentiation between lifestyle and labor migration, the authors excavate an underlying ethnic-national elitism within the self-classifications of migrants from the UK and northern countries to Spain who are claiming mainly non-economic factors as motivations for their residential mobility. However, the quantitative comparison of their residential mobility patterns over time brings the dependence on economic factors to the fore, rendering their mobility patterns strikingly similar to the ones of the so-called

The Mobile Subject? 135

labor migrants. Thus, using multilevel data can help to correct for blind spots, preconscious knowledge, biased accounts, or assumptions of one-dimensional effects on one level.

On this token, another interesting technique of analysis could be social network analysis extended by a spatial dimension, applied to micro data as well as survey data. Larsen et al. (2006), for example, outline a form of qualitative spatial network analysis for individual cases, whereas the works of Axhausen et al. (Axhausen 2007; Frei et al. 2009) are pioneering in the field of visualization and analysis of geographies of social networks based on standardized survey data. They suggest some analytical techniques in order to compare network geographies between different social groups that form the backdrop for their differing mobility practices. These methods of spatial network analysis seem promising tools to account more systematically for the socio-spatial embedding of mobile actors and the network effects of mobile practices.

These few suggestions may suffice to show that, besides the development of further qualitative methods for mobilities research, it may also be worth it to re-discover standardized techniques which are suitable to contextualize mobility practices and thus re-embed the solitary mobile subjects into spatial and social structures in a non-deterministic way. Taken together, the suggested advancements within this discussion of mobile methods and methods for mobilities research may contribute to the discursive deconstruction of the modern automobile subject and, at the same time, an understanding of networked mobile agency.

Conclusions

Realities do not exist independently of their representation and these representations of the social world are highly contested and continuously changing. Taking mobilities studies as a standpoint within the contestation of the mobile social order, my point is the critique of the mobile subject as a rational autonomous actor characteristic of Western modernity and paradigmatically manifest as the automobile subject. From its very beginnings, the mobilities paradigm challenged this conception which pervades social sciences in general and transportation studies and policymaking in particular. Taking the order of knowledge—to which scientific discourses continuously contribute—as a cultural space of definitions and productions of specific subjectivities (Reckwitz 2008, 26ff.), research practices should be understood not only as descriptors of empirical worlds but also as techniques to effect and coproduce these very realities.

With the aim of methodologically translating networked agency and their embedding into material, infrastructural, social, cultural, and historic settings, I suggested to look more closely at the tool boxes of ANT and STS research. Especially technography, as well as selected multilevel statistics which allow the contextualization of individual practices within broader

136 *Katharina Manderscheid*

structural backgrounds, can be taken as sources for further development of methods for mobilities research.

However, I am not claiming that mobilities research can change mobility realities simply by broadening their methodologies and analytical techniques. Socio-cultural discourses and fields of knowledge suggest and impose specific patterns and subjectivities. Yet, they do not determine the empirical individual, who is always faced with multiple and contradicting expectations, forces, and patterns. As part of the social struggle for the 'true' view on the social, mobilities studies contribute to the way we conceive mobility. And by doing so, this also might help changing mobility itself.

References

Ahas, R. 2011. "Mobile positioning". In *Mobile Methods*, edited by Büscher, M., Urry, J. and Witchger, K. London: Routledge.

Akrich, M. and Latour, B. 1992. "A summary of a convenient vocabulary for the semiotics of human and nonhuman assemblies". In *Shaping Technology/Building Society Studies in Sociotechnical Change*, edited by Bijker, W. E. and Law, J., 259–64. Cambridge, MA: MIT Press.

Axhausen, K. W. 2007. "Activity spaces, biographies, social networks and their welfare gains and externalities: Some hypotheses and empirical results". *Mobilities*, 2(1), 15–36.

Bachelard, G. 2002. *The Formation of the Scientific Mind*. Bolton: Clinamen.

Bennett, T. and Joyce, P., eds. 2013. *Material Powers: Cultural Studies, History and the Material Turn*. London and New York: Routledge.

Bissell, D. 2010. "Narrating mobile methodologies: Active and passive empiricisms". In *Mobile Methodologies*, edited by Fincham, B., McGuinness, M. and Murray, L., 53–68. New York: Palgrave Macmillan.

Bourdieu, P. 1986. "The (three) forms of capital". In *Handbook of Theory and Research in the Sociology of Education*, edited by Richardson, J.G., 241–58. New York and London: Greenwood Press.

Bourdieu, P. 2000. *Distinction: A Social Critique of the Judgment of Taste*. Cambridge, MA: Harvard University Press.

Büscher, M. and Urry, J. 2009. "Mobile methods and the empirical". *European Journal of Social Theory*, 12(1), 99–116.

Büscher, M., Urry, J. and Witchger, K. 2011a. "Introduction: Mobile methods". In *Mobile Methods*, edited by Büscher, M., Urry, J. and Witchger, K., 1–19. Oxon and New York: Routledge.

Büscher, M., Urry, J. and Witchger, K., 2011b. *Mobile Methods*. Oxon and New York: Routledge.

Cass, N., Shove, E. and Urry, J. 2005. "Social exclusion, mobility and access". *Sociological Review*, 53(3), 539–555.

Cresswell, T. 2006. *On the Move: Mobility in the Modern Western World*. New York and London: Routledge.

Cresswell, T. 2010. "Towards a politics of mobility". *Environment and Planning D: Society and Space*, 28(1), 17–31.

D'Andrea, A., Ciolfi, L. and Gray, B., 2011. "Methodological challenges and innovations in mobilities research". *Mobilities*, 6(2), 149–60.

The Mobile Subject? 137

Dant, T. 2004. "The driver-car". *Theory, Culture & Society*, 21(4/5), 61–79.

Diaz-Bone, R. 2015. "Die Sozio-Epistemologie als methodologische Position Foucaultscher Diskursanalysen". *Zeitschrift für Diskursforschung*, 3(1), 43–61.

Fincham, B., McGuinness, M. and Murray, L. 2010. *Mobile Methodologies*. London: Palgrave Macmillan.

Foucault, M. 1972. *Archeology of Knowledge and the Discourse on Language*. New York: Pantheon Books.

Frei, A., Axhausen, K. W. and Ohnmacht, T. 2009. "Mobilities and social network geography: Size and spatial dispersion—the Zurich case study". In *Mobilities and Inequality*, edited by Ohnmacht, T. Maksim, H. and Bergman, M. M., 99–120. Aldershot: Ashgate.

Frello, B. 2008. "Towards a discursive analytics of movement: On the making and unmaking of movement as an object of knowledge". *Mobilities*, 3(1), 25–50.

Freudendal-Pedersen, M. 2007. "Mobility, motility and freedom: The structural story as an analytical tool for understanding the interconnection". *Schweizerische Zeitschrift für Soziologie*, 33(1), 27–43.

Goodman, A., Jones, A., Roberts, H., Steinbach, R. and Green, J. 2013. "We can all just get on a bus and go: Rethinking independent mobility in the context of the universal provision of free bus travel to young Londoners". *Mobilities*, 9(2), 275–93.

Graham, S. and Marvin, S. 2001. *Splintering Urbanism. Networked Infrastructures, Technological Mobilities and the Urban Condition*. London and New York: Routledge.

Hannam, K., Sheller, M. and Urry, J. 2006. "Editorial: Mobilities, immobilities and moorings". *Mobilities*, 1(1), 1–22.

Hilti, N. 2009. "Here, there, and in-between: On the Interplay of multilocal living, space, and inequality". In *Mobilities and Inequality*, edited by Ohnmacht, T., Maksim, H. and Bergman, M. M., 145–64. Aldershot: Ashgate.

Huete, R., Mantecón, A. and Estévez, J. 2013. "Challenges in lifestyle migration research: Reflections and findings about the Spanish crisis". *Mobilities*, 8(3), 331–48. doi:10.1080/17450101.2013.814236.

Ingold, T. 2004. "Culture on the ground: The world perceived through the feet". *Journal of Material Culture*, 9(3), 315–40.

Jansen, K. and Vellema, S. 2011. "What is technography?" *NJAS—Wageningen Journal of Life Sciences*, 57(3–4), 169–77.

Jensen, O. B., Sheller, M. and Wind, S. 2015. "Together and apart: Affective ambiences and negotiation in families' everyday life and mobility". *Mobilities*, 41(4), 363–82.

Katz, C. 1994. "Textures of global change: Eroding ecologies of childhood in New York and Sudan". *Childhood*, 2(1–2), 103–10.

Kazig, R. and Weichhart, P. 2009. "Die Neuthematisierung der materiellen Welt in der Humangeographie". *Berichte zur deutschen Landeskunde*, 83(2), 109–28.

Kien, G. 2008. "Technography = technology + ethnography: An introduction". *Qualitative Inquiry*, 14(7), 1101–9.

Kuhm, K. 1997. *Moderne und Asphalt. Die Automobilisierung als Prozeß technologischer Integration und sozialer Vernetzung*. Pfaffenweiler: Centaurus.

Kuhn, T. S. 1962. *The Structure of Scientific Revolutions*. Chicago: University of Chicago Press.

Larsen, J., and Jacobsen, M. H. 2009. "Metaphors of mobility—Inequality on the move". In *Mobilities and Inequality*, edited by Ohnmacht, T., Maksim, H. and Bergman, M. M., 75–96. Aldershot: Ashgate.

138 *Katharina Manderscheid*

Larsen, J., Urry, J. and Axhausen, K. W. 2006. *Mobilities, Networks, Geographies.* Hampshire: Ashgate.

Latour, B. 2005. *Reassembling the Social: An Introduction to Actor-Network-Theory.* Oxford: Oxford University Press.

Law, J. 2002. "Objects and spaces". *Theory Culture Society*, 19(5–6), 91–105.

Law, J. and Urry, J. 2004. "Enacting the social". *Economy and Society*, 33(3), 390–410.

Malkki, L. 1992. "National Geographic: The rooting of peoples and the territorialization of national identity among scholars and refugees". *Cultural Anthropology*, 7(1), 24–44.

Manderscheid, K. 2012. "Automobilität als raumkonstituierendes Dispositiv der Moderne". In *Die Ordnung der Räume*, edited by Füller, H. and Michel, B., 145–78. Münster: Westphälisches Dampfboot.

Manderscheid, K. 2014a. "Criticising the solitary mobile subject: Researching relational mobilities and reflecting on mobile methods". *Mobilities*, 9(2), 188–219.

Manderscheid, K. 2014b. "The movement problem, the car and future mobility regimes: Automobility as dispositif and mode of regulation". *Mobilities*, 9(4), 604–26.

Manderscheid, K. 2016. "Mobile Ungleichheiten. Eine sozial- und infrastrukturelle Differenzierung des Mobilitätstheorems". *Österreichische Zeitschrift für Soziologie*, 41(1), 71–96.

Merriman, P. 2013. "Rethinking mobile methods". *Mobilities*, 9(2), 1–21.

Mikkelsen, M. R. and Christensen, P. 2009. "Is children's independent mobility really independent? A study of children's mobility combining ethnography and GPS/mobile phone technologies". *Mobilities*, 4(1), 37–58.

Murdoch, J. 2001. "Ecologising sociology: Actor-network theory, co-construction and the problem of human exemptionalism". *Sociology*, 35(1), 111–33.

O'Brian, M., Jones, D., Sloan, D. and Rustin, M. 2000. "Children's independent spatial mobility in the urban public realm". *Childhood*, 7(3), 257–77.

Otto, M. 2014. *Der Wille zum Subjekt. Zur Genealogie politischer Inklusion in Frankreich (16.–20. Jahrhundert).* Bielefeld: Transcript.

Paterson, M., 2007. *Automobile Politics: Ecology and Cultural Political Economy.* Cambridge: Cambridge University Press.

Peck, J. and Tickell, A. 2002. "Neoliberalizing space". *Antipode*, 34(3), 380–404.

Pel, B. 2014. "Interactive metal fatigue: A conceptual contribution to social critique in mobilities research". *Mobilities* (online), 1–19.

Pooley, C., Turnbull, J. and Adams, M. 2005. *A mobile century? Changes in everyday mobility in Britain in the twentieth century.* Hampshire: Ashgate.

Rajan, S. C. 2006. "Automobility and the liberal disposition". *Sociological Review*, 54, 113–29.

Rammert, W. and Schubert, C., eds. 2006. *"Technographie." Zur Mikrosoziologie der Technik.* Frankfurt am Main: Campus.

Reckwitz, A. 2008. *Subjekt.* Bielefeld: Transcript.

Sassen, S. 2001. *The Global City: New York, London, Tokyo* (Second Edition). Princeton: Princeton University Press.

Schad, H. and Duchêne-Lacroix, C. 2013. "Multilokales Wohnen als hybride Praxis—Implikationen der 'mobilities studies' und der Akteur-Netzwerk-Theorie". In *Mobilitäten und Immobilitäten. Menschen—Ideen—Dinge—Kulturen—Kapital*, edited by Scheiner, J., Blotevogel, H.-H., Frank, S., Holz-Rau, C. and Schuster, N., 259–374. Essen: Klartext Verlag.

The Mobile Subject? 139

Schneider, N. F., Limmer, R., and Ruckdeschel, K. 2002. *Mobil, flexibel, gebunden. Familie und Beruf in der mobilen Gesellschaft*. Frankfurt and New York: Campus.

Shaw, B., Watson, B., Frauendienst, B., Redecker, A., Jones, T. and Hillman, M. 2013. *Children's Independent Mobility: A Comparative Study in England and Germany (1971–2010)*. London: Policy Studies Institute.

Sheller, M. and Urry, J. 2006. "The new mobilities paradigm". *Environment and Planning A*, 38(2), 207–26.

Sheppard, E. 2001. "Quantitative geography: Representations, practices, and possibilities". *Environment and Planning D: Society and Space*, 19, 535–54.

Sheppard, E. (2002). "The spaces and times of globalization: Place, scale, networks, and positionality". *Economic Geography*, 78 (3), 307–30.

Taipale, S. 2014. "The dimensions of mobilities: The spatial relationships between corporeal and digital mobilities". *Social Science Research*, 43(1), 157–67.

Urry, J. 2000. "Mobile sociology". *The British Journal of Sociology*, 51(1), 185–203.

Urry, J. 2004. 'The 'system' of automobility". *Theory, Culture & Society*, 21(4/5), 25–39.

Urry, J. 2003. "Social networks, travel and talk". *The British Journal of Sociology*, 54(2), 155–175.

Urry, J. 2007. *Mobilities*. Cambridge: Polity.

Vannini, P. and Vannini, A. S. 2008. "Of walking shoes, boats, golf carts, bicycles, and a slow technoculture: A technography of movement and embodied media on protection island". *Qualitative Inquiry*, 14(7), 1272–301.

Weiss, A. 2005. "The transnationalization of social inequality: Conceptualizing social positions on a world scale". *Current Sociology*, 53(4), 707–728.

Wolff, J. 1993. "On the road again: Metaphors of travel in cultural criticism". *Cultural Studies*, 7(2), 224–239.

Zeiher, H. 1990. "Organisation des Lebensraum bei Großstadtkindern—Einheitlichkeit oder Verinselung?" In *Lebenslauf und Raumerfahrung*, edited by Bertels, L. and Herlyn, U., 35–57. Opladen: Leske + Budrich.

9 Mobility and the Cosmopolitan Perspective

Ulrich Beck

This chapter raises the following questions: What is new about mobility in the cosmopolitan perspective? How does the cosmopolitan gaze, or to be more precise, 'methodological cosmopolitanism,' change the conceptual frame, the realities, and relevance of mobility?

I shall develop my argument in five steps: First I would like to locate the cosmopolitan perspective in the discourse of globalization. Second I want to draw a distinction between philosophical cosmopolitanism and social scientific cosmopolitanism. My third part focuses on the opposition between methodological nationalism and methodological cosmopolitanism. The fourth step outlines the research program of the cosmopolitan social science, especially in relation to issues of mobility. And finally, in the fifth step I discuss different ways of perceiving, analyzing, and coping with the local-global nexus.

Cosmopolitan Perspective and the Discourse on Globalization

Globalization has exploded into the sociological agenda in the last 10 to 15 years. We can distinguish three reactions: first *denial*, second *conceptual and empirical explorations*, third *epistemological turn*. The first reaction was and is nothing new. There has been quite a sophisticated defense of conventional economics, sociology, political science, etc., which tries to demonstrate that the evidence which has been brought up in favor of globalization is not really convincing.

But this strategy lost its credibility when a second reaction became prominent, that is a generation of globalization studies, which were concerned with how to define globalization; which aspects of globalization represented historical continuity and discontinuity; and how to theorize the relationship between globalization and modernity, postmodernity and postcolonialism. These studies primarily concentrated on understanding the character of globalization as a social phenomenon; there were important conceptual innovations, operationalizations, and empirical studies, represented for example by David Held and his group ('Global Transformations') or, in Germany, Michael Zürn and his group ('Im Zeitalter der

Globalisierung?'); Held used the basic term of 'interconnectedness,' Zürn the term of 'denationalization.'[1]

More recently, however, scholars started to ask what implications these socio-historical changes may have for social science itself: When fundamental dualisms—the national and the international, we and the others, inside and outside, fixity and motion—collapse, how does this affect the units of analysis in special fields of social science? In this 'epistemological turn' globalization poses a challenge to existing social scientific methods of inquiry. To be more radical: Sociology, political science, and ethnography rely on fixed, immobile, and comparable units of analysis (like surveys and comparative research), but they lose their subject of inquiry (see e.g. Urry 2000, 18–20). They all face significant challenges in reconfiguring themselves for the global era. In order to do this one needs a new standpoint of observation and conceptualization of social relations and consequently a paradigmatic shift from the dominant national gaze to a cosmopolitan perspective is enforced.

Philosophical Cosmopolitanism and Social Scientific Cosmopolitanism

As a first step on this way of change we have to distinguish between different versions of 'cosmopolitanism' (Beck 2006a; Beck and Sznaider 2006): The first, most commonsense meaning refers to a plea for cross-cultural and cross-national harmony; this is what I mean by '*normative* cosmopolitanism' or '*philosophical* cosmopolitanism.' During the era of enlightenment, European intellectuals heatedly fought over what today would be called two 'passwords': 'citizen of the world' and 'cosmopolitanism.' Both terms were always discussed in relation to the then nascent nationalism. What we need to do now is what Walter Benjamin called a 'saving critique' of the Enlightenment's distinction between nationalism and cosmopolitanism so we can usefully apply it to twenty-first-century reality: The normative notion of cosmopolitanism has to be distinguished from the *descriptive-analytical social science* perspective, which is no longer consistent with thinking in national categories. This I call 'analytical-empirical cosmopolitanization.' From such a perspective we can observe the growing interdependence and interconnection of social actors across national boundaries, more often than not as a side effect of actions that are not meant to be 'cosmopolitan' in a normative sense; this is '*real existing cosmopolitanism*' or the '*cosmopolitanization of reality*.' This last type of cosmopolitanization refers to the rise of global risks, global publics, global regimes dealing with transnational issues: '*institutionalized cosmopolitanism*.'

The philosophical debates on cosmopolitanism have tended to neglect actual existing cosmopolitanism or cosmopolitanization. My favorite neglected Kant quote to demonstrate what I mean comes from his popular lectures on anthropology and is about the German character: "[The Germans] have no nation

142   Ulrich Beck

pride, and are too cosmopolitan to be deeply attached to the homeland" (1974, 180). Is this only further evidence that philosophers know themselves least? Perhaps. But it also suggests that philosophy is of limited use in thinking about real existing cosmopolitanism, because the cosmopolitan challenges are not in theory, but in practice, and—even more important—the 'cosmopolitanization of reality' is quite a different thing than imagining cosmopolitanism philosophically.

What are some actually existing cosmopolitanisms? Most of them are not intended but unintended, not a matter of free choice but a matter of being forced. Cosmopolitanism may be an elite concept, cosmopolitanization is *not* an elite concept. Cosmopolitanization, for example, derives from the dynamics of global risks, of mobility and migration, or from cultural consumption (music, dress styles, food), and the media impact leads—as John Urry and others showed—to a shift of perspective, however fragile (Hannam, Sheller, and Urry 2006). And it leads to a growing awareness of relativity of one's own social position and culture in a global arena. Cosmopolitanization also leads to new relations, new connectivities, and new mobilities, as Tomlinson (1999) puts it.

All of these actually existing cosmopolitanisms involve individuals with limited choices. The decision to enter a political realm larger than the local one may sometimes be made voluntarily, but it often results from the force of circumstances.

More narrowly market-driven choices usually derive from the desire not to be poor, or simply not to die. Entertainment choices are based on a range of options frequently beyond the control of individual consumers. Such compulsions may explain in part why the mass of really existing cosmopolitanization doesn't enter into scholarly discussions of cosmopolitanism: To argue that the choice of cosmopolitanism is in some sense self-betraying and made under duress takes away much of its ethical attractiveness. If cosmopolitanization is both indeterminate and inescapable, it becomes difficult to conceptualize and theorize. Yet such is normally the case in a world where the boundaries are deeply contested.

Conceptualizing these different types of cosmopolitanization raises many questions and objections. I want to pick up only one: What do the vastly different variants of 'cosmopolitanization' have in common? To what point is it meaningful to classify, for example, 'Kant's Ewiger Friede,' the Rio conference on sustainable development, and white New York teenagers listening to the 'black' rap as variants of 'cosmopolitanism'? There is a big difference between Kant's philosophical vision of a cosmopolitan order and the Rio conference, but through the backdoor of 'side effects'—that is of the global perception and acceptance of the global risk dynamics—global problems offer options for cosmopolitan solutions and institutions Kant had in mind. And the New York teenager is, of course, not a cosmopolitan. Listening to 'black' rap doesn't make him a cosmopolitan, but an active part of an ever denser global interconnectedness, interpenetration, and mobility of

Mobility and the Cosmopolitan Perspective   143

cultural symbols and flows. From Moscow to Paris, from Rome to Tokyo people live in a network of interdependencies, which are becoming tighter by everybody's active participation through production and consumption. At the same time we are all confronted with global risks—economically, environmentally, and by the terrorist threat—which bind underdeveloped and highly developed nations together. There is a global mobility of risks where people, ideas, concepts, and things travel from one side of the world to the other and infect or affect at any place that no one can predict (see e.g. Kaplan 2006; Law 2006; Urry 2002, 2004, and Chapter 4, this volume).

One big difference between the classical philosophy debate on cosmopolitanism and sociological cosmopolitanization is: The cosmopolitan philosophy is about free choice, the cosmopolitan perspective informs us about a *forced* cosmopolitanization, a passive cosmopolitanism produced by side effects from radicalized modernization. And in this context the distinction between globalism and cosmopolitanization is very important.

Globalism involves the idea of the world market, of the virtues of neoliberal capitalist growth, and of the need to move capital, products, and people across a relatively borderless world. Cosmopolitanization is a much more multidimensional process of change that has irreversibly changed the very nature of the social world and the place of states within that world. Cosmopolitanization thus includes the proliferation of multiple cultures (as with cuisines from around the world), the growth of many transnational forms of life, the emergence of various non-state political actors (from Amnesty International to the World Trade Organization), the paradox generation of global protest movements against globalization, the formation on international or transnational states—like the European Union—and the general process of cosmopolitan interdependence and global risks. In terms of contemporary politics one might pose these as conflicts between the United States and the UN: The United States represents globalism, the UN cosmopolitanization. These two visions of second modernity haunt contemporary life, each trying to control and regulate an increasingly turbulent new world.

Opposition Between Methodological Nationalism and Cosmopolitanization

My third argument starts with making a distinction between normative and methodological nationalism. Normative nationalism is about the actor's perspective, methodological nationalism is about the social scientific observer's perspective. The conventional post-war social science regards the nation as a huge container, while international relations are assumed to account for all relations outside that national container.

Even in world-systems theory, the subunits of the system are almost always nations, whose relations to each other are ordered by capitalist development and interstate competition. Most political scientists and political theories

144   *Ulrich Beck*

still do equalize state with nation-state; political parties monopolize the representation of political conflicts and so on.

Anthropology takes the local for the site of culture, which is often analyzed in terms of its relationship to the world of nations (colonialism, nation building, etc.). It often takes the established hierarchies of the local, the national, and the international for granted. This critique of methodological nationalism is only possible from a cosmopolitan point of view. It is the first step of methodological cosmopolitanism.

Critique of methodological nationalism includes reflecting and questioning the basic background assumptions and distinctions. One can explain this very shortly in the field of mobility research, which often presupposes the distinction between *mobility* and *migration*.

Of course, on the level of the social actor (mainly the nation-state and its citizens) there is a big difference between mobility and migration. 'Mobility' stands for a fact and a positive value inside national societies and it is a general principle of modernity (see Kesselring 2008a). 'Migration' stands for movements of actors across national borders, which is negatively valued and often criminalized. In the national perspective it is both legal and legitimate to stop or regulate 'migration' while at the same time 'mobility' is to be enforced. But if this distinction becomes part of the social science vocabulary and theory, this is a clear case of the consequence of methodological nationalism. The problem of this substantial treatment of 'migration' and 'mobility' is that it adopts categories of *political actors* as categories of *social scientific analysis*. It takes a conception inherent in the practice of nationalism and in the workings of the modern state and state system and makes this conception a center for social theory, philosophy, and research about mobility and migration (aliens and citizens).

In social and political theory and philosophy one has to ask: What justifies closed borders? What justifies the use of force against many poor and depressed people, who wish to leave their countries of origin in the Third World to come to Western societies? Perhaps borders and guards can be justified as a way of keeping out criminals, subversives, or armed invaders. But most of those trying to get in are not like that. They are ordinary, peaceful 'mobile' people, seeking only the opportunity to build decent secure lives for themselves and their families. What gives anyone the right to point guns at them?

It was Niklas Luhmann who argued in his system theory that communication knows no borders. This is one of the main reasons why he criticizes the conception of *many* national societies and argued for one and only one society, namely 'world society.' There are three contemporary approaches to political theory—Rawls, Nozick, and liberalism—to construct arguments to oppose the social scientific distinction between mobility and migration. It is, especially, the liberal tradition of Western societies which contradicts this distinction. Liberalism emerged with the modern state and presupposes it. Liberal theories are deeply rooted in methodological nationalism. They

Mobility and the Cosmopolitan Perspective 145

were not designed to deal with questions about migration. They assumed the context of the sovereign state. As a historical observation this is true. But liberal principles (like most principles) have implications that the original advocates of the principles did not entirely foresee. This is one of the reasons why radicalized liberalism can argue for a cosmopolitan perspective and becomes part of methodological cosmopolitanism.

The Cosmopolitan Perspective on Mobility

Methodological cosmopolitanism, therefore, is not only about new concepts but about a new *grammar of the social and political*. Methodological cosmopolitanism is *not* justified in itself; it only justifies itself by producing—as Imre Lakatosz calls it—a 'positive problem shift.' It justifies it by opening up new fields for research, theoretical interpretation, and political action. This shift of perspective from methodological nationalism to methodological cosmopolitanism allows a focus upon quite a lot of different theoretical and empirical landscapes:

- Global risk dynamics: The rise of a global public arena results from the reaction to non-intended side effects of modernization (Beck 1992; Böschen, Kratzer, and May 2006). More precisely, the risks of modern society—terrorism, environment, etc.—are inherently transnational and global in nature and attempts at controlling them lead to the creation of global fora of debate, if not necessarily to global solutions, too.
- Cosmopolitan perspective allows us to go beyond '*international relations*' and to analyze a multitude of interconnections not only between states, but also between other actors on different levels of aggregation. More than this: It opens up a new space for understanding trans- or post-international relations.
- Sociology of inequality: A de-nationalized social science can research into the global inequalities that were covered by the traditional focus on national inequality and its legitimation.
- Different forms of 'banal cosmopolitanism': Finally, everyday cosmopolitanization on the level of cultural consumption (music, dress styles, food), everyday traveling and connecting between distant places and people in the world (Lassen 2006; Kesselring 2006), and media representation lead to a shift of perspective, however fragile, in growing awareness of relativity of one's owns social position and culture in a global arena.

But here I want to discuss the question: What kind of innovations derive from a cosmopolitan perspective on mobility?

My first argument relates to a *macro perspective*: What is the 'subject' of mobility? Not only individuals or groups within or across borders, but also whole national societies and nation-states. This 'society mobility' or 'state-migration' is a kind of *immobile mobility* of a territorialized unit. It

146   *Ulrich Beck*

can be studied in the case of the European Union and relates to the mobility between membership and non-membership countries. Europe is not a static unit (like a national society), but a process of *Europeanization*. That means one of the basic secrets of the European Union is the *dialectics of integration and expansion*. The mobility of societies as a whole is one of the main characteristics of Europeanization. The intensified integration within the European Union alters the communities' external relationships. The affluent core becomes more and more directly involved in stabilizing political and economic conditions in the neighboring regions. EU integration intensifies and more inner-EU borders vanish, the common interest of EU states maintaining the patterns of concentric circles outside the communities' borders becoming even more apparent. In a certain sense this expresses the European Union's capacity to alter and to change the shape of its social and political configurations and it signifies its liveliness. Its capacity to be mobile, its '*motility*' (see Canzler, Kaufmann, and Kesselring 2008), is a decisive factor in the whole process of making Europe.

Since the non-members of the European Union have to adjust their structures and institutions to EU norms (open markets, human rights, democratic values), the EU integration of variable geographies includes the excluded: the non-members but potential members. Thus this kind of macro-mobility, which is grounded on consensus and free choice of the non-member states, is not a product of war, imperialism, and colonialism—but it operates with a specific inside-outside nexus. Borders are at the same time there and not there; they do function and don't function, because the anticipated future of the EU membership becomes a real existing force for institutional reforms in the non-member state (e.g. Turkey).

Are there other conceptual innovations looking at mobility from a cosmopolitan perspective? Yes. And I would like to distinguish between the concept of a *cosmopolitan place* and the concept of *cosmopolitanization of places*. What I define as 'cosmopolitan place' is pretty much related to 'urban space' or 'global city,' but it has to be clearly distinguished from methodological nationalism. I suggest there are two aspects to what makes 'being cosmopolitan' different from 'being national.'

First, one does not exist in the cosmopolitan place in the same way as one exists as part of the nation. If the nation is fundamentally about belonging to an abstract community, then the cosmopolitan place or space is about immersion in a world of multiplicity and implicates us in the dimension of embodied cultural experience. In cosmopolitan places cultural differences are experienced *at ground level* and involve *bodily-materialized engagement* with the complex realities of the 'excluded others.' The co-existence of cultural differences provokes questions like: *Who am I? What am I? Where am I? Why am I where I am?*—very different questions from the national questions: Who are we? and What do we stand for? The nation, we may say, is a space of identification and identity, whilst a cosmopolitan place is an existential and experimental space of difference. Here the concern is

Mobility and the Cosmopolitan Perspective 147

no longer with the culture as a binding mechanism—'what binds people together into a single body'; cosmopolitan places are regarded as a huge cultural reservoir and resource—valued for its complexity and its incalculability. While the nation is about stability and continuity, the cosmopolitan place offers important possibilities for cultural experimentation: How can strangers live together? It is a complex of specially distributed cultures, side-by-side, overlapping, hustling, negotiating, constantly moving and jostling—a physical and embodied co-existence that defies any abstract (national) schemes of integration and assimilation.

This understanding of the cosmopolitan place has implications for the understanding of citizenship and vice versa. Again it undermines the distinction of mobility and migration in relation to specific places. In the first nation-state-centered modernity three distinct components of citizenship are being combined: citizenship as a political *principle of democracy*, citizenship as a *juridical status of legal personhood*, and citizenship as a form of *membership* in an exclusive social category. Republic or democratic theorists stress the active participatory dimension, liberals mostly concentrate on personal rights and methods of justice, and communitarian theorists are concerned with the dimension of collective identity and solidarity. What characterizes cosmopolitan places is the *de-composition* of the first modern paradigm of citizenship and the evolving of new as-well-as categories with a new set of choices and dangers.

The clear-cut dualisms between members and non-members of a (national) category or between humans and citizens collapse. This does have several implications. For example: The juridical dimension of citizenship—the citizen in this approach is not a political actor but a legal person, free to act by law and under the protection of law. It can be more 'fluid' and potentially inclusive, since it is not tied to particular collective identities or a membership in a *demos*. Consequently the citizen does not need to be territorially bound. But consequences could be a loss of politicization and solidarity. Universalizing legal personhood undermines the will to political participation as well as the strong identification with the social solidarity that the democratic-republic concept presupposes. On the other hand, cosmopolitan places open spaces to invent and amalgamate in crucial experimentation the combination of human rights and citizenship, legal status, social identity, and political-democratic participation.

From a conceptual sociological point of view this experimentation combines elements which seem to be analytically exclusive (at least in a Weberian perspective): the principles of legality and legitimation or illegality and illegitimation. The border-crossing world of cosmopolitan places and spaces is, relative to specific perspectives, at the same time legal and non-legal, legitimate and non-legitimate, depending on a national or cosmopolitan perspective, a methodological nationalism or methodological cosmopolitanism.

In reality, what characterizes cosmopolitan places is their structural and topographical overlapping and their to some extent contrary frames

148 Ulrich Beck

of reference related to the position and the power of social and political actors. The first modern paradigm of citizenship was never normatively satisfactory. It promised to resolve the tensions between democracy, justice, and identity if only it was institutionalized in the right way. Cosmopolitan places are an empirical falsification to this claim: The exclusive territoriality and sovereignty inherent in the nation-state model are being transformed due to the emergence of transnational economic practices in super-national legal regimes, post-national political bodies, which intersect in cosmopolitan places. Thus cosmopolitan places are an experimental space about a new paradigm of citizenship that is both adequate to cultural diversity in cosmopolitan places and normatively justifiable.

Perceiving, Analyzing, and Coping With the Local-Global Nexus

Main differences between a *cosmopolitan place* and the *cosmopolitanization of places* are: the first is reflexive, the second is latent; the first is fixed to urban space, the second is open to many different configurations of 'place': the global context of *rural areas*, the global context of *regions*, the global context of *households*, and so on. All of these different 'politics of scale' (Swyngedouw 1997; Marston 2000; Brenner 2001) involve the question about the activity of the actors. In a second cosmopolitan modernity the social and the political has to be re-imagined and redefined. But this is a challenge for quite different theoretical approaches: system theory (in its distinct versions from Wallerstein to Luhmann), symbolic interactionism, or ethno-methodology (to name only a few). *Beyond* methodological nationalism the competition between theoretical positions and their framing of empirical research evolves anew.

I would like to make a distinction between a postmodern approach and a second-modern approach: Very much simplified, the postmodernists to some extent welcome the fluidity of an increasingly borderless world. They argue that the disembedded 'social' and 'political' are increasingly constituted by flows of people, information, goods, and cultural symbols (see e.g. Lash and Urry 1994; Urry 2000). From the point of view of second-modernist theory and research they underestimate the importance and contradiction of 'boundary management' in a world of flows and networks (see Beck, Bonß, and Lau 2003). This has to be studied both in cosmopolitan places and the cosmopolitanization of places. A postmodern vocabulary of flows and networks, despite recognizing that networks can be exclusionary, provide little analysis of power relations within cosmopolitan places and networks. And therefore it finds it difficult to explain reproduction into change in cosmopolitan places. The question is: Does thinking in 'flows' and 'networks' neglect the *agency* of the actors and their sense-making activities as forces in shaping the flows themselves?

In order to go beyond the false opposition between the space of flows versus the space of places (Manuel Castells), social theory has to develop an

Mobility and the Cosmopolitan Perspective 149

understanding of how cosmopolitan places (or the cosmopolitanization of places) constitute an *active relationship of actors to space and place*. Thinking along this line, reflexive modernists see globalization as a repatterning of fluidities and mobilities on the one hand and stoppages and fixities on the other, rather than an all-encompassing world of fluidity and mobility. Since if the whole world became mobile and liquid this would be a certain form of linear and first-modern modernization. Mobility research in the context of the theory of reflexive modernization shows an active mobility politics of actors on every scale from the body to the global. Also in contexts of hypermobility and hyperactivity there is a need for stability and reliability. People actively develop sophisticated strategies of coping with mobility constraints. Kesselring (2006, 2008b) describes patterns such as the centered, the de-centered, and the reticular mobility management where people actively deploy stability cores in contexts of mobility and fluidity which enable them to manage a huge amount of movements and travels. Surprisingly, the most effective strategy seems to be the centered mobility management. In this type people circulate around a clearly defined place of belonging. They practice an active relation to space and place without losing social and cultural contact and identity. In a certain way this exemplifies what I call a cosmopolitan identity of 'roots with wings' (Beck 2006a).

From a standpoint of mobility research in a cosmopolitan perspective the main issue is not, as Lefebvre puts it, the 'production of space' (Lefebvre 2000). If we take actors as powerful players in the process of the social construction of the global age we shall talk and think about the 'production of place.' More than this we need to talk about the social production of interfaces between spaces of globality and spaces of territoriality. The 'world city network' (Taylor 2004) represents the visible structure of globalization and cosmopolitanization. It rests on powerful infrastructures and machines that enable individuals, groups, companies, and whole nations to be connected with other places and spaces around the world. Together with complex systems of IT infrastructures and the Internet, these networks of mobility, such as airports, road systems, the worldwide system of vessels and ports, etc., build the backbone of the cosmopolitan society and the process of globalization. This constitutes a specific constellation of 'fixity and motion' (David Harvey) and the dialectics of (im)mobility and a strained relationship between moorings and flows. The modern open society is a mobile society and as such it is a 'mobile world risk society' (Beck 1992; Kesselring 2009).

From the discussion of flows, we see the need to redefine places in the light of the multiple connections cutting across places. From the study of transnationalism, we see the critical importance of the emergence of a new politics of scales of social action and the reconfiguring of relationships among the multiple scales within which places are embedded. Finally, from the study of borders, we see the vital importance of seeing place as politically produced and contested. In a second-modern perspective we have to merge these various perspectives into a concept of the social as increasingly embroiled in

150   Ulrich Beck

place-making projects that seek to redefine the connection, scales, borders, and characters of particular places and particular social orders. What methodological cosmopolitanism looks for is to replace the national ontology by methodology, a methodology which helps to create a cosmopolitan observer-perspective to analyze the ongoing dialectics between cosmopolitanization and anti-cosmopolitanization of places.

These ongoing dialectics can be observed in so called 'places of flows' where the ambivalences of the process of cosmopolitanization come together, interact, and create new mobilities, stabilities, and fixities. These places of flows like global cities, airports, train stations, museums, cultural sites, etc., are locally based but transnationally shaped, connected, and linked with cosmopolitan networks and structures. Understanding power in the global age needs a mobility-related research that focuses on places of flows and the power techniques and the strategies of boundary management that define and construct places and scapes where cosmopolitanization is possible. From these places we can learn how the cosmopolitan society works. The cosmopolitanization of modern societies does not happen in an abstract space of flows. It happens where and when the local meets the global and the channeling and the structuration of flows has to be made and organized. It is the hidden 'power of the local in a borderless world' (Berking 2006) that structures and gives shape to global flows and mobilities.

Note

1. See Held, McGrew, Goldblatt, and Perraton (1999); Zürn (2005).

References

Beck, U. 1992. *Risk Society*. London: Sage.
Beck, U. 2006a. *The Cosmopolitan Visions*. Cambridge UK, and Malden, MA: Polity Press.
Beck, U. 2006b. *Power in a Global Age: A New Global Political Economy*. Oxford: Blackwell.
Beck, U. and Sznaider, N. 2006. "Unpacking cosmopolitanism for the social sciences: A research agenda". *The British Journal of Sociology*, 57(1), 1–23.
Beck, U., Bonß, W. and Lau, C. 2003. "The theory of reflexive modernization: Problematic, hypotheses and research programme". *Theory, Culture & Society*, 20(2), 1–34.
Berking, H., ed. 2006. *Die Macht des Lokalen in einer Welt ohne Grenzen*. Frankfurt and New York: Campus.
Böschen, S., Kratzer, N. and May, S. 2006. *Nebenfolgen—Analysen zur Konstruktion und Transformation moderner Gesellschaften*. Weilerswist: Velbrück.
Brenner, N. 2001. "The limits to scale? Methodological reflections on scalar structuration". *Progress in Human Geography*, 25(4), 591–614.
Canzler, W., Kaufmann, V. and Kesselring, S., eds. 2008. *Tracing Mobilities: Towards a Cosmopolitan Perspective*. Aldershot: Ashgate.
Hannam, K., Sheller, M. and Urry, J. 2006. "Mobilities, immobilities and moorings: Editorial". *Mobilities*, 1(1), 1–22.

Mobility and the Cosmopolitan Perspective   151

Held, D., McGrew, A., Goldblatt, D. and Perraton, J. 1999. *Global Transformations: Politics, Economics and Culture*. Cambridge: Polity Press.

Kant, I. 1974. *Anthropology from a Pragmatic Point of View*. Dortrecht: Springer Netherlands.

Kaplan, C. 2006. "Mobility and war: The cosmic view of US air power". *Environment and Planning A*, 38, 395–407.

Kesselring, S. 2006. "Pioneering mobilities: New patterns of movement and motility in a mobile world". *Environment and Planning A*. Special Issue "Mobilities and Materialities", 269–79.

Kesselring, S. 2008a. "The mobile risk society". In *Tracing Mobilities: Towards a Cosmopolitan Perspective*, edited by Canzler, W., Kaufmann, V. and Kesselring, S., 77–102. Aldershot: Ashgate.

Kesselring, S. 2008b. "Skating over thin ice. Pioneers of the mobile risk society". In *The Social Fabric of the Networked City*, A book in honour of Manuel Castells, edited by Pflieger, G., Pattaroni, L., Jemelin, C. and Kaufmann, V., 17–39. Lausanne: EPFL Press.

Kesselring, S. 2009. "Global transfer points: The making of airports in the mobile risk society". In *Aeromobilities*, edited by Cwerner, S., Kesselring, S. and Urry, J., 39–60. London and New York: Routledge.

Lash, S. and Urry, J. 1994. *Economies of Signs and Space*. London: Sage.

Lassen, C. 2006. "Aeromobility and work". *Environment and Planning A*, 38(2), 301–12.

Law, J. 2006. "Disasters in agriculture: Or foot and mouth mobilities". *Environment and Planning A*, 38(2), 227–39.

Lefebvre, H. 2000. *The Production of Space*. Oxford: Blackwell.

Marston, S. 2000. "The social construction of scale". *Progress in Human Geography*, 24(2), 219–42.

Swyngedouw, E. 1997. "Neither global nor local: 'Glocalization' and the politics of scale". In *Spaces of Globalization: Reasserting the Power of the Local*, edited by Cox, K. R., 137–66. New York: Guildford.

Taylor, P. J. 2004. *World City Network: A Global Urban Analysis*. London: Routledge.

Tomlinson, J. 1999. *Globalization and Culture*. Oxford: Oxford University Press.

Urry, J. 2000. *Sociology Beyond Societies: Mobilities of the Twenty-First Century*. London: Routledge.

Urry, J. 2002. "The global complexities of September 11th". *Theory, Culture & Society*, 19(4), 57–69.

Urry, J. 2004. "Connections". *Environment and Planning D: Society and Space*, 22(1), 27–37.

Zürn, M. 2005. *Globalizing Interests: Pressure Groups and Denationalization*. Albany, NY: State University of New York Press.

Index

Abercrombie, Sir Leslie Patrick 2
Actor-Network Theory (ANT) 133, 135
Adey, Peter 28
Aerial Life (Adey) 28
agency, networked 124–9
Aguiléra, Anne 113
Allen, Woody 86
American Association of Geographers 82
Amin, Ash 21
Amnesty International 143
anonymous strangers, modern
    metropolis 36–7
anthropology 45, 85, 141, 144
Ascher, Francois 117
Australia's Gold Coast elevator 88

Bachelard, Gaston 129
Ballard, J. G. 85
Barthes, Roland 129
Beck, Ulrich 11, 12, 15–16, 140–50
Being John Malkovich (film) 85
Beirut bombings 71
Benjamin, Walter 141
Bernard, Audreas 98
Bhopal disaster 66
Bhopal Group for Information and
    Action 61
Bilderberg Group 55
Boltanski, Luc 109
Brechin, Gray 98
Buffett, Warren 50
Burj Khalifa, Dubai 91, 93–4, 95, 100, 102
Büscher, Monika 14, 59–75
Business Week (journal) 81

Canguilhem, Georges 129
Carey, James 20
cars: changing desires relative to
    115–16; driverless 12; freedom of

choice and individuality 126; history
in Western Europe 111–13; mobility
110–11; polytopic living and 113–14;
structural decline of use 116, 120;
travel time budgets 114–15
Castells, Manuel 148
Charlie and the Great Glass Elevator
    (Dahl) 86
Chernobyl disaster 66, 72
Chiapello, Eve 109
Chicago heat wave (1995) 67
Chicago School 5, 6
children, independent mobility 131–2
CIAM (International Congress of
    Modern Architecture) 3
cities: historical perspective of mobilities
    2–4; social fabric of 4–6; time-space
    relations in 7–8
City, The (Park, Burgess and
    McKenzie) 5–6
city of strangers 36
communications: age of remote 118–19;
    local living 119; networked 60
communicative capitalism 71–2
communities of risk 63
commuting, widespread high
    mobility 118
connected mobility 20
consumption 9; global connector 10
container society logic 11
cosmopolitanism: banal 145;
    philosophical 141–3; social scientific
    141–3
cosmopolitanization: concept of 142;
    methodological nationalism and 143–5
cosmopolitanization of places: concept of
    146; cosmopolitan place and 148–50
cosmopolitan perspective: local-global
    nexus 148–50; mobility 140–1, 145–8

154   Index

cosmopolitan place: concept of 146; cosmopolitanization of places and 148–50
crisis informatics 30
critical mobilities theory 20
critical mobility thinking 27
cyberspace 22

Dahl, Roald 86
daily travel time budgets 114–15
dating site, web-based 39, 40
Death and Life of Great American Cities, The (Jacobs) 3
Deconstructing Harry (film) 86
de Jong, Johannes 81
Delaware: as tax haven 53–4
democracy: offshoring and 14, 56, 57, 58; principle of 147
De Quille, Dan 101
de Sola Pool, Ithiel 84
Diering, D. H. 103
digital access, democratizing 31
digital cityscapes 21
Digital Humanitarian Network 72
digital humanitarians 30, 68–72, 74
digital networks, wireless access to 19
Dilain, Claude 97
disaster and networked urbanism 59–61, 74–5; communications 59–61; difficulties and contradictions 70–2; difficulties in responsibility distribution 64–5; mobile publics 68–9; networked partnerships 61–4; networks of trust 72–4; technologies of articulation 72–4; technologies of humility 65–8
Dodgeball 38
Dragonquest 9 38, 41, 43
Dubai's Burj Khalifa 91, 93–4, 95, 100, 102
Durrheim, Ray 101

eBay 41
Economist, The (journal) 25, 26, 55
elevators 14–15; Atlanta's Hyatt Regency Hotel 86, 87; Australia's Gold Coast 88; broken, in Chicago 95, 96; colonization of the up 83–5; comparing mines and towers 100; location of fastest 89–91; Taipei Financial Center 89, 90; trapped crises 95–8; ultra-deep mining and 98–103; Volkswagen's Car Tower 91, 92; *see also* vertical mobilities

Energize the Chain 26
Engels, Friedrich 4, 5
Europeanization 146
European Union 28, 146

Facebook 60, 69, 71
familiar stranger 38
Federal Emergency Management Agency (FEMA) 63–4, 72
Ferguson, James 24
Finger Plan 2
flow management 10
Forbes (magazine) 89
Foucault, Michel 20, 31, 129
Foursquare 38, 42–3
Freudendal-Pedersen, Malene 1–16
Friedberg, Anne 21
Fukushima disaster (Japan) 66, 72–3

Garden City 2–3, 12
Garfinkel, Susan 86
geography 7; of mobility 29; of satellites 25; urban 19, 82
Germany, Volkswagen's Car Tower 91, 92
global economy, offshoring 50–8
globalization: discourse on 140–1; offshoring 51; optimism rooted in 13–14; *see also* networked urbanism
global metabolism 29
global network: cities as nodes 1, 9; 'network society' 1; *see also* networked urbanism
Global North 12, 20, 23, 24, 30
global optimism 51
global shadows 12–13, 20, 24, 25, 28, 29
Global South 12–13, 20, 30, 98
Goldman Sachs 53, 54
Goldman Sachs Structured Products (Asia) Limited 54
Google 20, 37, 55
government-civil society partnerships 64
Graham, Stephen 14–15, 80–104, 126
Greater London Plan 2
Great Pacific Garbage Patch 52
Greenfield, Adam 22
Grindr 38, 41–2
Guardian (newspaper) 13

Haiti earthquake (2010) 61, 68
Haiti, mobile communications 26
Hart, Matthew 102
Harvey, David 7, 149
Hayek, Friedrich 53

Index 155

health and social care 12
High-Rise (Ballard) 85
Hitachi G1 Tower 80–1, 84, 91
households: global context 148;
  motorized transport of 113, 116;
  transition of mobility 117–18
Howard, Ebenezer 2
Human-Computer Interaction (HCI) 37
Humanity Road (HR) 73
Hurricane Katrina, and New Orleans
  (2005) 61, 67
Hurricane Sandy (2012) 97
Hyatt Regency Hotel (Atlanta) 86, 87
hybrid ecologies 31–2; concept of 27;
  reflexive 43–4
hypertext society 117

IBM 20, 21
iLab/Haiti 30
immobile mobility 145–6
Inada, Yoriko 27
inequality, offshoring 54–5
Information and Communications
  Technologies for Development
  (ICTD) 26
infrastructural ideal, concept of 126
Ingress 37, 41
interactive metal fatigue, concept of 134
International Academy of Astronautics 91
International Consortium of Investigative
  Journalists 55
Internet 9, 22, 27
Internet of things 12, 20

Jacobs, Jane 3
Jeddah, Kingdom Tower 91, 100

Kant, Immanuel 142
Kathmandu, Nepal, crisis mappers 69, 70
Kaufmann, Vincent 15, 108–21
Kerasidou, Xaroula 14, 59–75
Kesselring, Sven 1–16
Keynesianism 53
Kingdom Tower (Jeddah) 91, 100
Kingwell, Mark 93
Kittler, Friedrich 20
Kone elevator company 81

Lakatosz, Imre 145
Law, John 129
Le Corbusier's 'Radiant City' 3–4
Lefebvre, Henri 29
Le Monde (newspaper) 97
LesinRocks (magazine) 97

liberalism 53, 144–5
Licoppe, Christian 13, 27, 36–47
local-global nexus, analyzing and coping
  with 148–50
local living, quality of 119
locative media 13; encounters with
  pseudonymous strangers 47; types of
  mobile 37–8; virtual acquaintances
  and pseudonymous strangers 41–3
Long-Term Evolution (LTE) wireless 61
Luhmann, Niklas 144

Manderscheid, Katharina 15, 124–36
many-to-many network partnerships
  64; communication 60–1, 70
Marvin, Simon 126
Marx, Karl 4, 5, 6
Mauss, Marcel 108
Mavhunga, Clapperton 27
methodological cosmopolitanism 15,
  140, 144–5, 147, 150
methodological nationalism 15;
  opposition with cosmopolitanization
  143–5
metropolis, anonymous strangers in
  modern 36–7
migration 11, 32: labor 134; long-distance
  125; mobility and 142, 144, 147;
  state- 145
mining, ultra-deep elevators 98–103
Mining Weekly (magazine) 103
Mitchell, William 22
mobile measuring 72
mobile mediality 20, 22–3; phenomenon
  of 12, 13
mobile methods 124; links with theory
  129–32
mobile money 26
mobile phones, reconfiguration of 25
mobile public, disaster response 68–9
mobile risk society and urban age 9–11
mobile subjects, networked agency and
  124–9
Mobile Technologies of the City (Sheller
  and Urry) 20–1
mobilities 6, 125, 144; actors 110–11;
  age of remote communication and
  mobile goods 118–19; cars 110–11;
  changing car use 116; changing
  desires relative to car 115–16;
  children's independent 131–2;
  contemporary ideology of 109;
  cosmopolitan perspective 140–1,
  145–8; cycling 132; definition of 6;

156 *Index*

factors explaining changing 113–16; history of urban transport in Western Europe 111–13; kinds of 31–2; local-global nexus 148–50; missing links between theory and methods 129–32; networked urban 11–16; networks in the city 8–9; paradigm 129; polytopic living 113–14; production factors 110; quality of local living 119; social phenomenon 108–9; subjects 124–9; transition scenarios 116–19; travel time budgets 114–15; understanding the urban 6–8; urban perspective 1; vision of futures 120–1; walking 27, 93, 110–11, 117, 126–7, 132; widespread high 118; *see also* networked urbanism; vertical mobilities

mobility methods, politics of 132–5
modal shift policies, history in Western Europe 111–13
modern subject 125
Mogi 37, 45
Momo 38
Mont Pèlerin Society 53
Moses, Robert 3
motility 146
Mountz, Alison 29
Mponeng Mine, South Africa 100, 101–3
Mumford, Lewis 10, 101
Murphy, Richard 56

National Geographic (magazine) 103
National Union of Mineworkers (NUM) 103
Neighborhood, The (McKenzie) 5
neoliberal capitalism 56–7
networked agency, mobile subjects and 124–9
networked intelligence 22
networked objects, notion of 23
networked partnerships, disasters 61–4
networked place 21, 22
networked urbanism 1, 14; emergent 19; global urbanizations 19–20; hybrid global third spaces 28–31; kinetic elites 20–4; mobilities and communication 31–2; subaltern appropriations 24–8; urban mobilities 11–16; *see also* disaster and networked urbanism
networks of trust 66, 72–4
'New Towns' 2–3

offshoring 50–8; democracy and 14, 56, 57, 58; generic principle of contemporary societies 57–8; getting around rules 55; inequality 54–5; neoliberalism 56–7; practices 52; processes of 52; tax havens 53–4; tax shaming 55–6
Oliphant, Rachel 14, 59–75
Open Data Cities 21
Open Street Map 68
Otis Company 89
Otis, Elisha 83
Oxfam 55

Paris attacks (2015) 60, 69, 71, 74
Parks, Lisa 26, 27
Patton, Phil 86, 88
Paumgarten, Nick 85
Peru earthquake (2011) 73
Petersen, Katrina 14, 59–75
"Place: Networked Place" (Varnelis and Friedberg) 21
planetary urbanization 19–20, 27, 31–2
planned face-to-face encounters, virtual acquaintances 38–41
politics, mobility methods 132–5
polytopic living, mobility 113–14
Portman, John 86, 89
Post-Petroleum (Urry) 118, 119
power of the local 11
principle of democracy 147
pseudonymous strangers 37, 46–7; enabling encounters between virtual acquaintances and 41–3; timid encounters 43–6
Public Protection and Disaster Response (PPDR) 61, 63, 75

'Radiant City' 3–4
Reader, Sharon 68
Red Cross 68, 71
ride sharing 40–1
Rifkin, Jeremy 9
Russian dolls 54, 117

'Safety Check' (Facebook) 69, 71
Sarvajal 26
saving critique 141
Sayre, Ryan 80, 83, 89
science and technology studies (STS) 59, 133, 135; technologies of humility 65–8
SecInCoRe project 63, 71
secrecy jurisdictions 53

Index   157

sentient cities 20, 21, 23
Sheller, Mimi 8, 12–13, 19–32, 71
Sheshoka, Lesiba 103
signal traffic 24
Simmel, Georg 1, 5, 29, 36
Simmen, Jeannot 85
Singaporean Housing Development
   Board 85
sky lobby, World Trade Center 93
Skype 118
skyscrapers 14; elevators in 82
smart cities 20; concept of 12
social collective intelligence 30
social fabric, cities 4–6
social mobility 108–9; immobile
   mobility 145–6
social networking platforms 40
sociology of inequality 145
South Africa: Mponeng mine 100,
   101–3; Vaal Reefs Mine 103
South Asian tsunami (2004) 61, 67
sovereign terrain for movement 31
spatial fixes 1, 8
Star Trek transporter device 93
state interventionism 53
stranger, concept of 36; *see also* virtual
   acquaintances
Süddeutsche Zeitung (newspaper) 13

Taipei Financial Center 89, 90
tax havens 53–4
Tax Information Exchange
   Agreements 54
Tax Justice Network 57
tax shaming 55–6
taxwash 56
technologies of articulation 72–4
technologies of humility, science and
   technology studies (STS) 65–8
Thill, Jean Claude 83
Things to Come (film) 86
Thrift, Nigel 21, 23
time budgets 114–15
time-space compression 10, 82, 84, 89,
   93–4, 110
timid encounters 13, 47; unfolding
   encounters with pseudonymous
   strangers 43–6
Tinder 38, 41
Tour Victor Hugo 97
Town and Country Planning Act 2
transportation 12, 14–15; cars for
   mobility 110–11; horizontal
   mobilities 81; intelligent highways

12, 22; vertical mobilities 81–3;
   widespread high mobility 118;
   see also vertical mobilities
treasure islands 13
Trendhunter (blog) 80
trusted traveler 28
Twitter disaster hashtags 68
Tzu Chi 64

Uberization 37, 40–1
ultra-deep mining: Belgian coal miners
   99; elevators going down 98–103;
   Mponeng mine 100, 101–3; *see also*
   vertical mobilities
uneven mobilities 31
Union Carbide India Limited 66
United Nations: Office for Disaster
   Risk Reduction 59; peacekeeping 30;
   *Sendai Framework for Disaster Risk
   Reduction 2015–2030* 62
United Way 95
urban age, mobile risk society and 9–11
urbanism *see* networked urbanism
urbanization 4, 104; global 19–20;
   planetary 19–20, 27, 31–2; process of
   10; *see also* networked urbanism
urban metabolism 29
urban transport, history in Western
   Europe 111–13
Urry, John 7–8, 13, 20, 50–8, 118, 119,
   129, 142
US Federal Emergency Management
   Agency (FEMA), 'Whole Community
   Approach to Emergency Management'
   63, 72
Ushahidi Haiti Project (UHP) 30, 68, 69

Vaal Reefs Mine, South Africa 103
Varnelis, Kazys 21
vertical mobilities: colonization of the
   up 83–5; comparing mines and towers
   100; crises for vertical transport
   trapping 95–8; Hitachi G1 Tower
   80–1, 84, 91; location of fastest
   elevators 89–91; postmodernities
   85–9; Street People and Air People
   91, 93–4; ultra-deep mining elevators
   98–103
virtual acquaintances 37; enabling
   encounters with pseudonymous
   strangers and 41–3; folded distance
   39, 40, 45; planned face-to-face
   encounters 38–41; pre-arranging
   visual cues 39–40

158   *Index*

Virtual Operations Support Teams (VOST) 72, 73
Volkswagen Car Tower 91, 92
'voluntweeters' 68

walking 27, 93, 110–11, 117, 126–7, 132
Wall Street Journal (newspaper) 55
Weber, Max 5
Weizman, Eyal 82
Wells, H. G. 86
Wenchuan earthquake (2008) 64
Western Europe, history of urban transport in 111–13

Woolworth Building (Manhattan) 84
World Social Forum 55
World Trade Center 93, 100; disaster (2011) 84–5
World Trade Organization 143
World War II 2
World Wide Web 7
Wright, Frank Lloyd 91

Young, Meghan 80

'Zahavi Conjecture' 114–15
Zahavi, Yacov 114
Zokwana, Senzeni 103